KUWABARA PAYNE McKENNA BLUMBERG

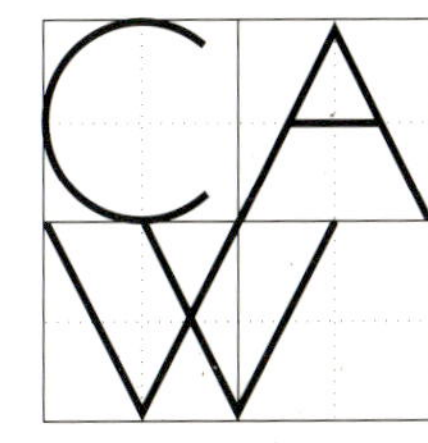

CONTEMPORARY
WORLD
ARCHITECTS

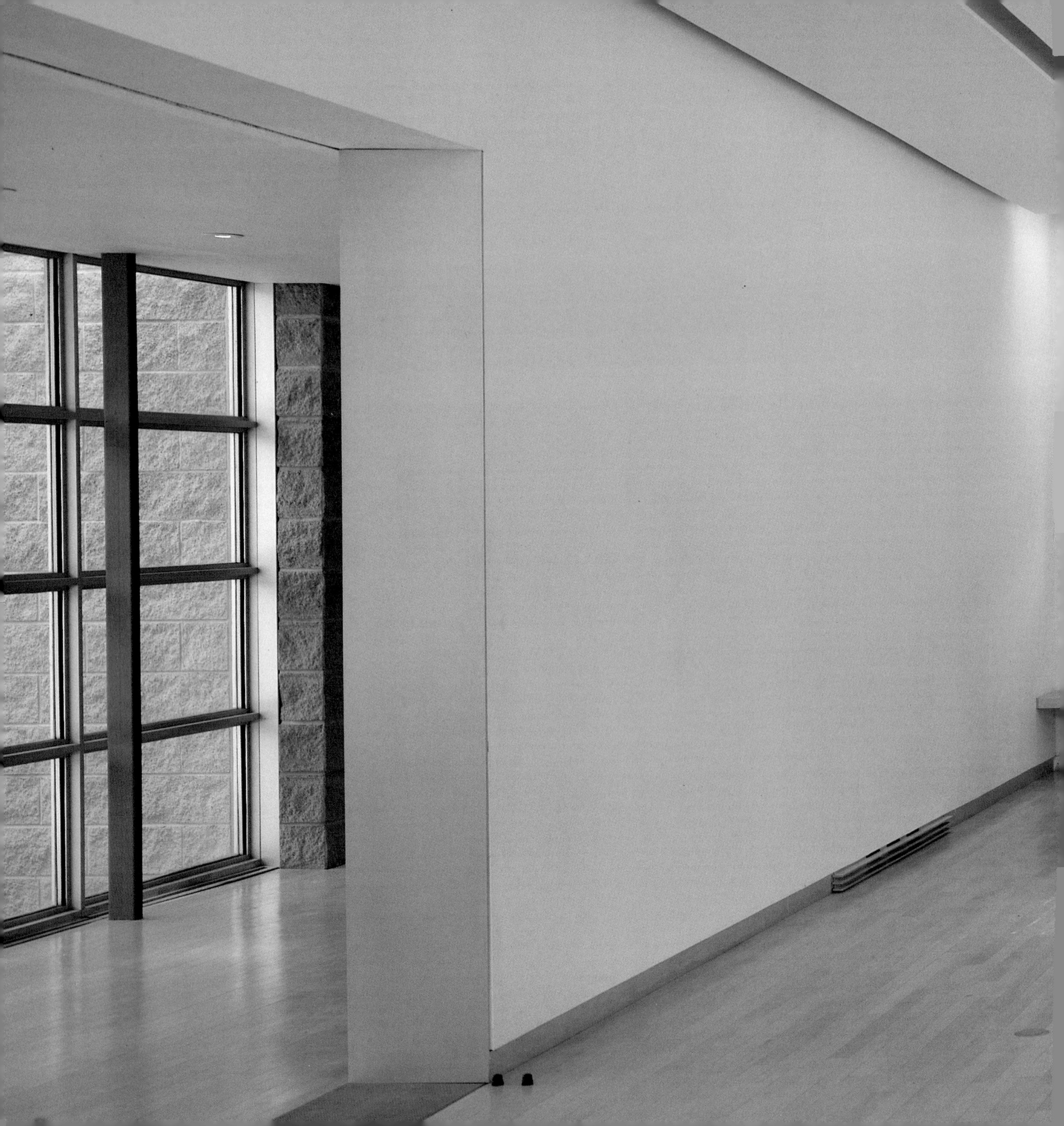

KUWABARA PAYNE McKENNA BLUMBERG

Foreword by
George Baird

Introduction by
Detlef Mertins

Concept and Design by
Lucas H. Guerra
Oscar Riera Ojeda

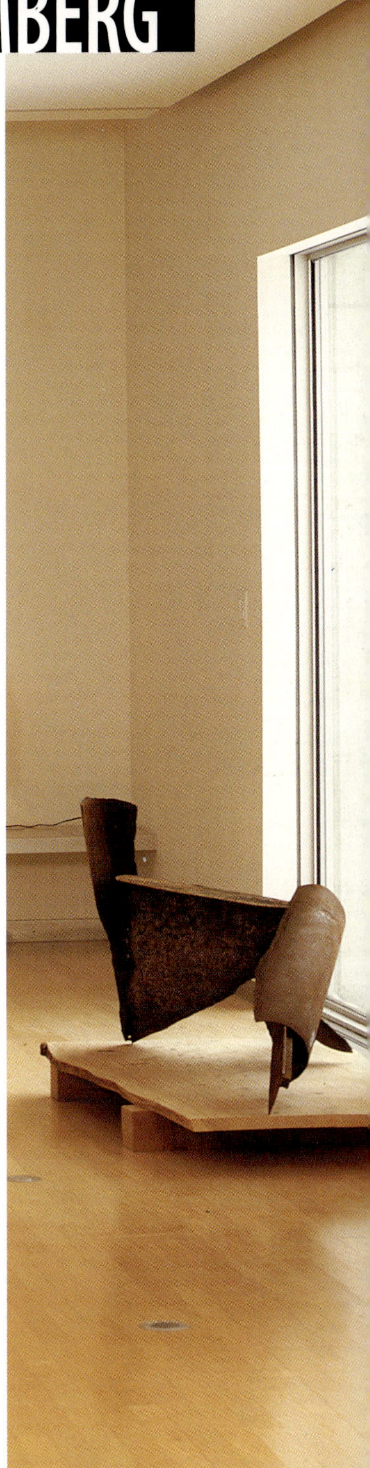

ROCKPORT PUBLISHERS
GLOUCESTER, MASSACHUSETTS
DISTRIBUTED BY NORTH LIGHT BOOKS
CINCINNATI, OHIO

First published in the United States of America by
Rockport Publishers, Inc.
33 Commercial Street
Gloucester, Massachusetts 01930-5089
Telephone: (508) 282-9590

Distributed to the book trade and art trade in the United States of America by
North Light Books, an imprint of
F & W Publications
1507 Dana Avenue
Cincinnati, Ohio 45207
Telephone: (800) 289-0963

Other Distribution by
Rockport Publishers, Inc.
Gloucester, Massachusetts 01930-5089

ISBN 1-56496-408-6

10 9 8 7 6 5 4 3 2 1

Printed in Hong Kong

Cover photograph: Kitchener City Hall by Steven Evans
Back cover photograph: Nicolas by Steven Evans (top); Gluskin Sheff & Associates by ESTO/Jeff Goldberg (bottom)
Back flap photograph: Ron Baxter-Smith
pp.1–3: Steven Evans; p. 6: Michael Awad; p.7: ESTO/Jeff Goldberg; p.9: ESTO/Jeff Goldberg; (left and center), Steven Evans (right); p.10: Michael Awad (top), Steven Evans (far left, far right), Robert Burley/Design Archive (center); p.11: Wolfgang Hoyt; p.12: Steven Evans; p.94: Steven Evans; p.134: Lenscape; p.141: Robert G. Hill; p.143: Ron Baxter-Smith

Graphic Design: Lucas H. Guerra/Oscar Riera Ojeda
Layout: Oscar Riera Ojeda
Composition: Gisella R. Onofre

CONTENTS

Foreword by George Baird   6
Introduction by Detlef Mertins   8

Public Realm

Kitchener City Hall   14
Joseph S. Stauffer Library   26
Woodsworth College   36
Fields Institute   42
Walter Carsen Centre for the National Ballet of Canada   46
The Design Exchange   50
King James Place   58
Marc Laurent   62
Creed's Interiors   70
Nicolas   74
Oasis Parfumerie   78
Creative Copy & Design   82
Sega City @ Playdium   84
Grand Valley Institution for Women   88

Private Realm

Tudhope Studios   96
Dome Productions   100
Hasbro Inc. Headquarters   104
Ammirati Puris Lintas   108
Alliance Communications Corporation   116
Gluskin Sheff + Associates   120
Reisman-Jenkinson House   128

Appendix

Selected Buildings   136
List of Works and Credits   140
List of Staff and Interns   143
Acknowledgments   144

Foreword

BY GEORGE BAIRD

For architects, a key professional pleasure over the past decade in Toronto has been to observe the remarkable career of the firm of Kuwabara Payne McKenna Blumberg unfold. Among both their local and international peers, KPMB's oeuvre has taken on a quite distinct and attractive coloration. It is not surprising, of course, that this precocious firm has chosen to eschew the formulaic production of mainstream corporate offices. What is more unexpected, perhaps, is that KPMB has at the same time avoided any systematic participation in the current, highly publicized professional avant-garde that usually forsakes the possibility of developing a body of locally based work. Such work gains strength and coherence from its evident geographical density, and establishes exemplary strategies of building that are—in principle—available to all.

Yet, such has been the accomplishment of this relatively young firm in the years of its remarkable production to date. The work of KPMB—sensuous in the assurance of its material palettes; civilized and urbane in its responses to the still only partially formed character of its home city; and astonishingly relaxed in the grace and ease of its tectonic plasticity and spatial character—constitutes a cultural accomplishment of a high order. More important, KPMB's built work also serves, in its local setting, as a broad, ongoing challenge to the general standards of practice today.

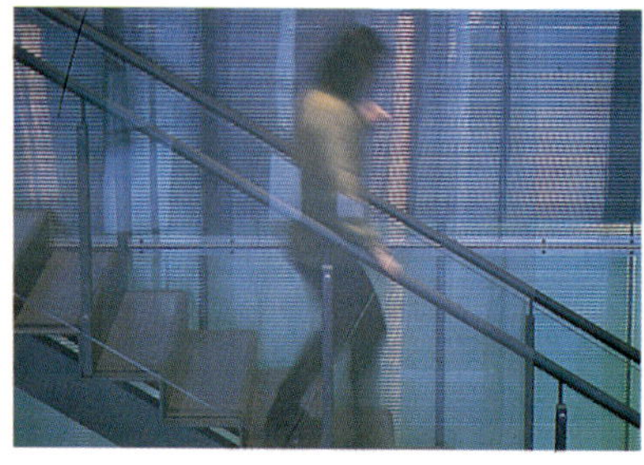
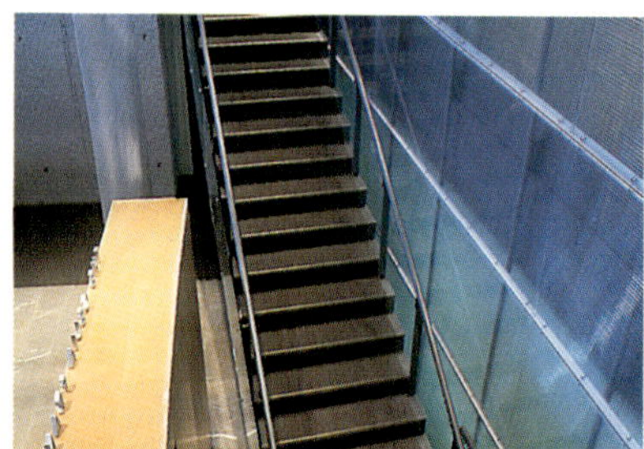

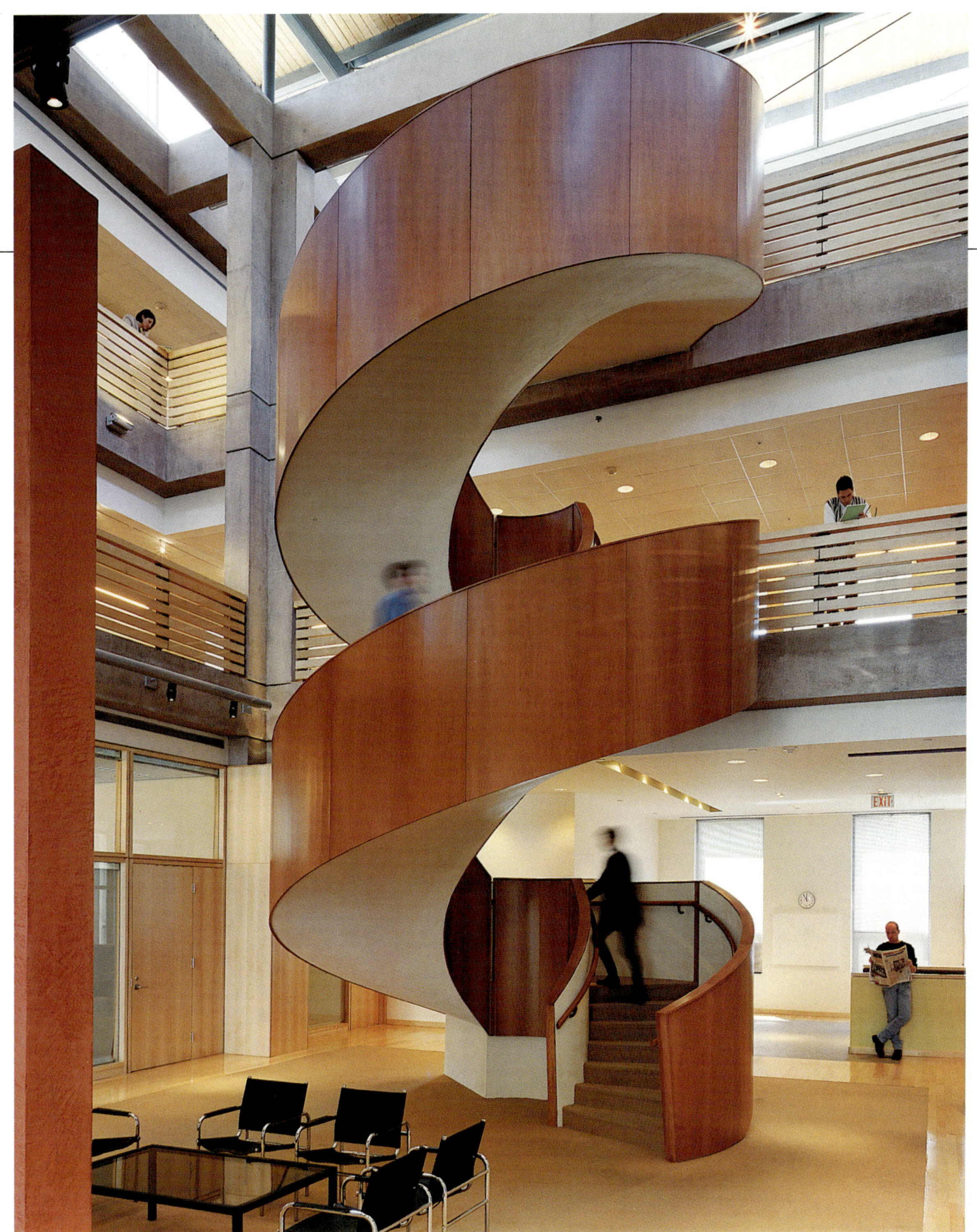

The spacious light-filled atrium of the Fields Institute at the University of Toronto organizes circulation and acts as a catalyst for intellectual and social exchange.

Introduction

BY DETLEF MERTINS

POETICS IN THE CITY OF BITS

One's first response to a work by Kuwabara Payne McKenna Blumberg is invariably astonishment at its rich assembly of sensory experiences, both haptic and optic. The insistent materiality of these projects draws one to touch the surfaces of things, to run the hand over the rough granite, precise steel, and lush wood. Even walls simply painted with sumptuous colors invite contact.

Yet, this compulsion to draw near is met with a double resistance. The materials, including the most humble, are so rich and luxurious in their effect, so beyond the ordinary, that they enforce a distance. They establish an aura. They look back at us. At the same time, every enticing surface, every translucent screen and intriguing group of elements begets another. The eye is drawn slowly into motion, the head compelled to turn, the body driven to wander by an insatiable desire to experience what waits around the corner, behind the screen, in the space beyond.

At every scale, this architecture creates such spaces of desire: in the composition of building masses and the arrangement of rooms; in the spiraling of stairs, the layering of planes, and the filtering of screens; in the intricate crevices of mechanical joints that make up canopies, desks, and room dividers; in the deep shadows where two materials meet. Everywhere, space opens between things—space to step into and move through, space that holds mystery, wonder, and potentiality.

The work is built up, rather than carved or molded; constructed, rather than grown. From structures to walls, ceilings, and doors, this is a building art of assemblage, montage, and installation. The discrete components of the Kitchener City Hall (1990–1993) and Woodsworth College (1990–1992) announce a playful, elemental, even toy-block approach to the composition of masses, capable of generating new and unexpected configurations. The kit of parts offered up by late twentieth-century building technology—the muscular, fleshy yet abstract and mechanical apparatus of cladding, window frames, and balcony railings—is augmented by custom fabrications to form buildings that are both familiar and fresh. Gestures of solidity and mass are countered by the explicit ways in which the thinness of materials, their transformation into products, and the resultant necessity of assemblage are acknowledged. The construction industry, whose drive for economy constantly reduces the amount of material and the complexity of processes used, is mastered by these architects to stage a play of substance and dissolution; image and abstraction; stasis and movement; permanence and transience.

The spatial implications of assemblage—the infinite openness of the column grid, the sublime space of the reveal, the convulsive vortex of hinges and joints—are drawn out to become a field of gaps within a landscape of continuity. Inside and out, lines of view and movement are cut through every mass, generating a labyrinth of partially dissolved volumes and interconnections, inviting the ambulations and appropriations of the imagination. The spatial paradigm of modernism is updated

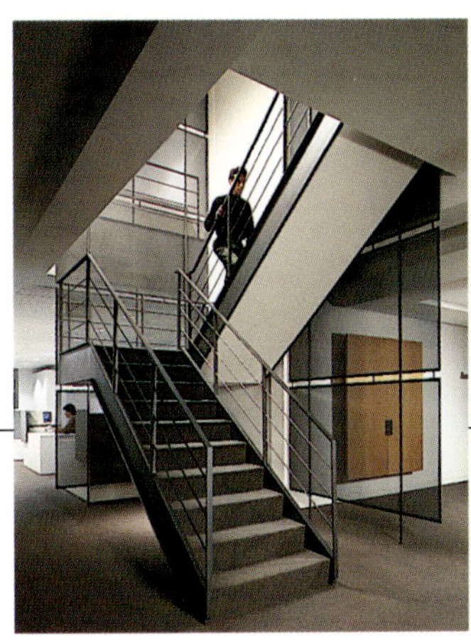 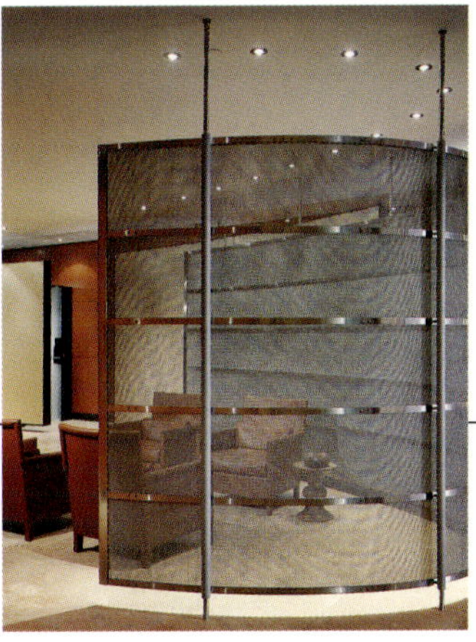 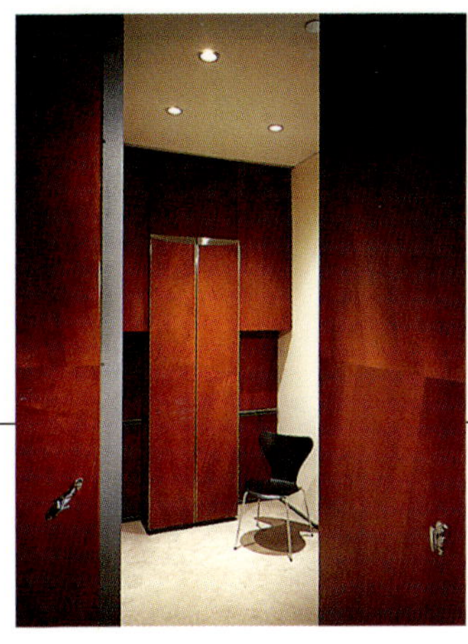

to the post-industrial age of information and communication, and rendered explicit. A city of bits provisionally composed in a swirl of space materializes a shared domain for performing everyday life. At its most remarkable, this domain provides the everyday with an expanded space of play and a heightened sense of perception and freedom that borders on exhilaration.

Two recent office projects demonstrate KPMB's ability to transmute work into play. Like the prototypical houses and cabinets of Charles and Ray Eames, KPMB designed a system of elements, together with templates for possible arrangements, that can be adapted for the various corporate offices of the advertising agency Ammirati Puris Lintas located around the world. KPMB's system creates room to play in response to the specific conditions of each situation, the size of the corporate office, and the nature of the space available. On the other hand, the Toronto offices of the investment firm Gluskin Sheff + Associates structures play not for the designers, but for the users. Here, offices and workstations adjust to the needs and changing desires of their occupants. Moveable components in tables and screen walls allow the apparatus of work to be customized, and the degree of privacy or openness to be self-regulated. Even boardrooms can transform, with moveable walls and audio-visual equipment that appears and disappears at the flick of a switch. In the best tradition of twentieth-century design, buildings, like furniture, are treated as flexible organisms capable of changing, growing, and empowering their users.

To promote creativity in children as they learned the fundamentals of geometry and developed small-scale muscle movements, the nineteenth-century educator Friedrich Froebel (inventor of the kindergarten) developed elemental toys that became widely disseminated by the turn of the century. Their principles were absorbed into the educational philosophy of Montessori schools and extended in the design of toys, children's furniture, and at the Bauhaus, even furnishings for adults. Now, at the end of the century, KPMB's reworking of modern abstraction takes this legacy of elementarism beyond the orthodoxy of purism. The world of images and popular culture—itself always engaged with modernization—enters into the imaginary at the Gluskin Sheff offices as work stations for the investment managers assume a character reminiscent of the control bridge on the starship *Enterprise*. Here, a performative mimetics takes its place beside pure, clear form as a strategy for stimulating creativity.

Following the lead of Pierre Chareau's suave and urbane modernism at the Maison de Verre in Paris (1928–1932), the relationship of KPMB's projects to the matrix of representation—the semiotic codes of building types, societal conventions, norms, and expectations—is subtle: both accepting and transformative. Woodsworth College, on the University of Toronto campus, reconfigures and extends an earlier house, drill hall, and officers' quarters into a cloister punctuated by gates and towers, while the Stauffer Library (1991–1994) at Queen's University recalls aspects of collegiate gothic architecture in forms more geometric and restrained. However, in mobilizing their craft in its elementalized, commodified, and globalized condition at the end of the twentieth century, the architects' reiteration of familiar forms and images opens them to new spatial relationships and extraordinary poetic effects. Closed rooms are partially dissolved without losing their enveloping

A new steel stair at the Ammirati Puris Lintas offices in New York City (top left). In the reception area at the offices of Gluskin Sheff + Associates (top center) and in the private dressing rooms at Creed's in Toronto (top right), meticulously crafted finishes and materials form translucent layers to slowly reveal, but not expose, intriguing elements and spaces beyond.

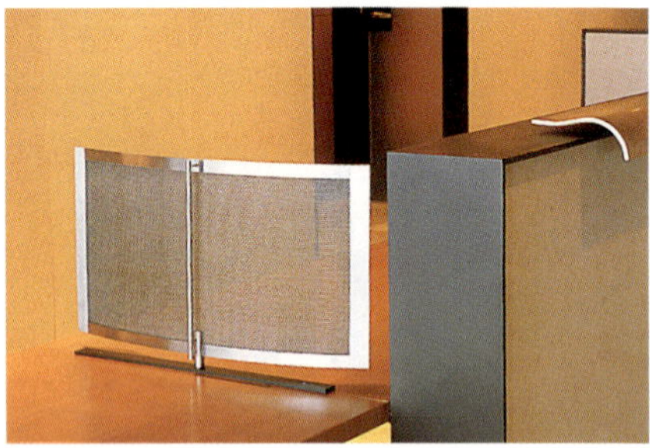

character. Sharp industrial materials—synthetic metals such as steel and aluminum, and various kinds of glass—are placed into everyday situations, simultaneously becoming domesticated and setting received domesticities on edge. Material substance is geometricized into pure surface and pure potential—an abstraction that absorbs materiality into the system of calculation and production, at the same time that it activates the senses and imagination.

Participating in normative networks of representation, these projects are accessible to popular expectations conditioned by the commodification and reification of familiar architectures. Yet, operating at the limit of legibility, these composite, hybrid, and ambiguous works stretch beyond familiar codifications toward an expanded space of possibility. In the minimal Reisman-Jenkinson House (1990–1991), for instance, the forms of the suburban home are emptied out, distilled, and reduced in order to concentrate perception and heighten the existential dramas of life. On the other hand, the hot television space of Sega City @ Playdium (1995–1996) presents a rich, fluid, and disorienting kaleidoscope of imagery contained only by the reticence of its architectural frame. Working to entirely different ends, each of these projects confronts the aura of the reified image with the aura of an abstracted and rarefied materiality, each corroding the other.

As the boundary between the virtual and real is renegotiated at the end of the century, the spaces of desire and potentiality of play that may be called out in the work of KPMB are signs of an idealist utopian impulse struggling for life. Like the distraction of montage cinema or the architecture of Mies van der Rohe, the discontinuities and dissociations in these projects are vehicles for the production of knowledge, and devices for recalibrating one's relationship to the world, caught in a seemingly endless process of modernization. They give pause and inspire hope that the system that reduces the objects and subjects it produces is open to transformation and the generative production of the work of art, which the romantics called poesie.

A work station behind metal screens at Tudhope Studios (opposite page). Fastidious detailing of the reception desk at Gluskin Sheff + Associates (top), the library stair at the Design Exchange (left), the staff lounge and kitchen area at Alliance Communications (center), and the facade and entrance to Creative Copy & Design (right).

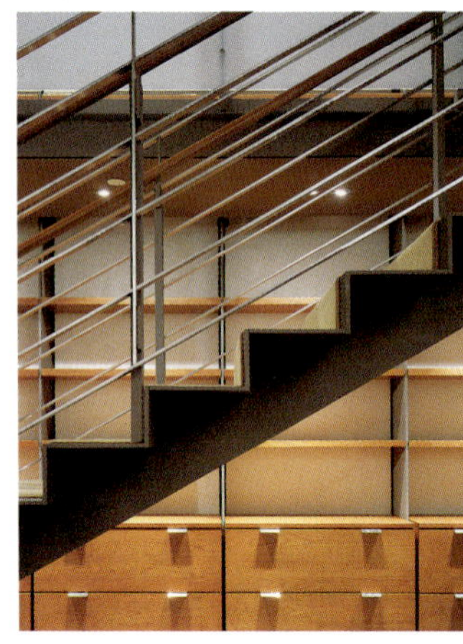

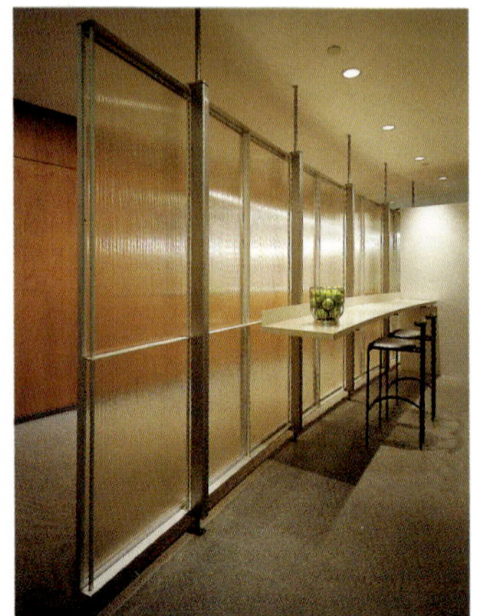

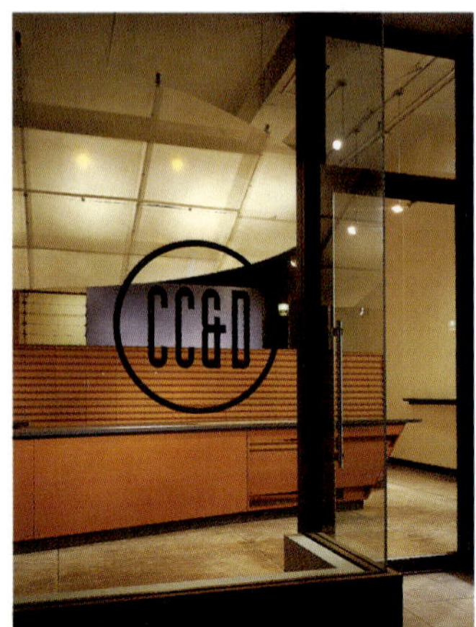

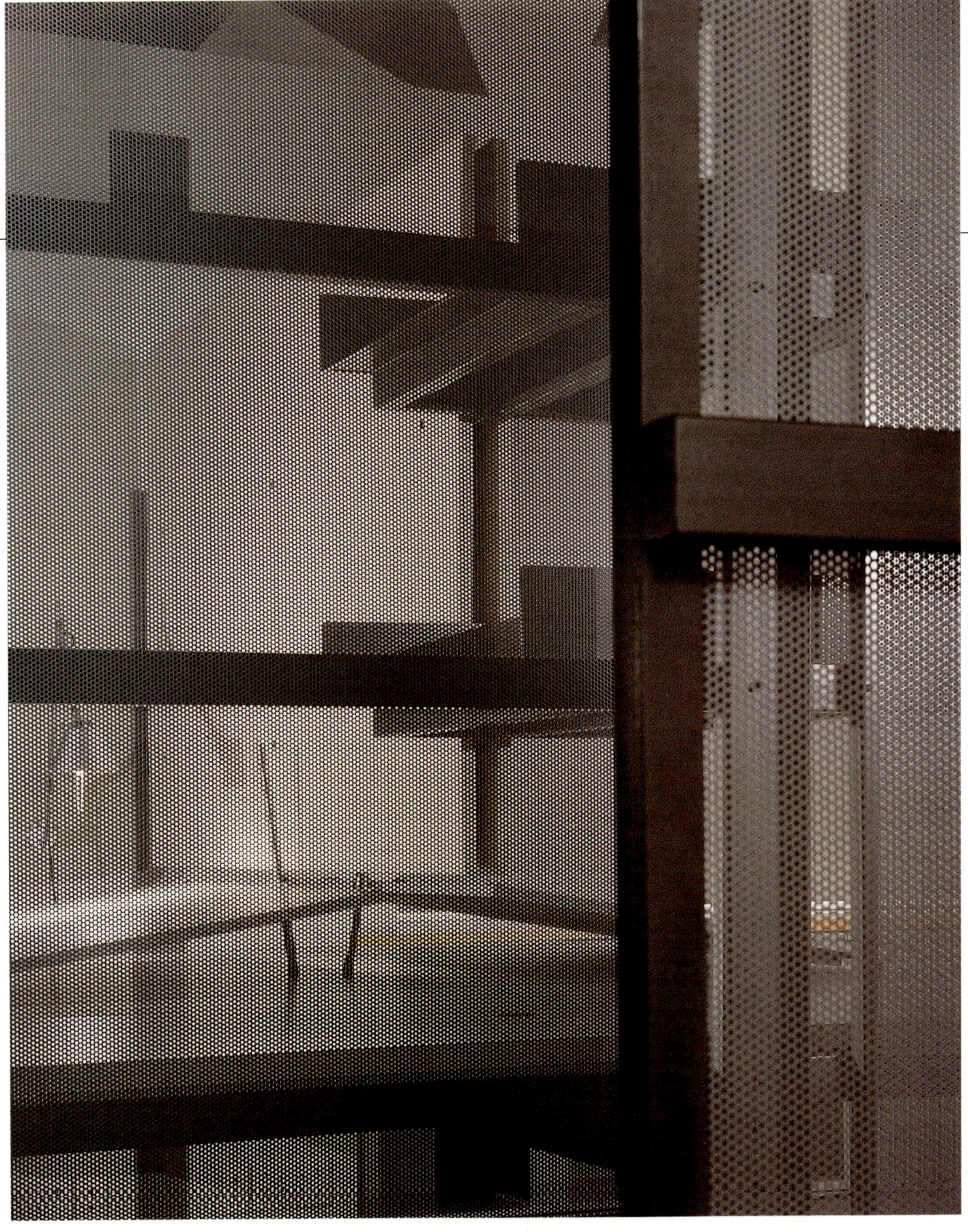

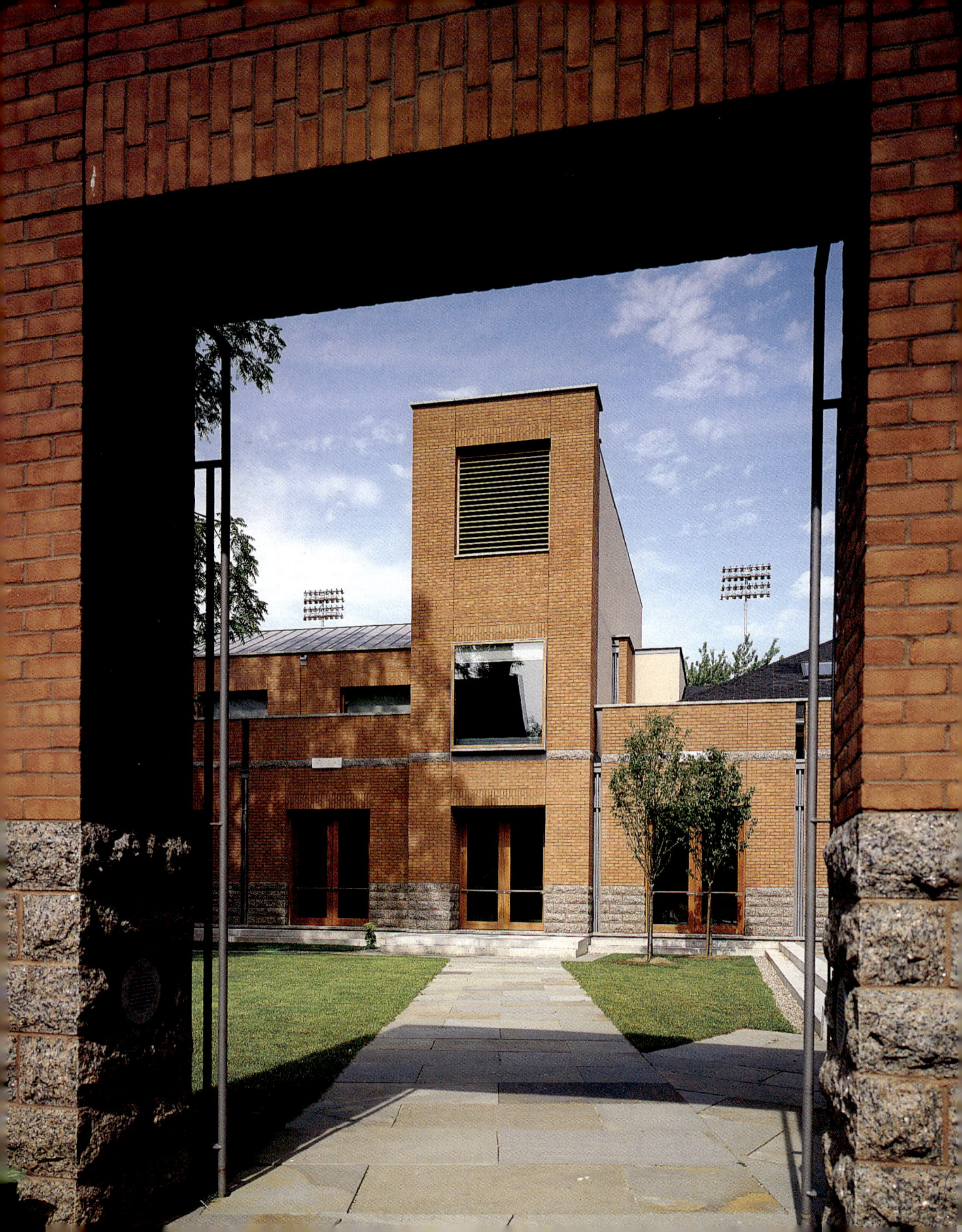

Public Realm ▶

Kitchener City Hall

The new Kitchener City Hall is the winning submission to a national design competition held in 1989. Located on a full city block fronting onto Kitchener's main street, King Street, the city hall and civic square constitute key elements in the city's downtown revitalization strategy.

To express the importance of the location, topography, program, and context in clear architectural terms, the design is conceived as an ensemble of spaces and volumes that create a public terrain for assembly and movement through the site. Defining urban edges along College and Young streets, the east and west wings contain the city hall and civic square, and act as a horizontal architectural datum as the site and city slope down toward historic Victoria Park, one of the city's major outdoor urban amenities.

Three principal volumes accommodate the city hall's main functions: the council chamber, which houses the offices of the mayor and councillors; the civic rotunda, which acts as a place of public assembly at the heart of the project; and the administrative office tower, which hold the city's departments and provides a public observation deck under its cubic top. The tower's spire acts as an illuminated weather-beacon that is visible from all parts of the downtown area. Evoking formal civic precedents such as the agora, amphitheater, plaza, and tower, the city hall is designed to function both as a continuous piece of the existing urban fabric, and as a self-sufficient civic space.

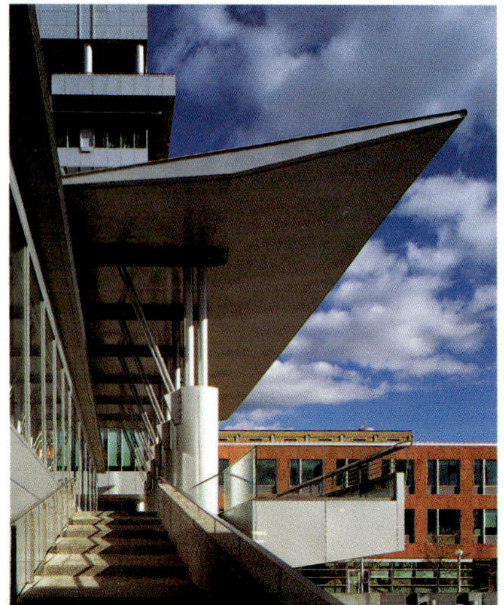

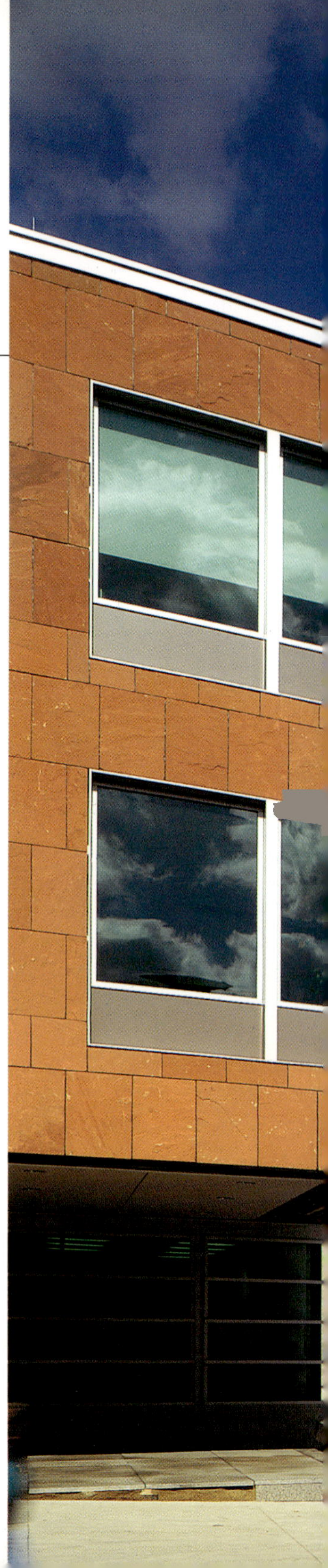

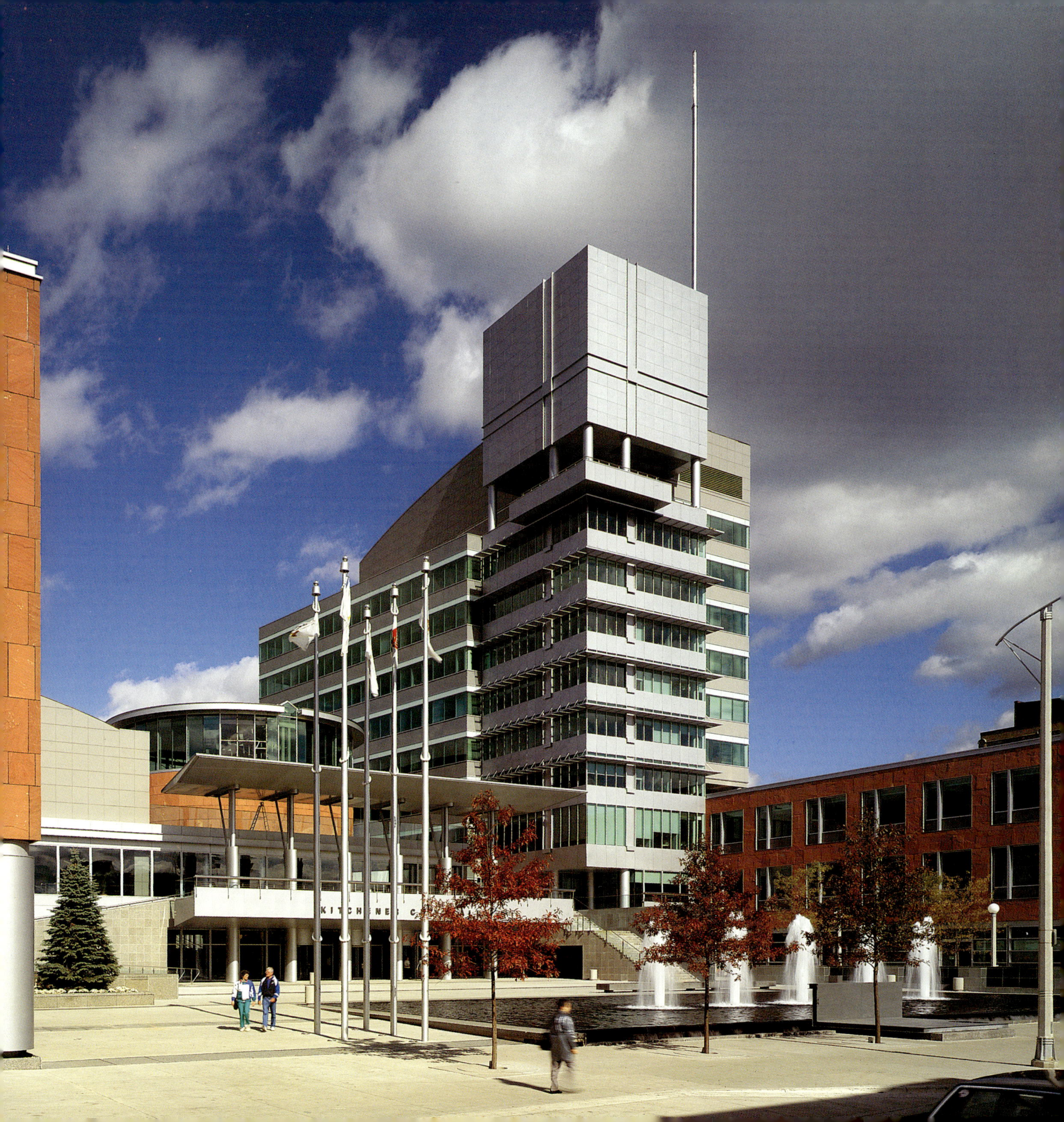

KITCHENER C

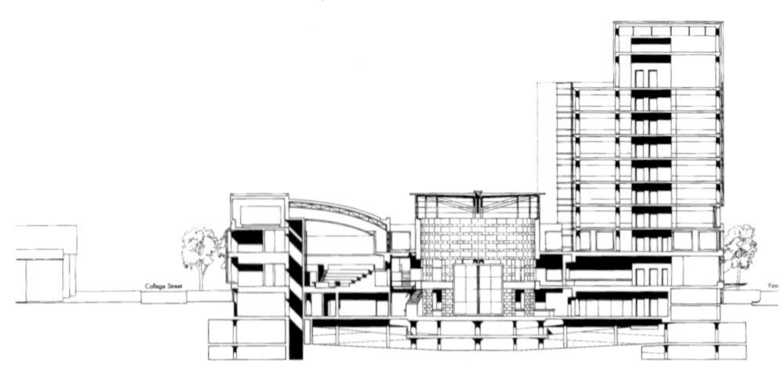

EAST-WEST SECTION

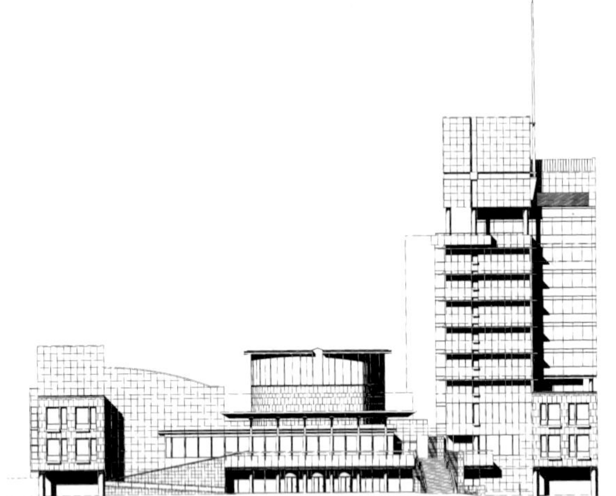

KING STREET ELEVATON

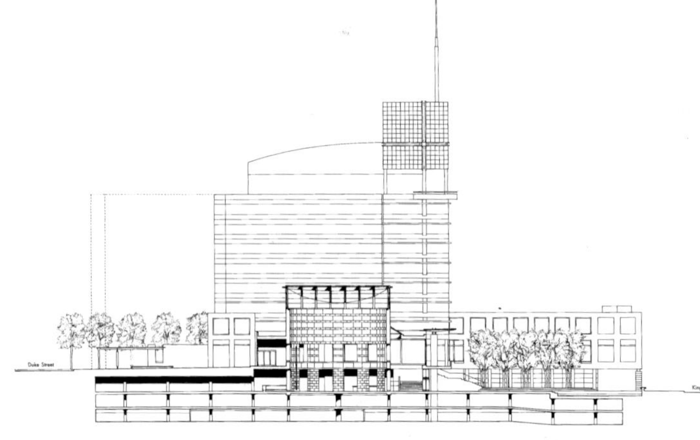

NORTH-SOUTH SECTION

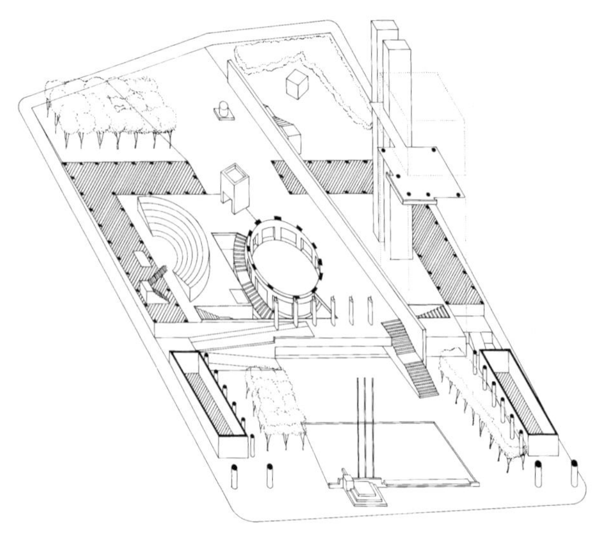

OBLIQUE PROJECTION OF PUBLIC SPACE

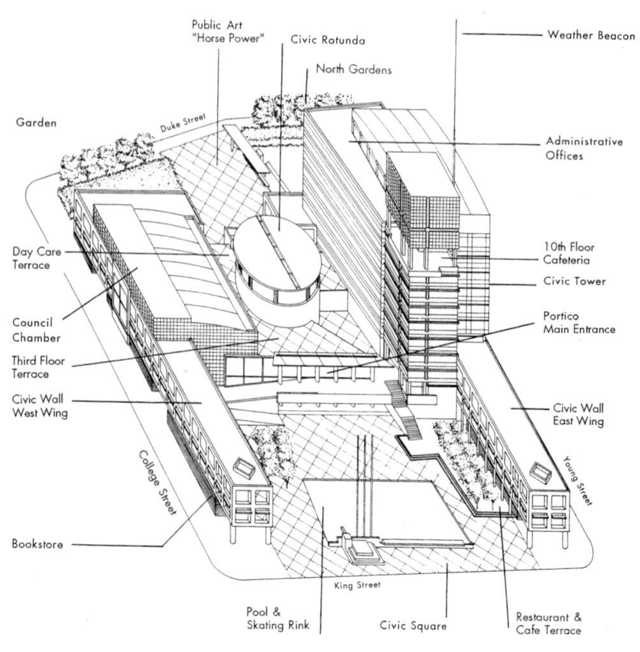

OBLIQUE PROJECTION OF COMPLEX

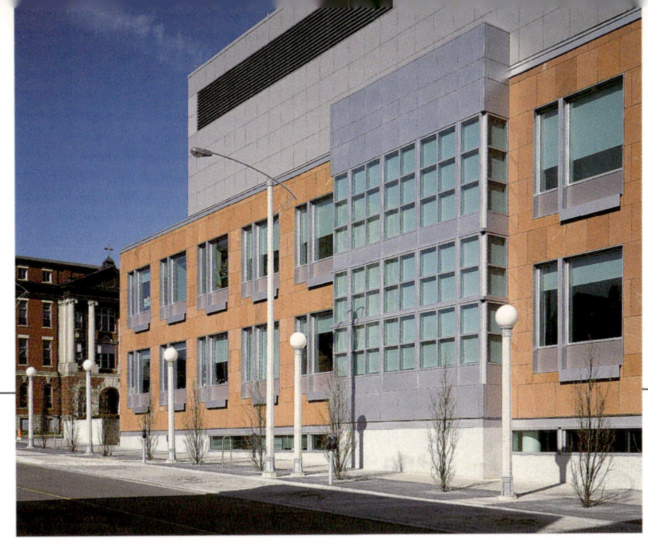

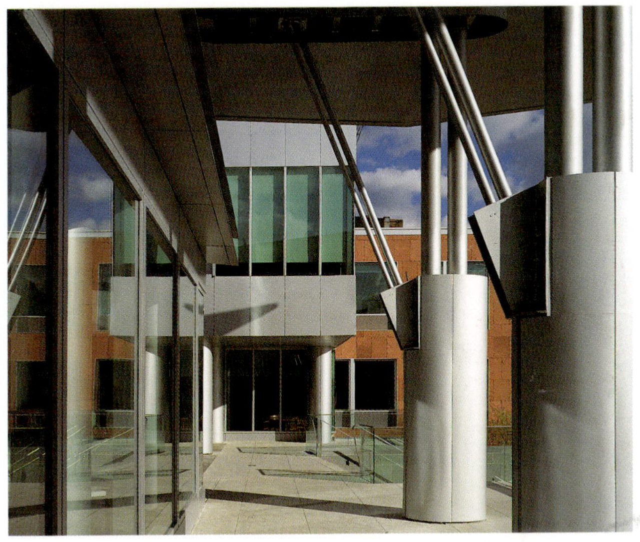

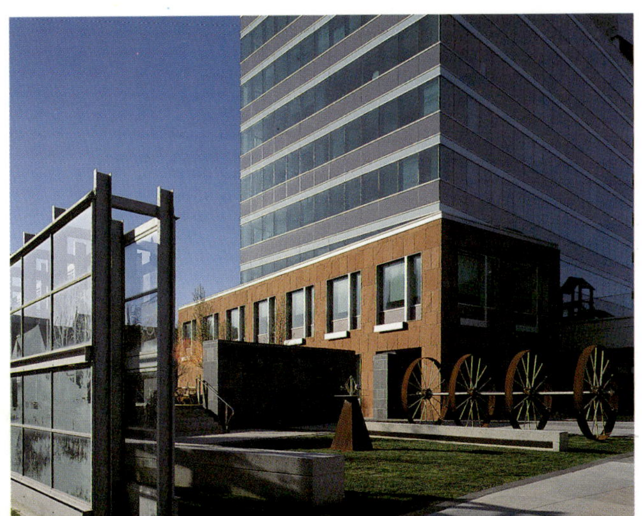

The perimeter elevations respond to the tone, character, and scale of the adjacent historic urban fabric (top). The upper-level public plaza offers views onto the civic square (center). Competition-winning public sculpture, "Horsepower," by Brad Golden and Lynn Eichenberg, alludes to the agricultural heritage of the Kitchener region (bottom).

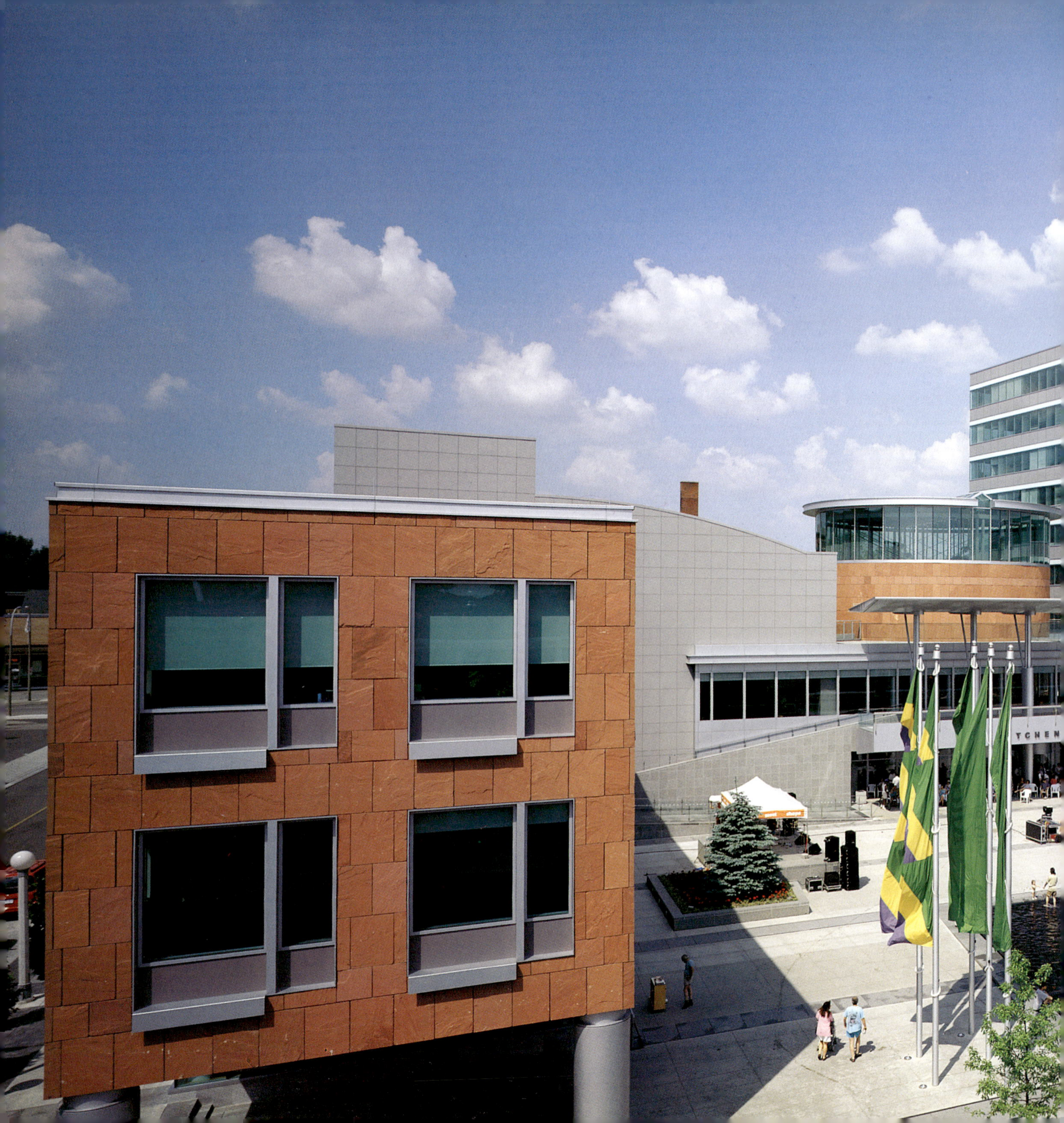

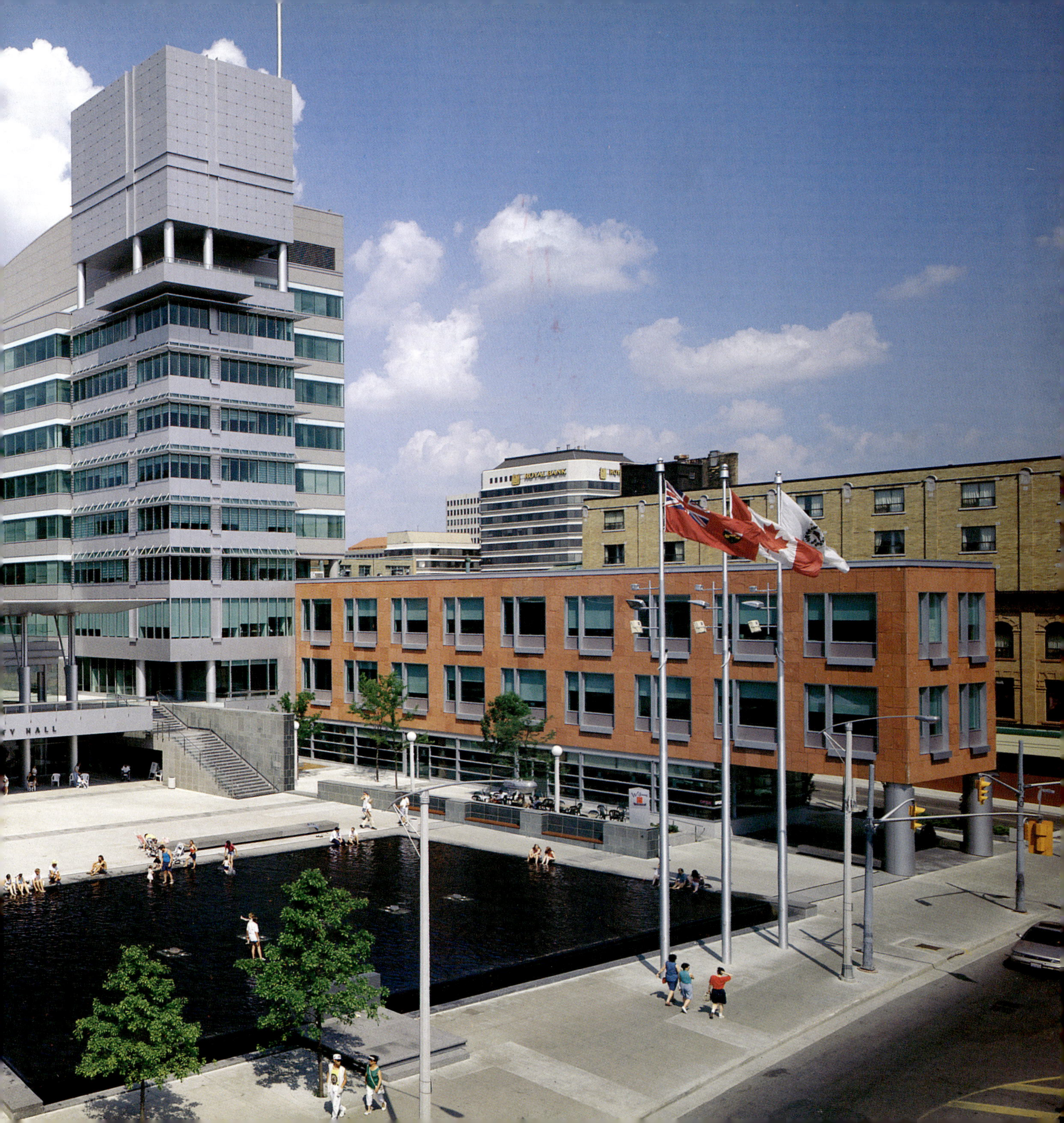

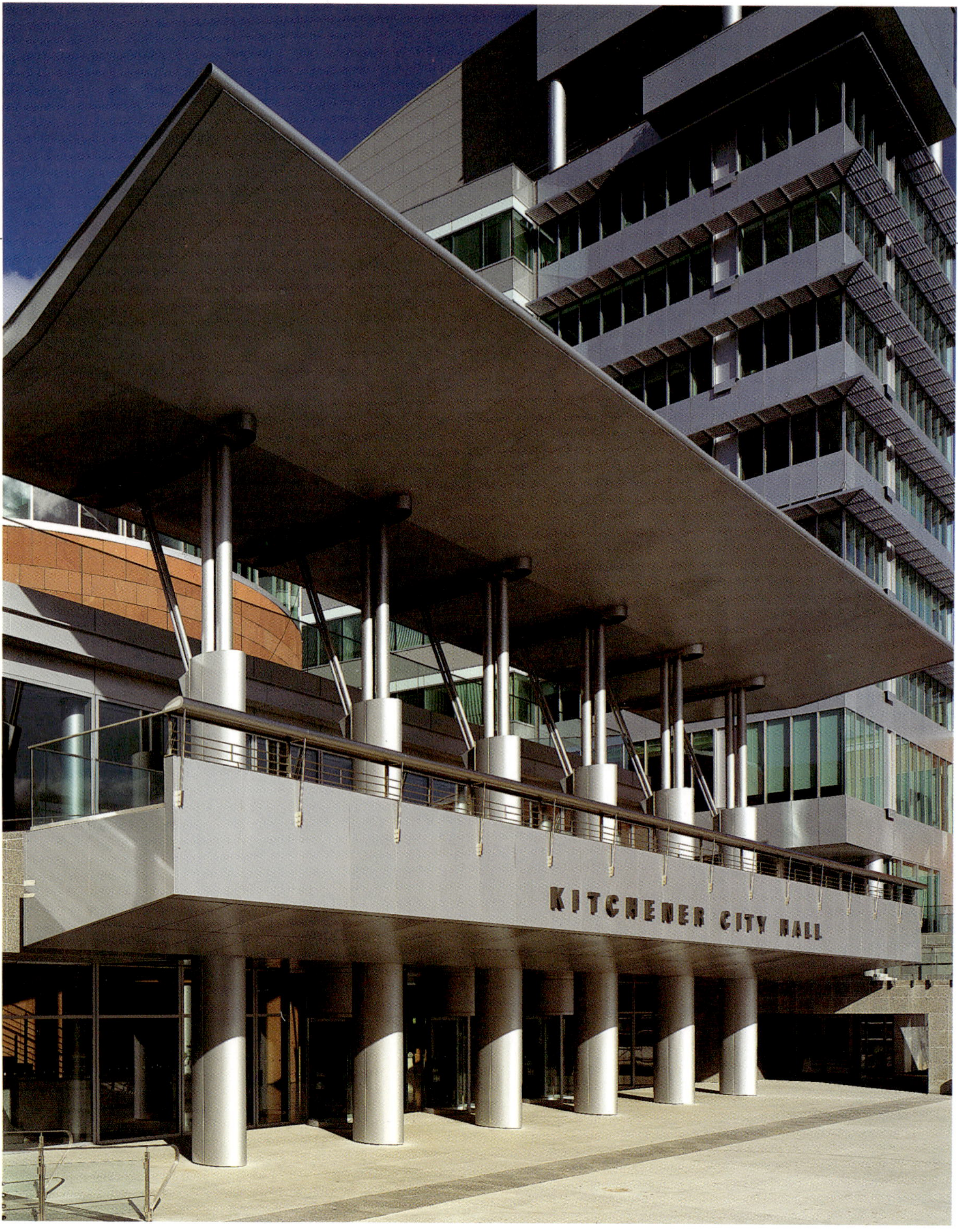

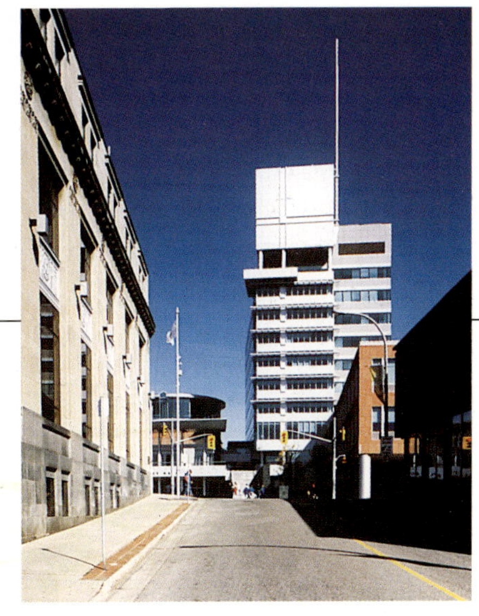

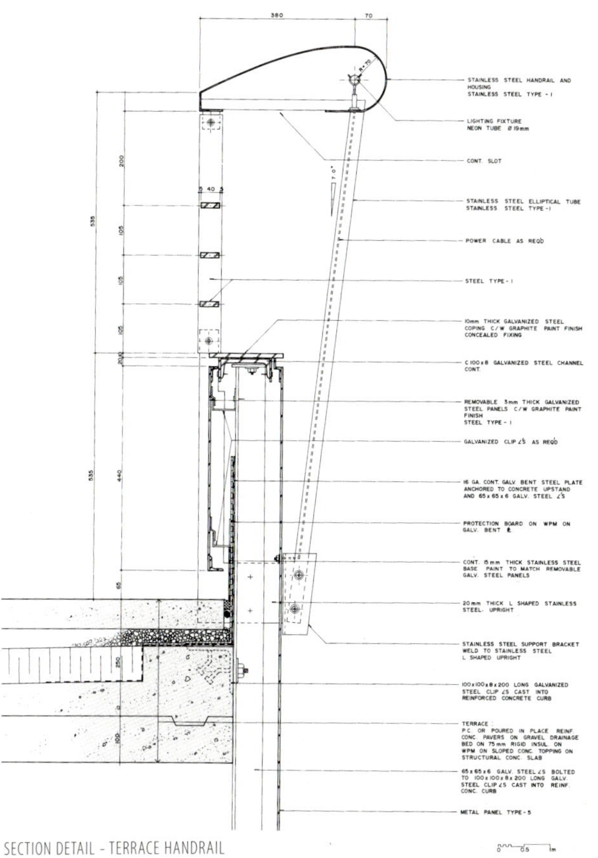

SECTION DETAIL - TERRACE HANDRAIL

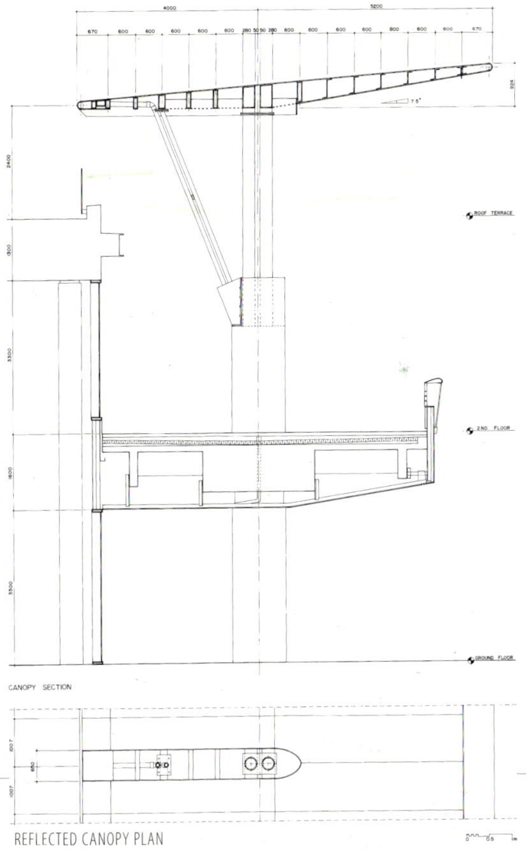

REFLECTED CANOPY PLAN

A monumental portico rises dramatically on steel columns over the entrance to the civic rotunda (opposite page). The city hall's main entrance and tower align with the urban axis from Victoria Park (top).

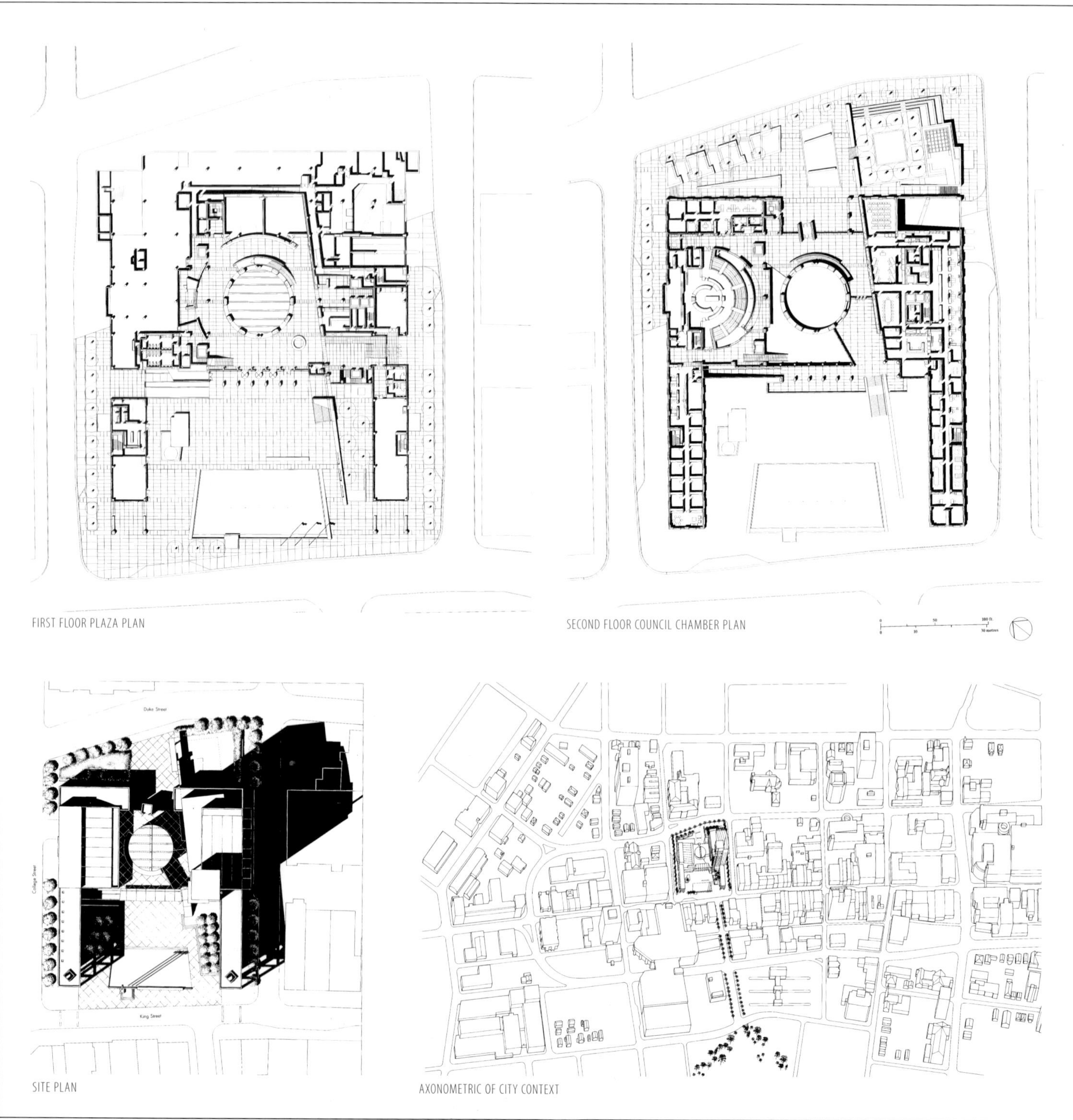

FIRST FLOOR PLAZA PLAN
SECOND FLOOR COUNCIL CHAMBER PLAN
SITE PLAN
AXONOMETRIC OF CITY CONTEXT
Duke Street
College Street
King Street

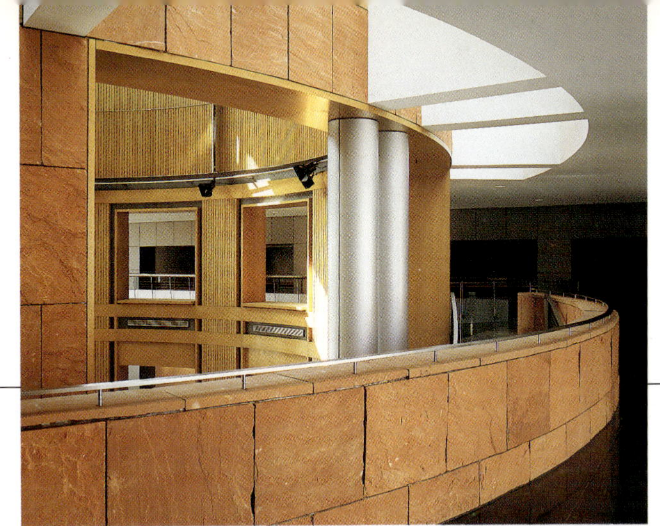

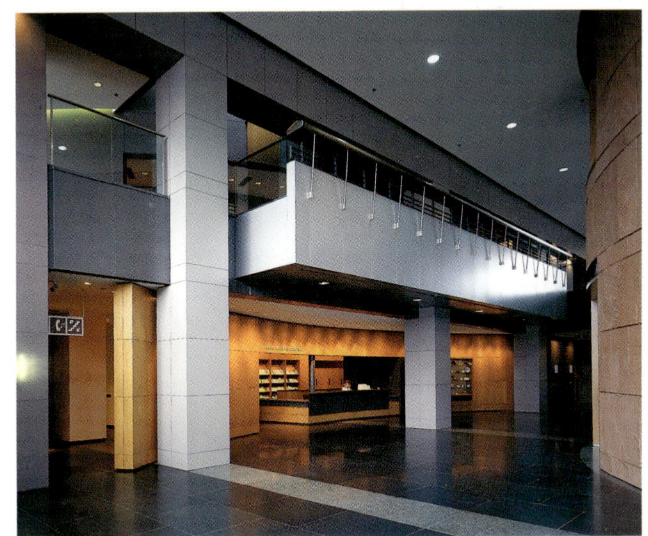

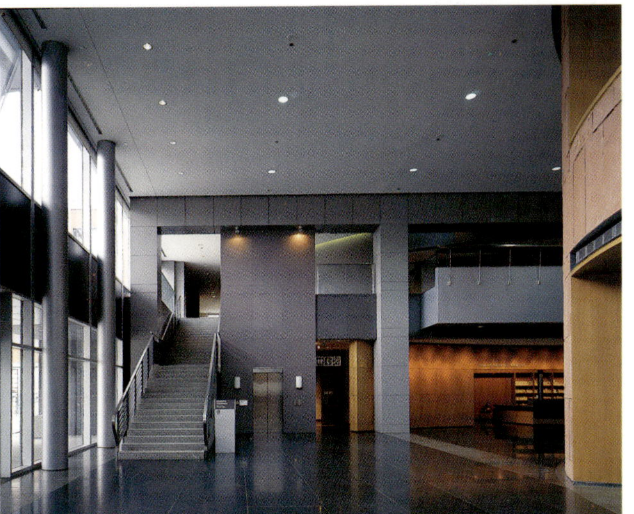

Public reception and information areas surround the civic rotunda, the literal and figurative center of the complex.

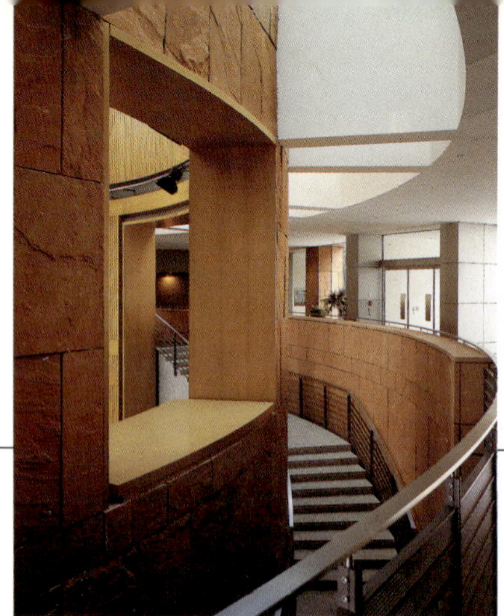

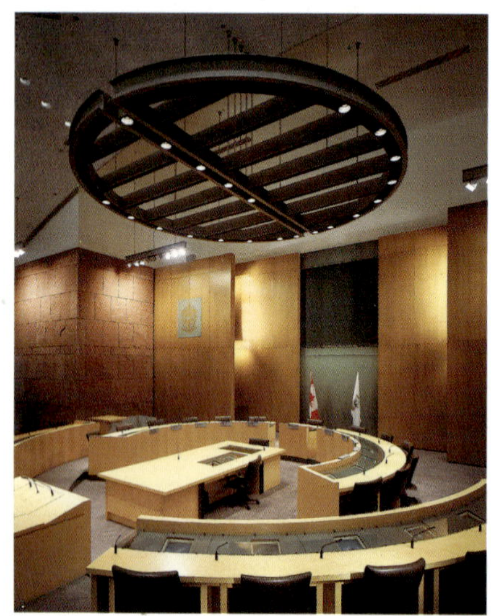

Skylit stairs lining the rotunda provide access to the mayor's office and committee rooms (opposite page). The council chamber (center) sits adjacent to the civic rotunda, which accommodates public assembly, performances, concerts, and exhibitions in the heart of the complex.

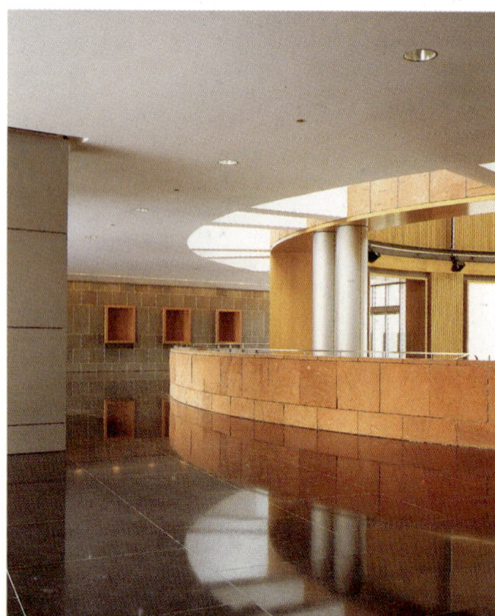

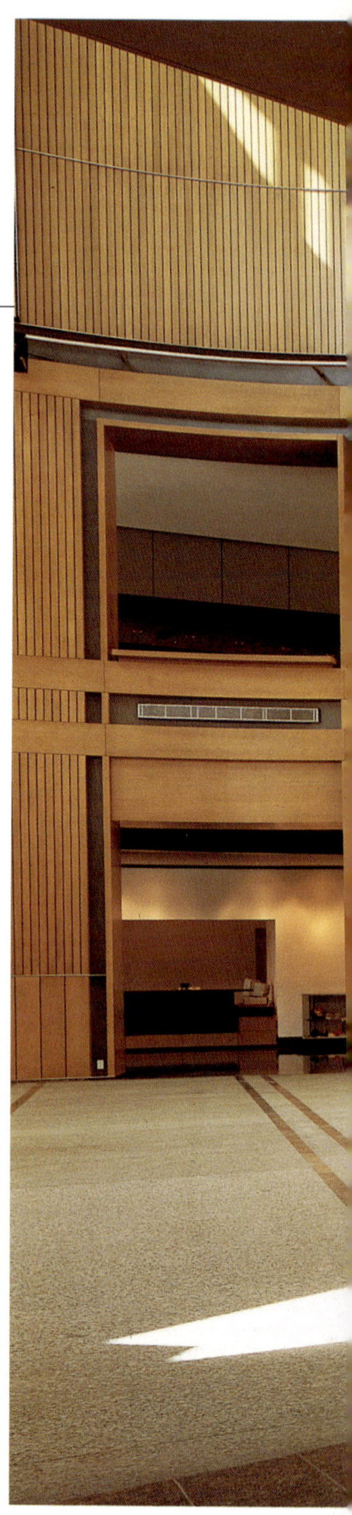

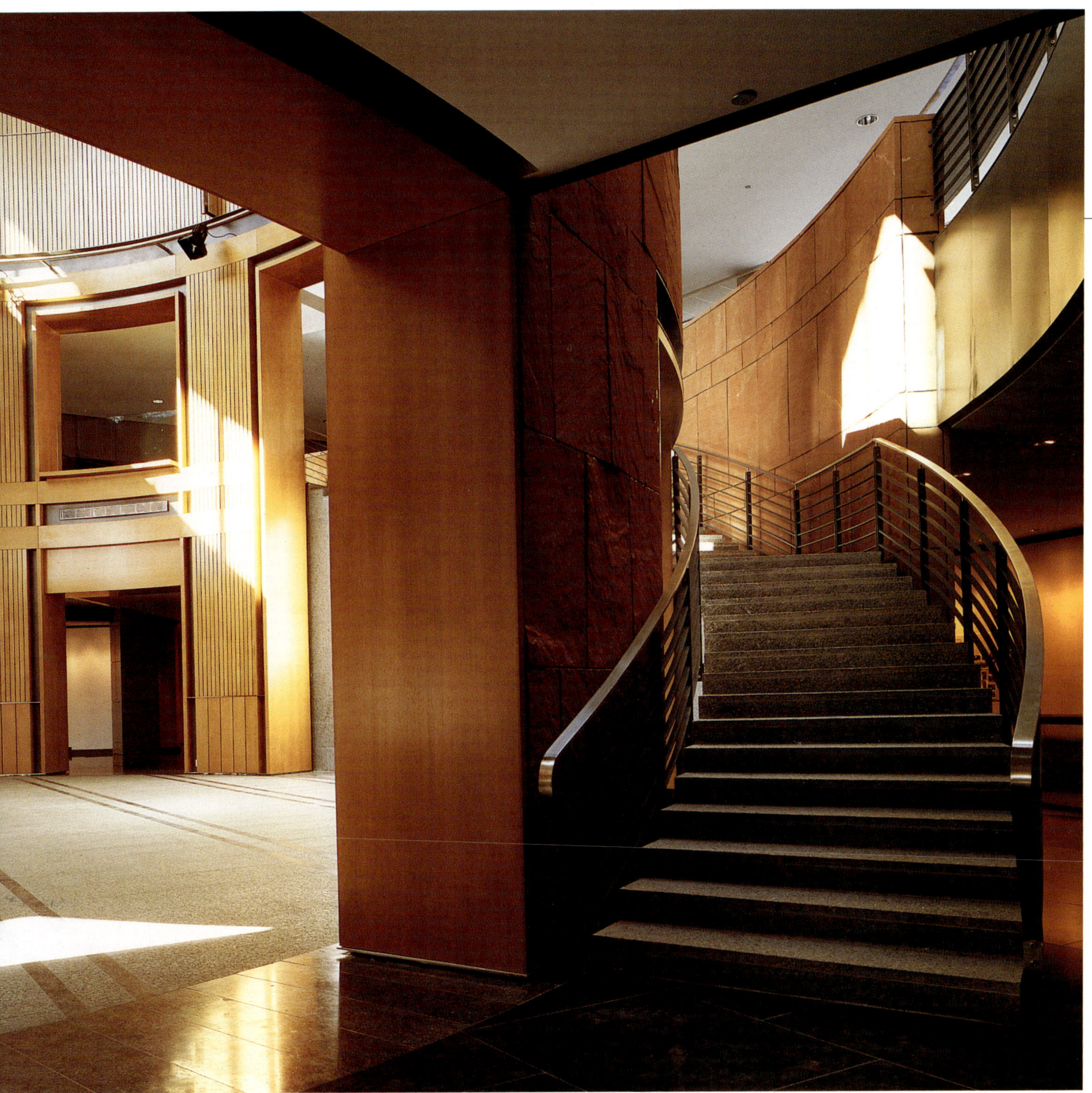

Joseph S. Stauffer Library, Queen's University

The winning design in a national competition, the Joseph S. Stauffer Library implements the vision of Queen's University to establish a library system for the twenty-first century, designed to house approximately one million volumes within a fully networked environment of digital information resources. Inspired by the vertical proportions and rich silhouettes of the university's architecture, as well as by other North American and European precedents, the project offers a contemporary interpretation of collegiate architecture while responding to its historic context.

The library occupies the northwest corner of the principal campus intersection at Union Street and University Avenue, with an octagonal stone-and-glass corner element serving as its main entrance. A four-story, skylit atrium forms the main ground-level circulation spine, running the length of the soaring central stack building and lighting large reading rooms on one side and small study carrels on the other.

Traditional and modern materials and forms are combined with building methods, and systems. The exterior material palette of limestone, wood, and metal refers to the history of limestone architecture in Kingston. Inside, cherry wood, painted metal, and stone banding evoke the warmth and richness of collegiate architecture. The color palette comprises buff yellow, lavender blue, and terra-cotta red, variations on the Queen's tricolor theme. Custom-designed furnishings incorporate wire management to provide desktop power and data delivery to all user stations.

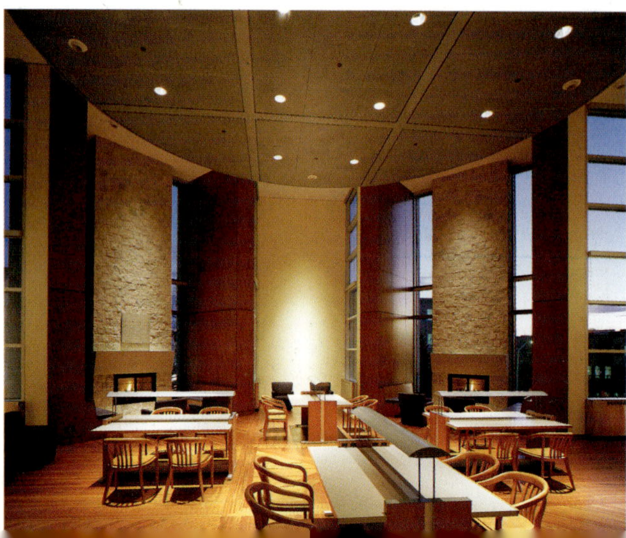

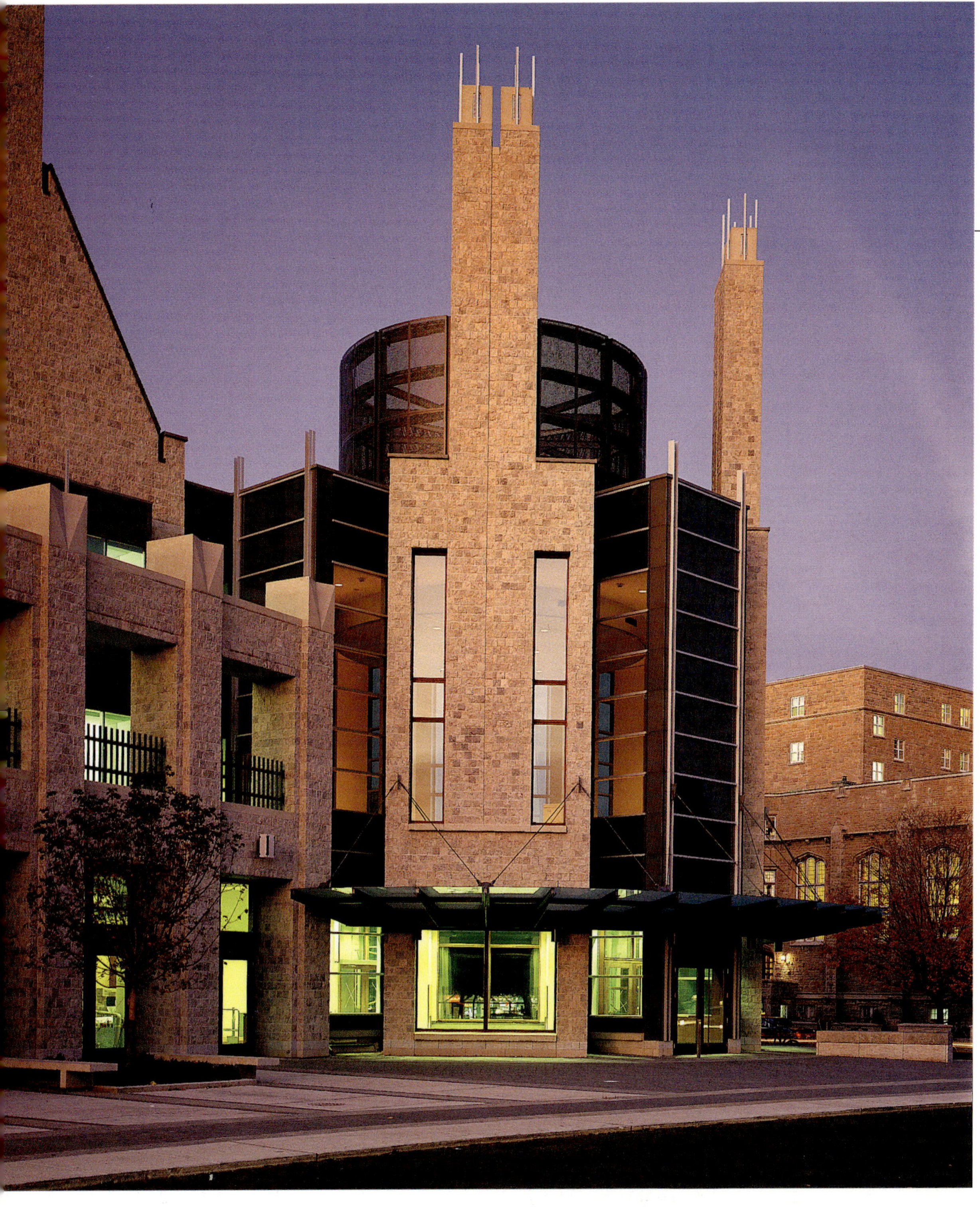

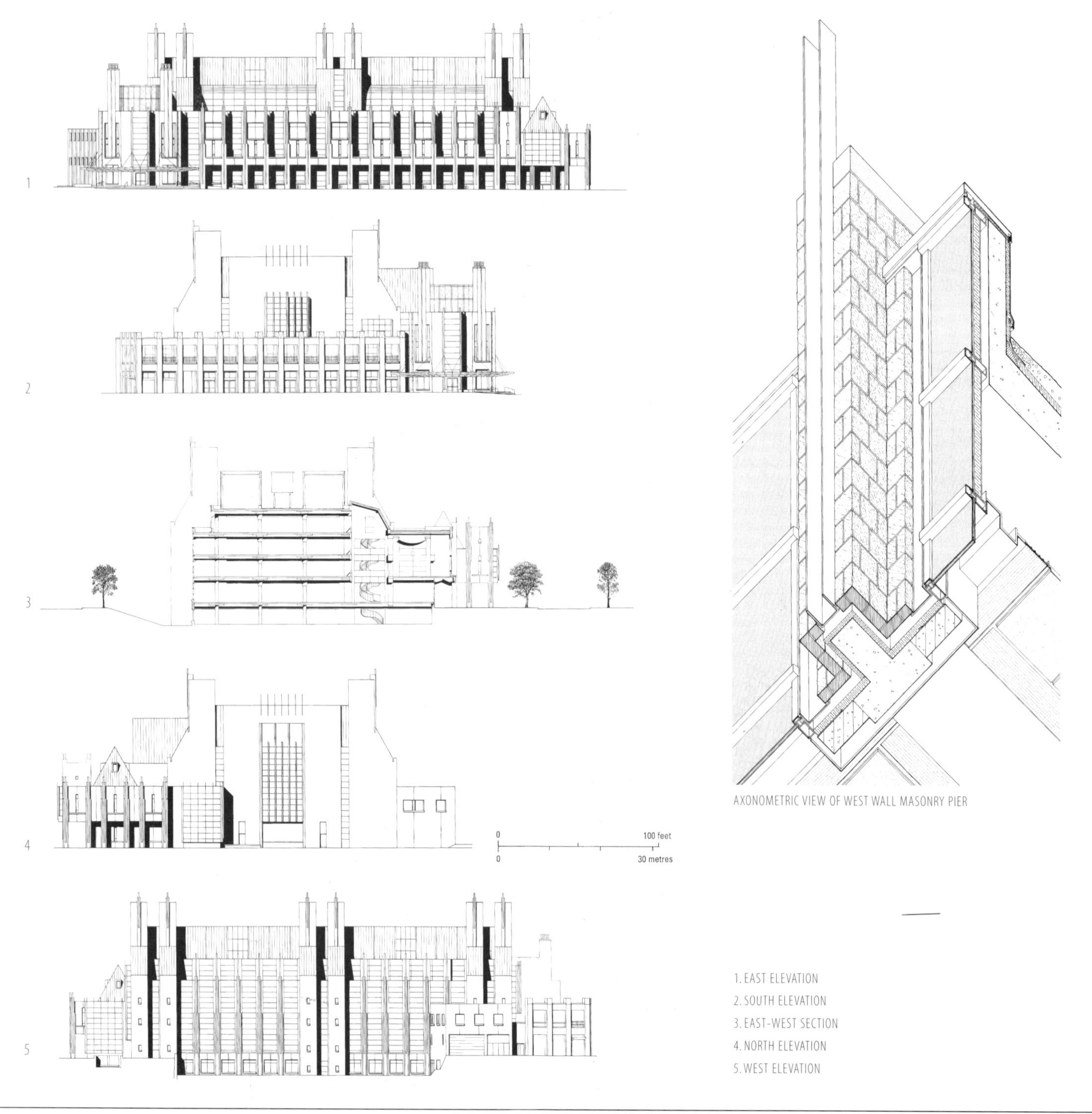

1
2
3
4
5
AXONOMETRIC VIEW OF WEST WALL MASONRY PIER
0
0
100 feet
30 metres
1. EAST ELEVATION
2. SOUTH ELEVATION
3. EAST-WEST SECTION
4. NORTH ELEVATION
5. WEST ELEVATION

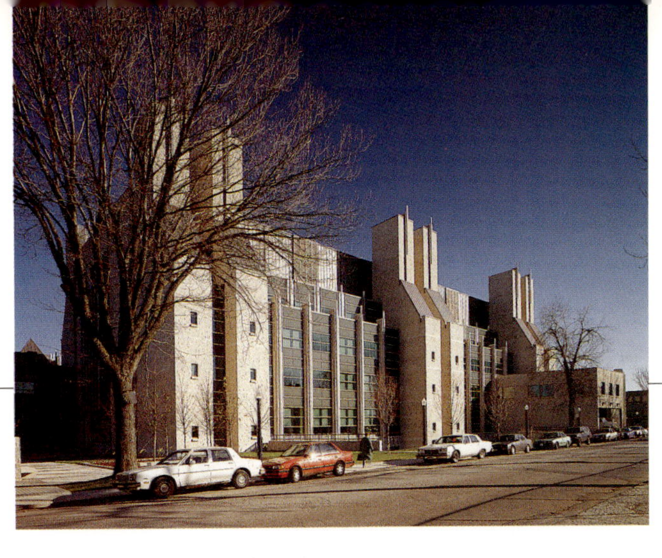

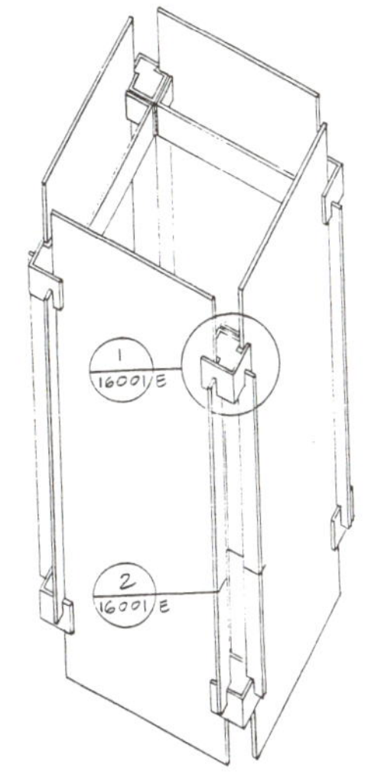

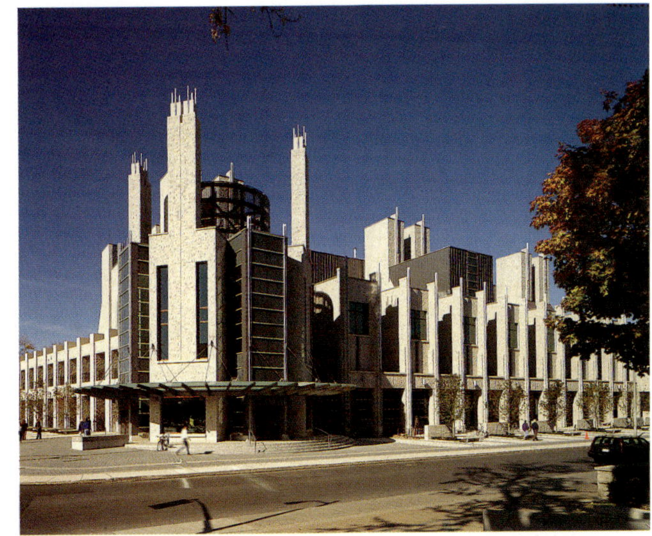

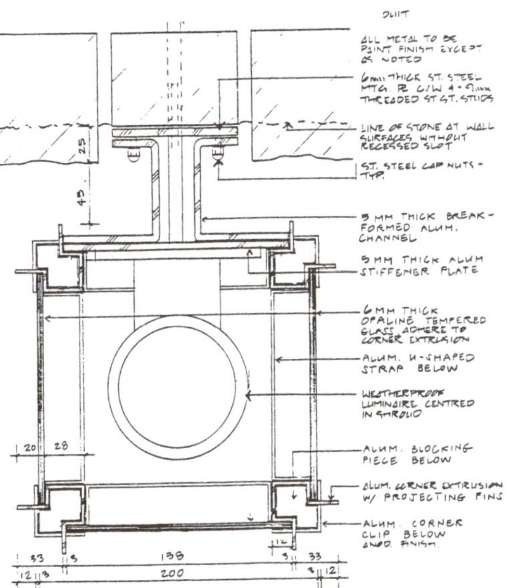

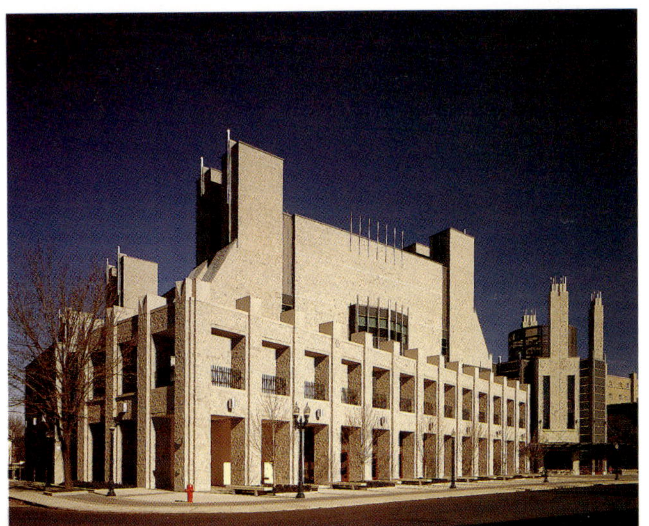

Split-faced limestone cladding harmonizes with the distinctive collegiate gothic character of the adjacent campus buildings. Piers and chimneys encircle the main corner entrance (center) and the Fireplace Reading Room above it.

DETAIL AND AXONOMETRIC OF CUSTOM LIGHT FIXTURE TYPE H3 USED OUTDOORS

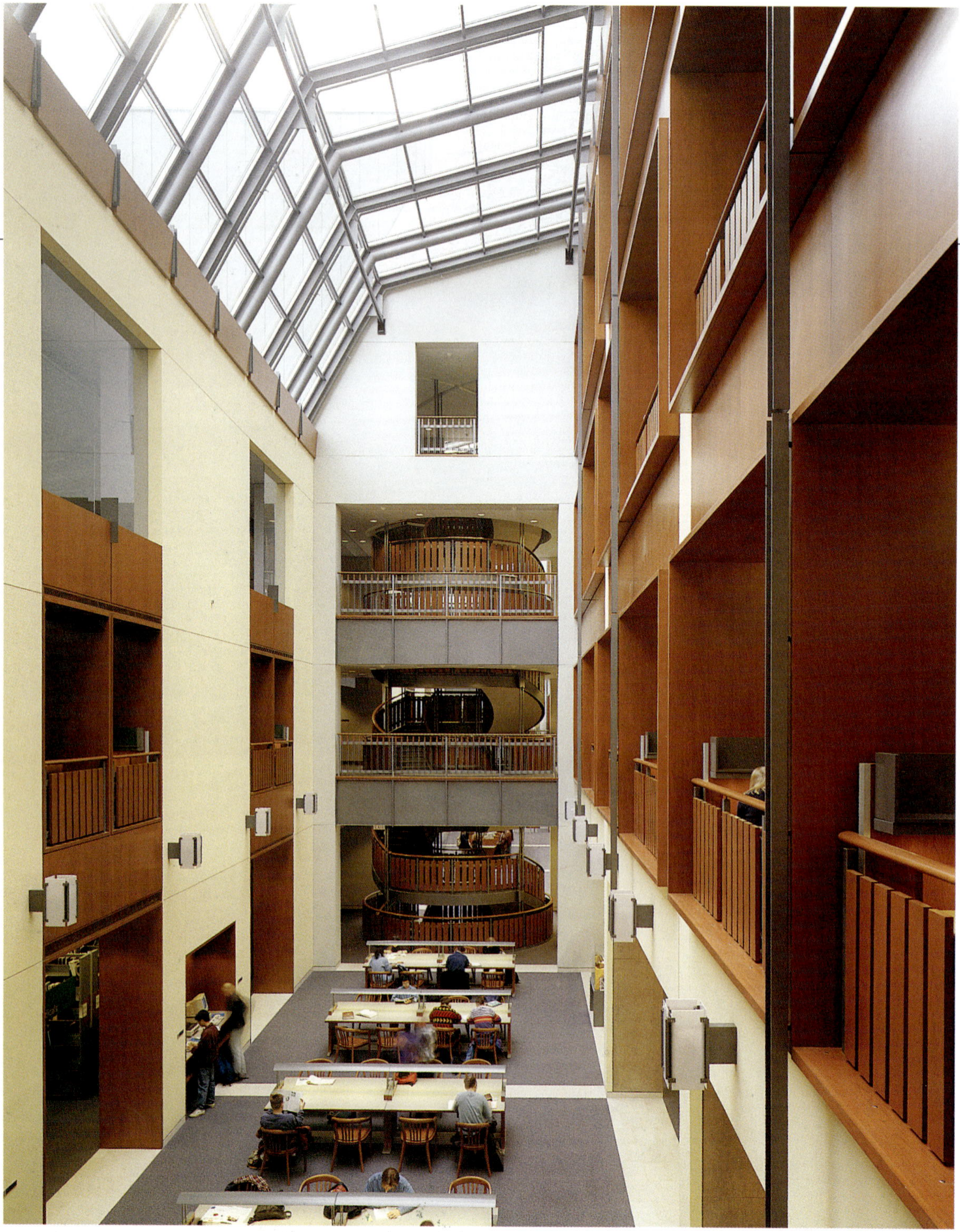

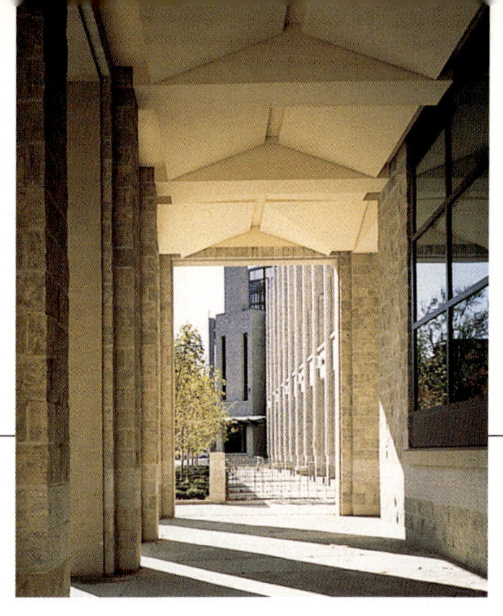

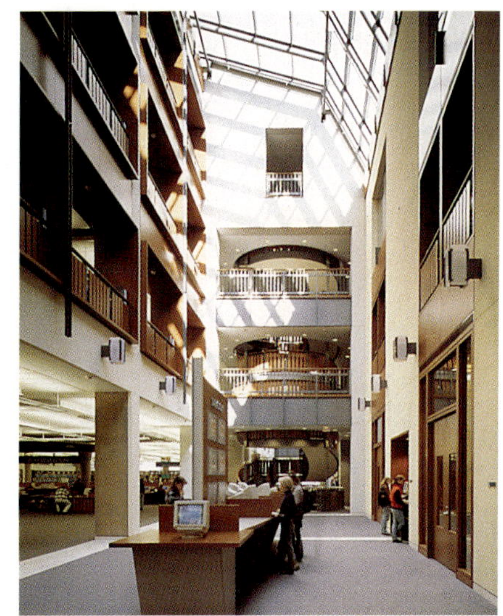

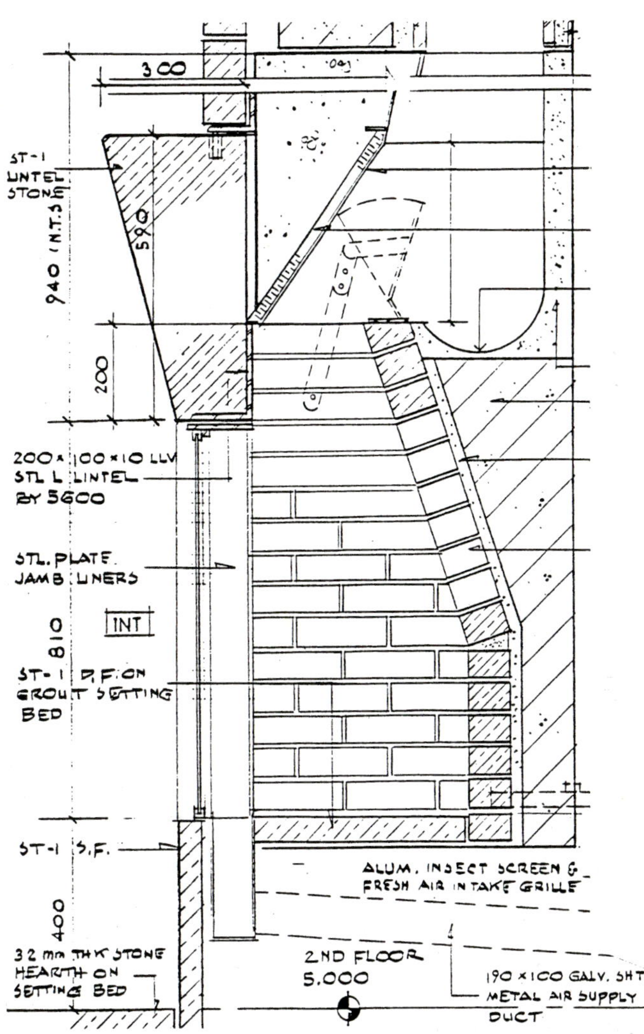

DETAIL OF READING ROOM FIREPLACE

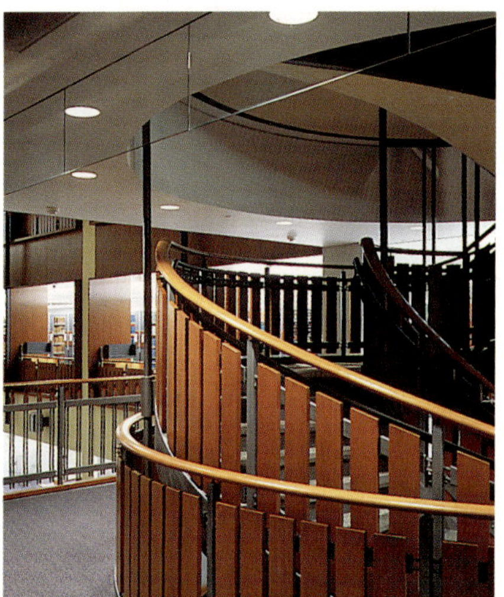

An exterior vaulted arcade leads to the octagonal main entrance (top). The soaring skylit atrium is lined with open carrels, work stations, and information desks (center, opposite page). A helical stair, suspended by cables from the roof, rises through the atrium to access the floors of the central stacks (bottom).

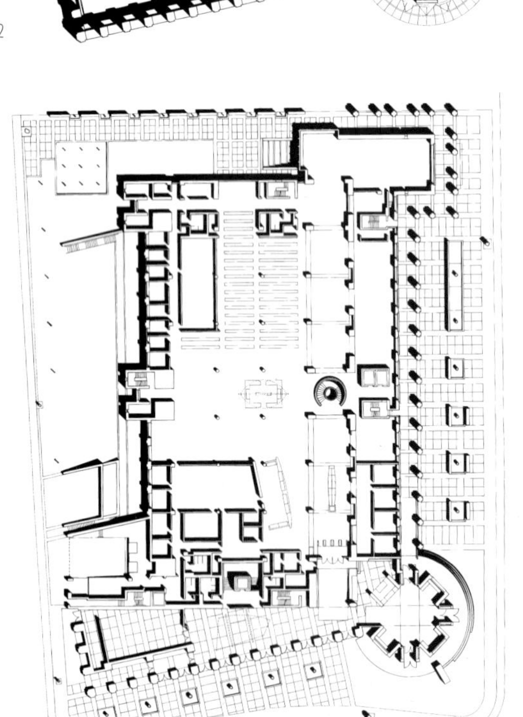

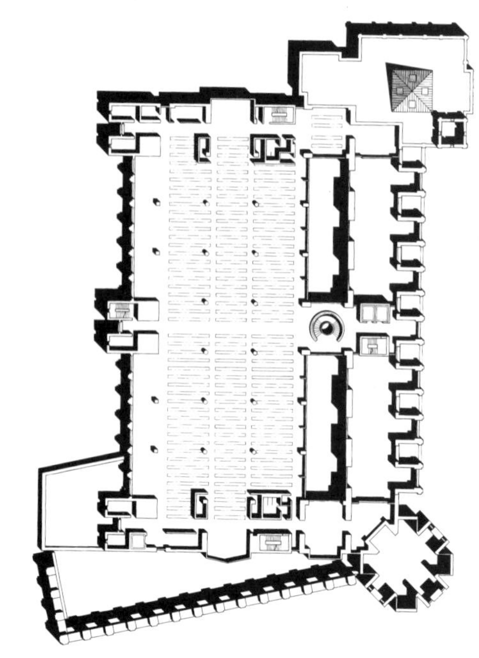

1. GROUND FLOOR PLAN
2. SECOND FLOOR PLAN
3. THIRD FLOOR PLAN
4. CONTEXT PLAN

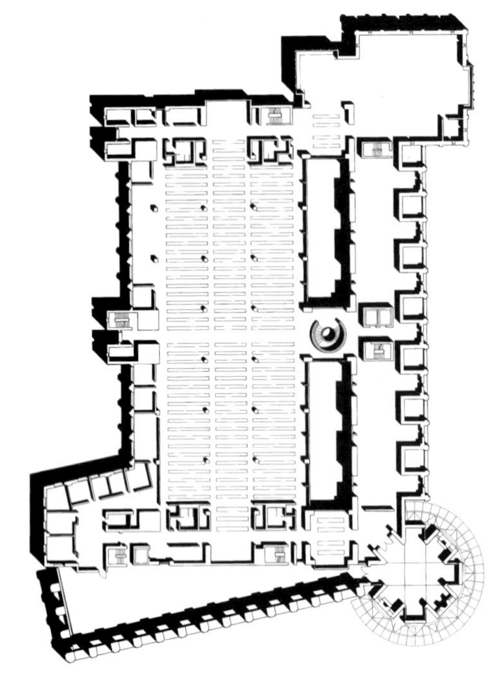

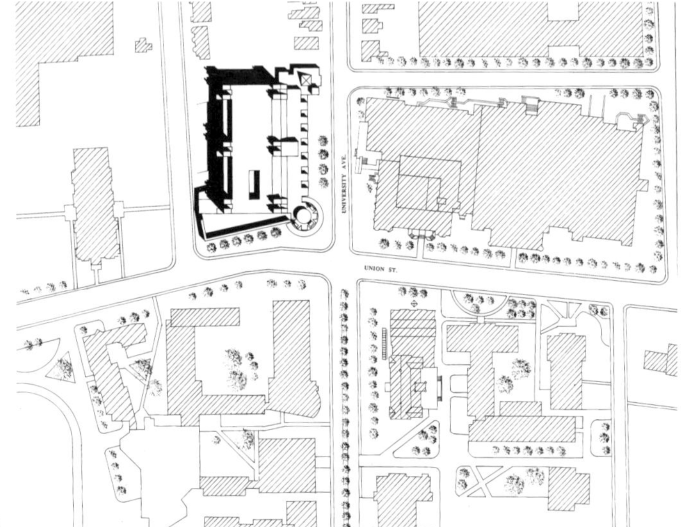

4

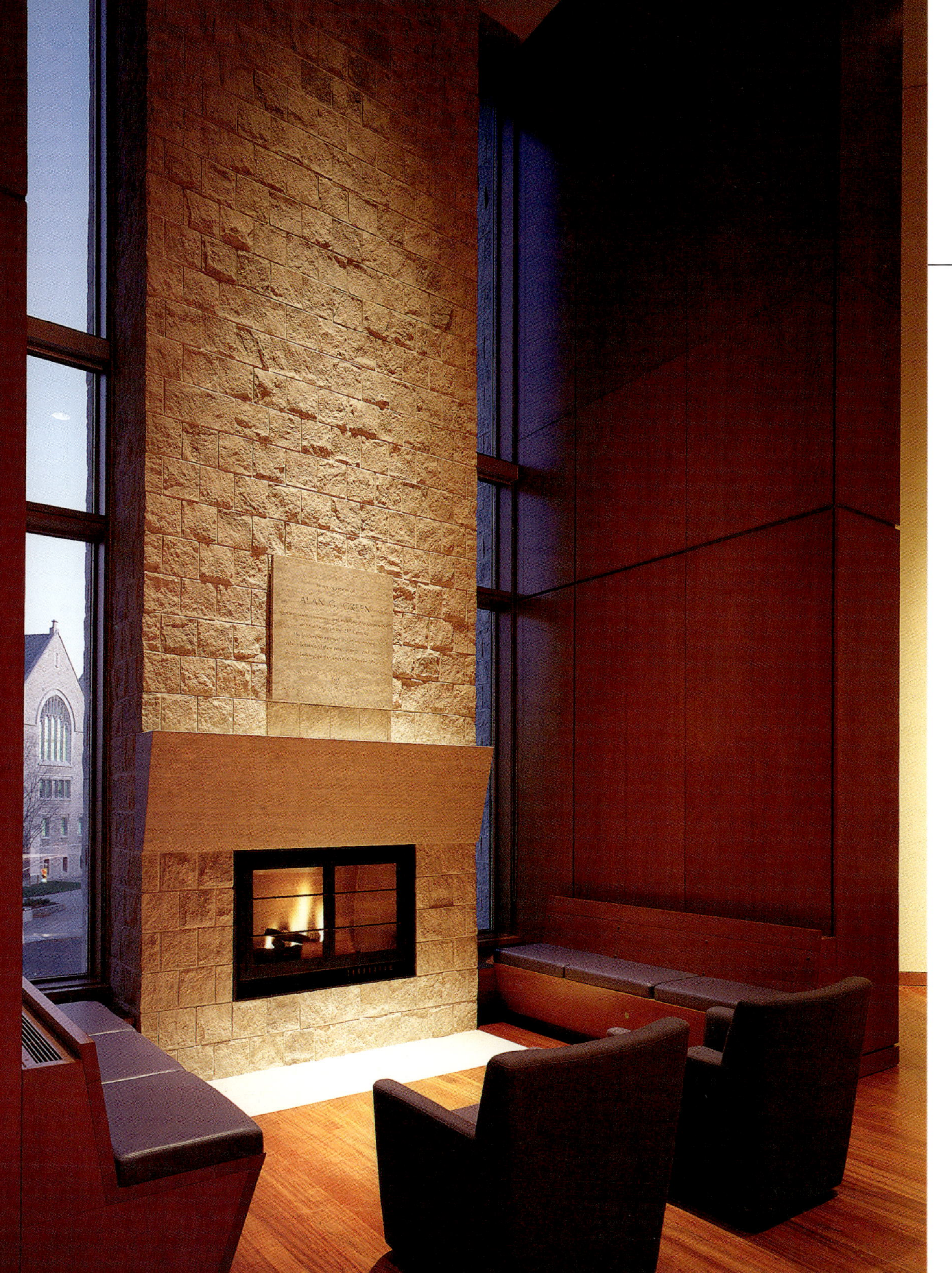

The Fireplace Reading Room exudes serenity for quiet, contemplative study, but can also function as a reception and meeting area for special events.

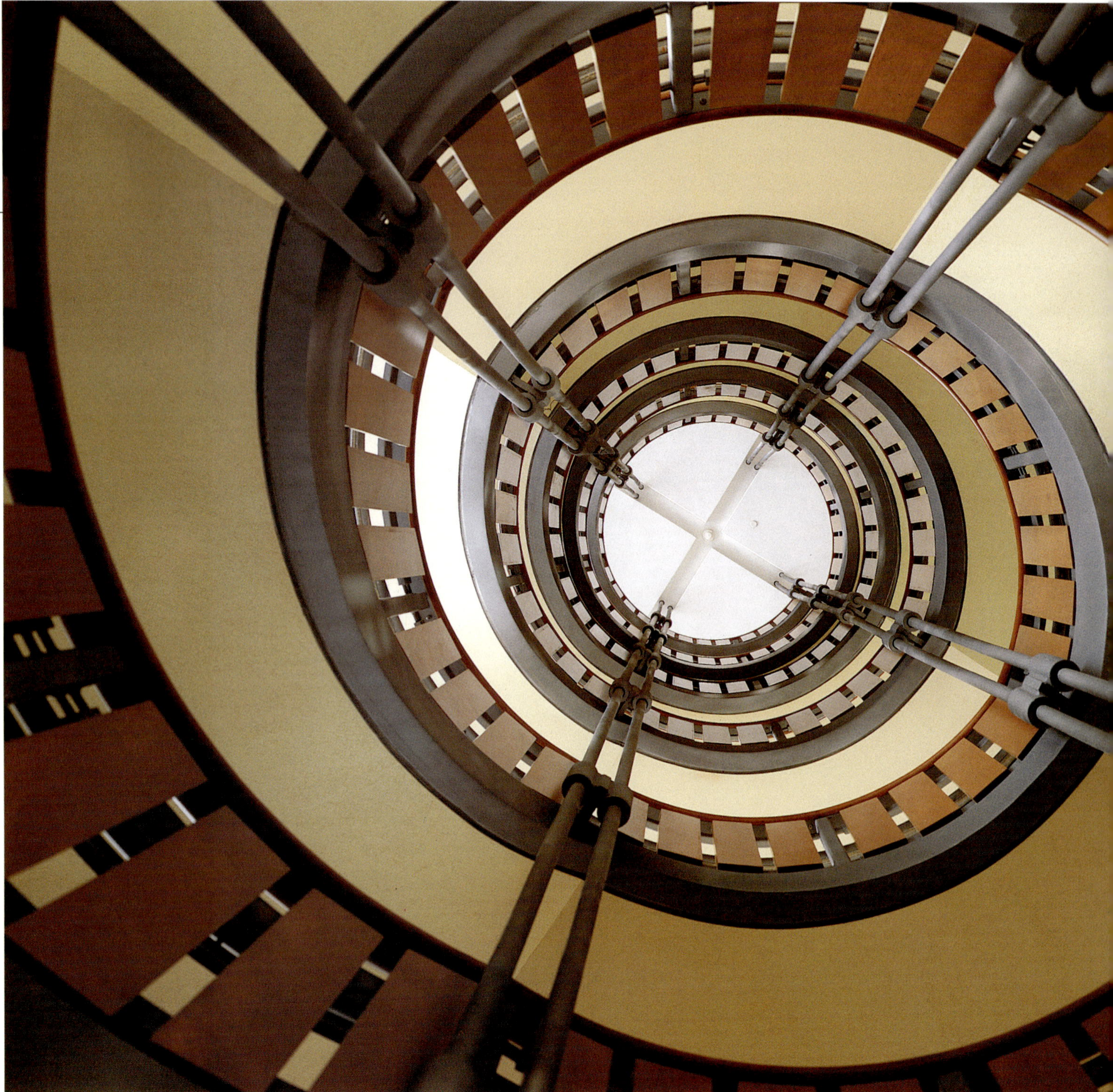

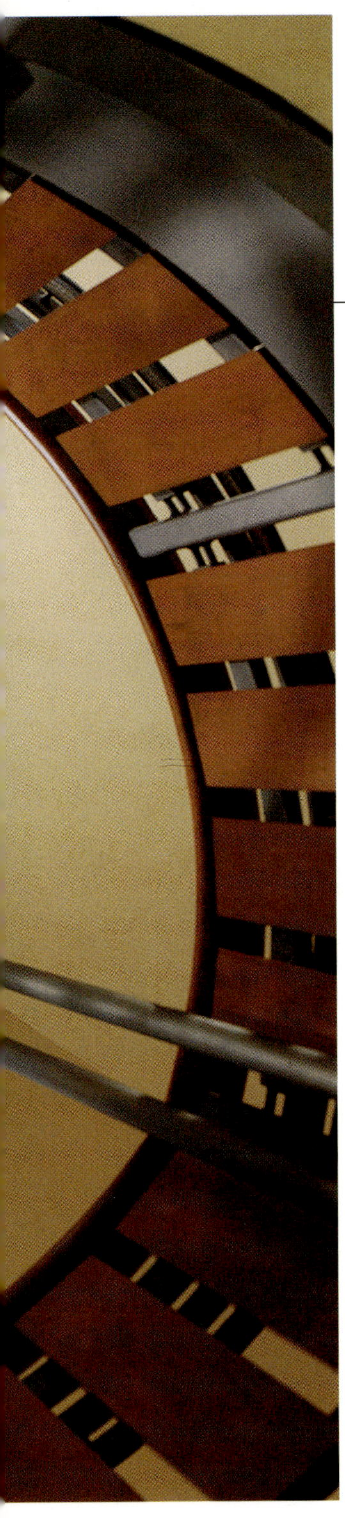

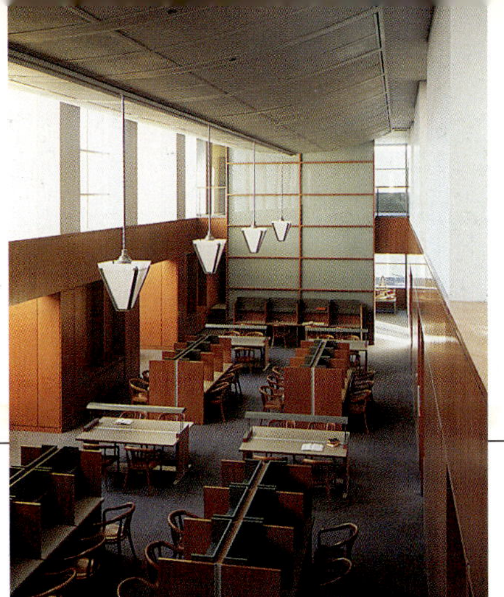

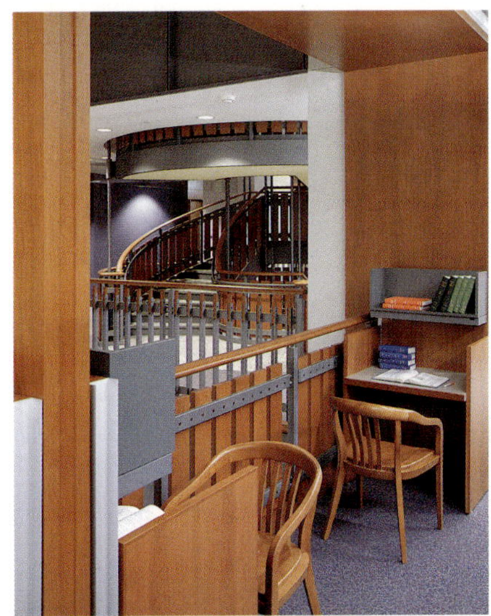

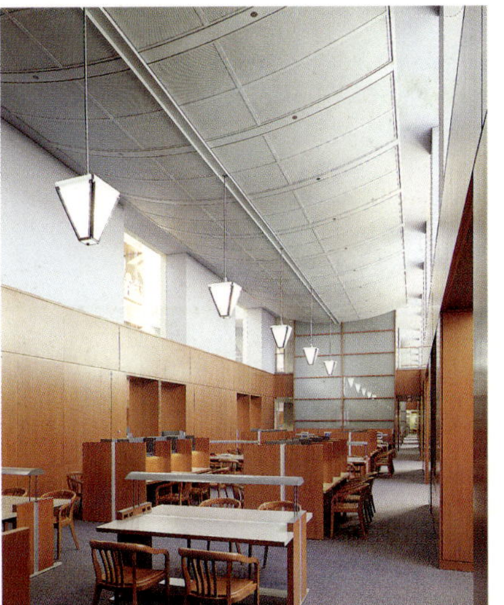

A detail of the helical stair's cherry wood balustrade (opposite page). Spacious reading rooms with natural light and high ceilings border one side of the atrium on several levels (top, bottom). Each level of the atrium itself is lined with study carrels adjacent to the book stacks (center).

Woodsworth College, University of Toronto

The renovations and additions to Woodsworth College culminate a long and passionate effort to establish the importance of part-time education at the University of Toronto, and reflect an intense collaboration between client and architect through all stages of the project.

Although generously funded by government and private sources, the project is distinguished by the unparalleled financial support of the student body. In a gesture of commitment to quality in design and materials, a self-imposed student levy provided more than half of the total construction cost.

To meet the needs of the College and its growing student population, the project unites three existing structures—a Victorian residence (1891), an ROTC Drill Hall (1939–1941), and an Officer's Mess—into one cohesive complex. A new L-shaped building defines a courtyard lined by a slightly raised, indoor-outdoor hall. A reinterpretation of the traditional academic quadrangle and cloister, the new complex connects the old and new structures both physically and symbolically.

As a reflection of the permanence of the institution and its noble goals, and in an effort to bring Woodsworth to a position of parity with the older, established colleges of the University of Toronto, an emphasis is placed on enduring value, material quality and craftsmanship. A material palette of red brick, Quebec granite, and limestone, and hand-crafted details of steel and wood elements, make subtle references to traditional collegiate architecture. The new facility is completely accessible to the physically challenged.

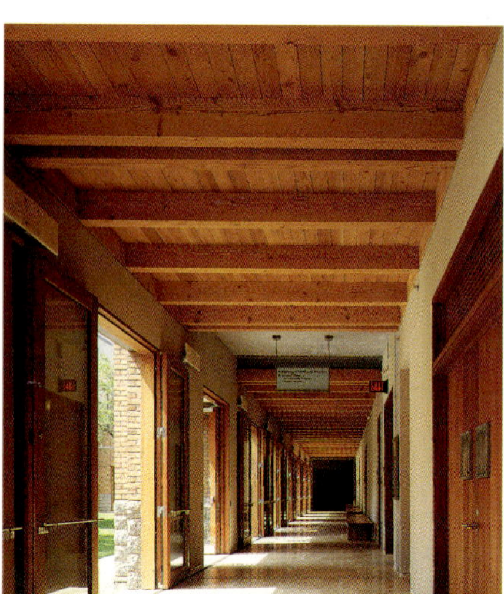

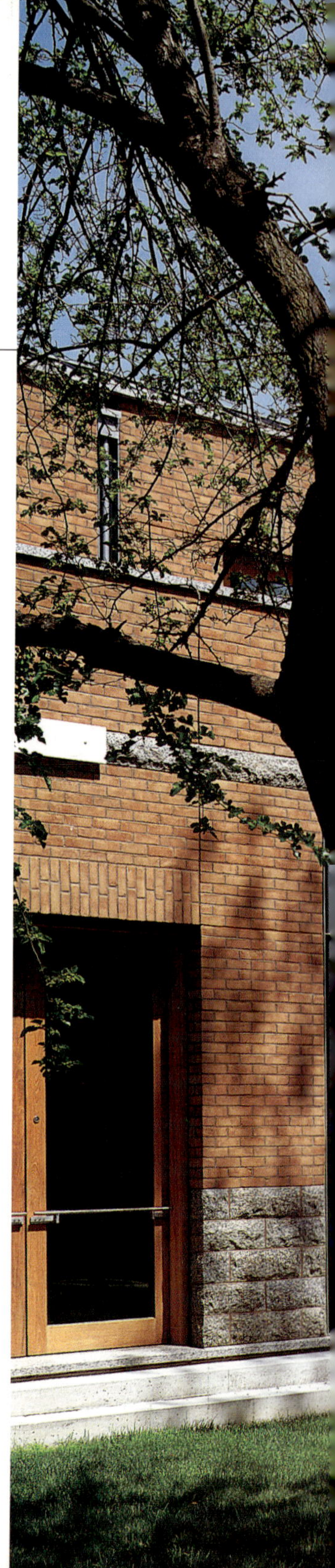

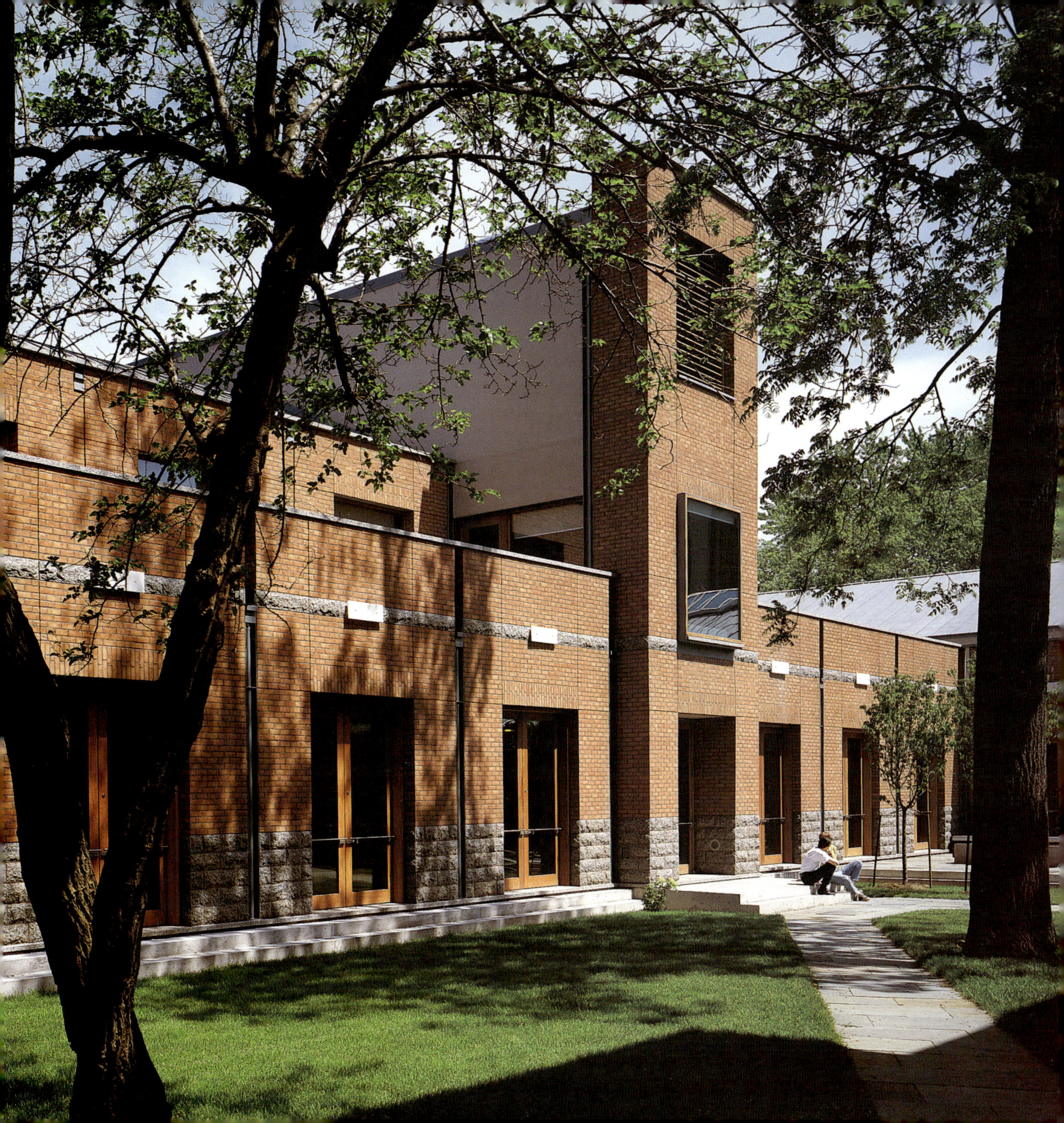

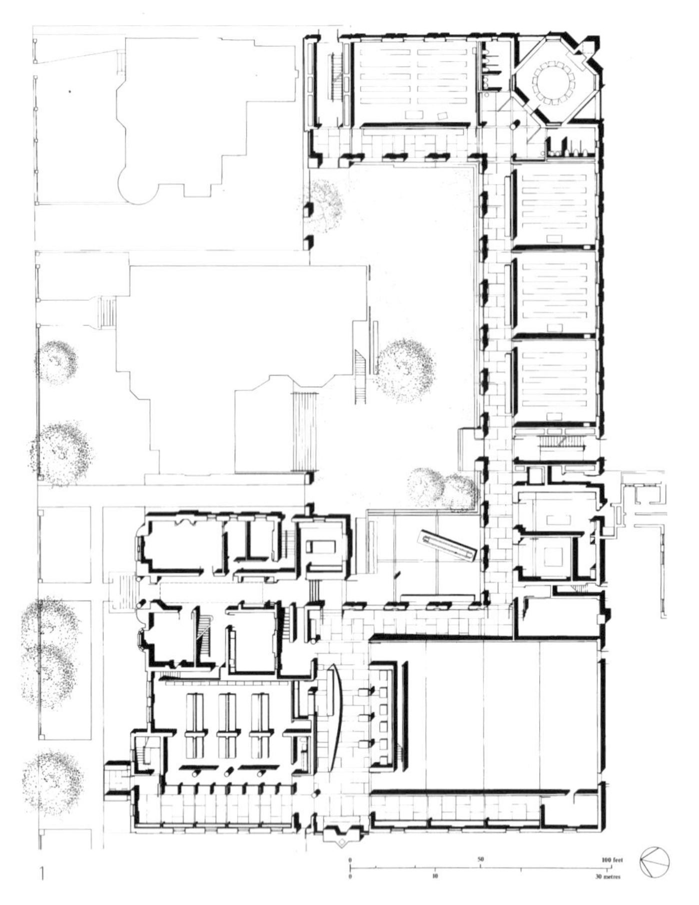

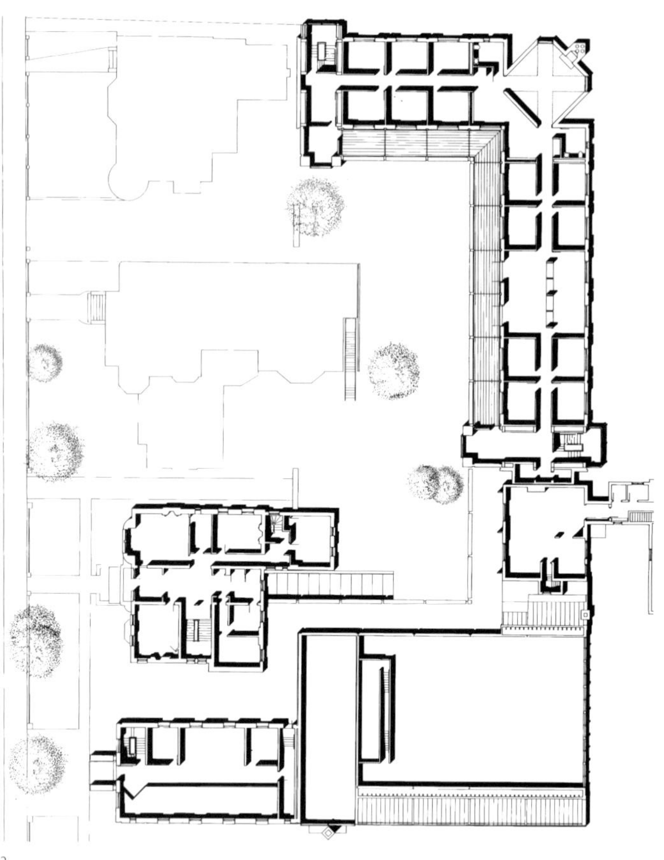

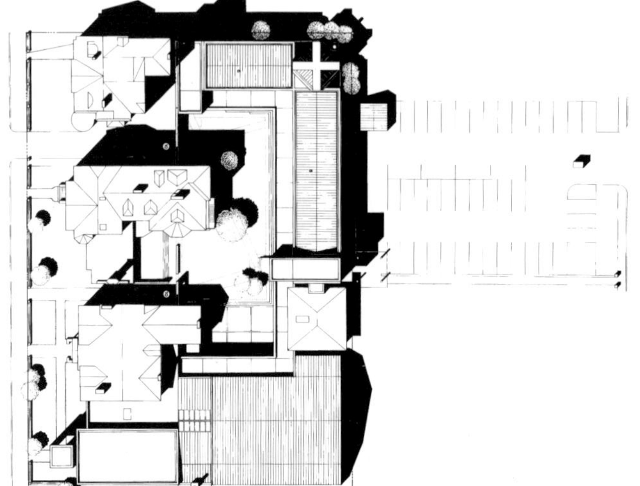

1. GROUND FLOOR PLAN
2. SECOND FLOOR PLAN
3. SITE PLAN

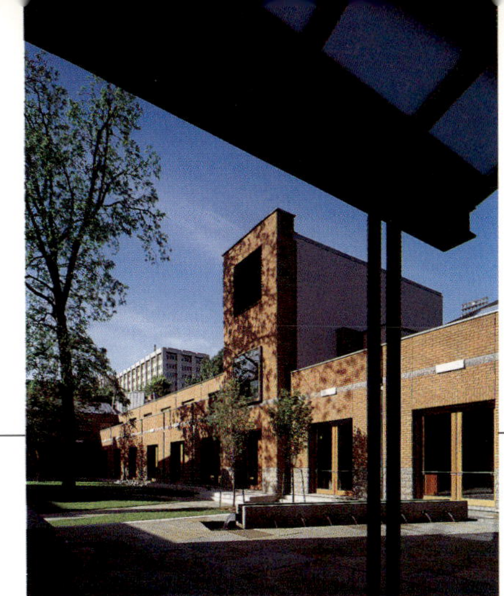

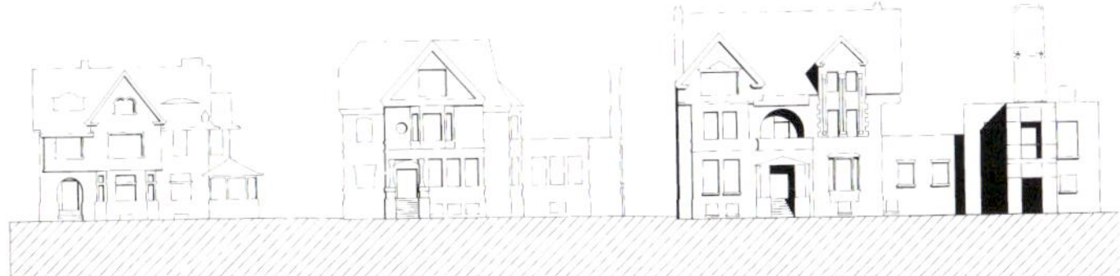

WEST ELEVATION

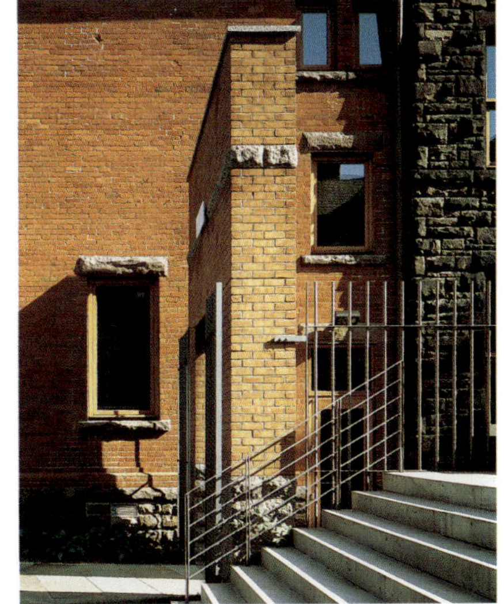

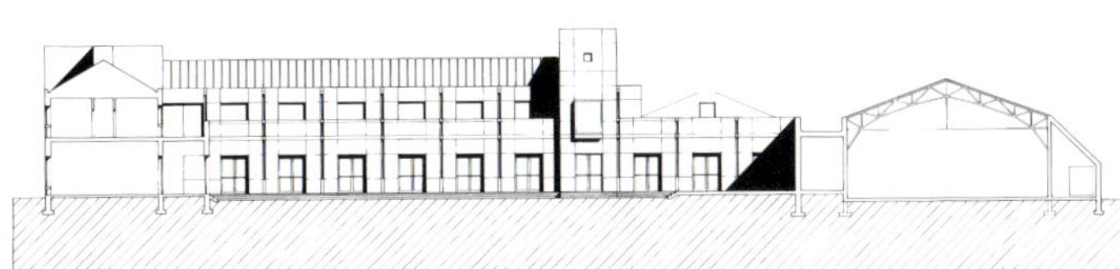

EAST COURT ELEVATION

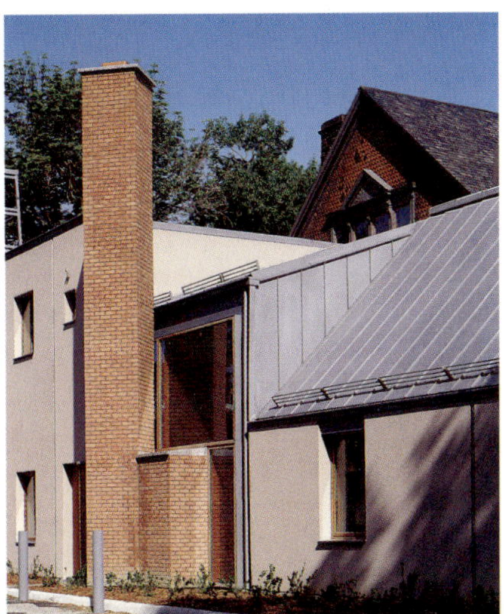

New buildings at Woodsworth College are integrated with three nineteenth-century historic houses and a 1941 ROTC Drill Hall. Together they form a new quadrangle reminiscent of the colleges at great British and American universities.

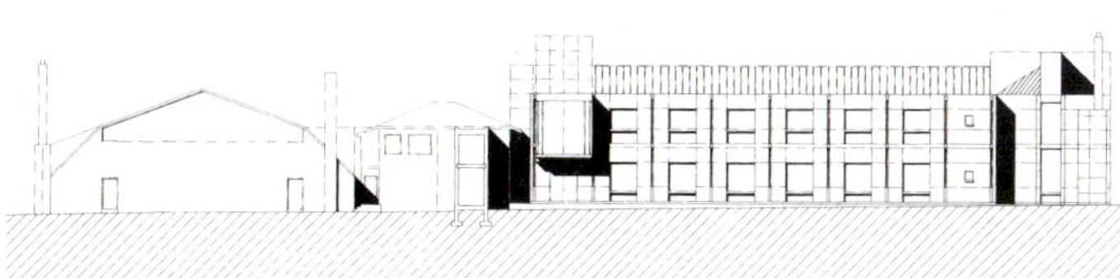

EAST ELEVATION

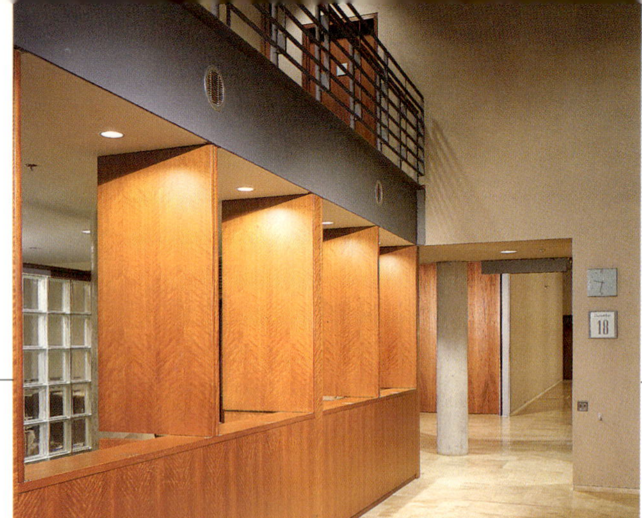

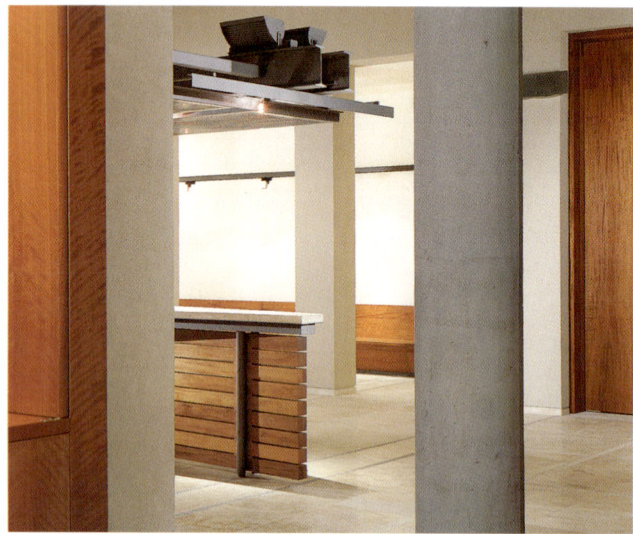

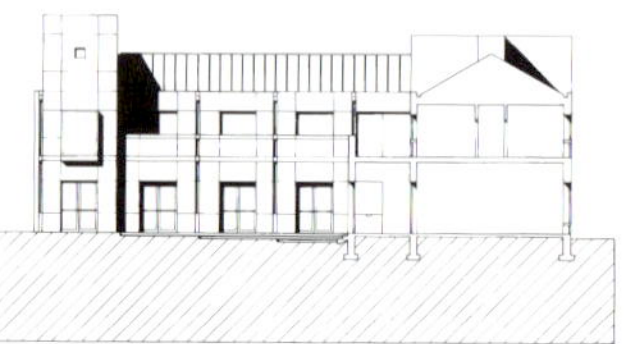

NORTH COURT ELEVATION

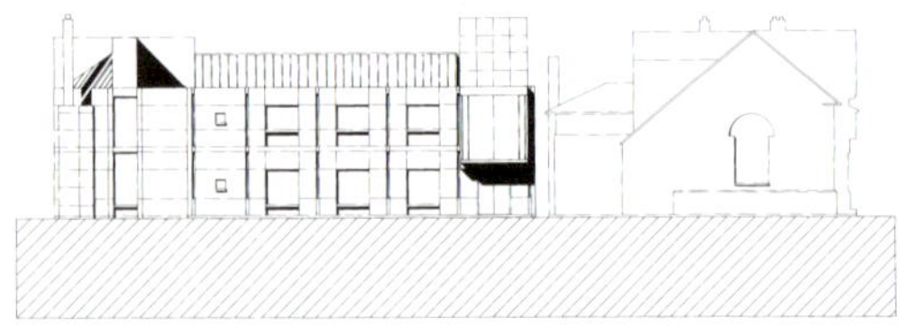

NORTH ELEVATION

The sequence of interior spaces begins at a reception desk with large mahogany shutters (top) and leads to the café and bar area, which has become the focus of social activity at the College (center, bottom, opposite page). Hand-crafted details of wood, glass, and stone punctuate and give texture to spaces throughout the complex.

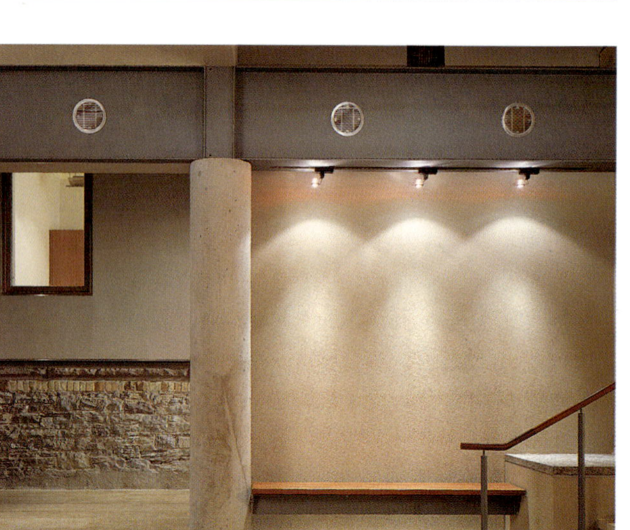

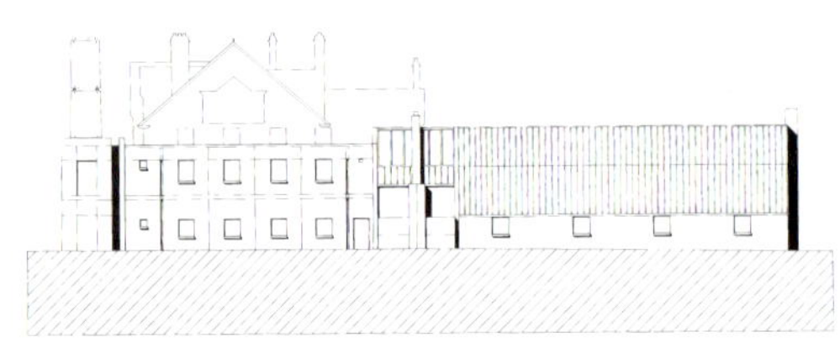

SOUTH ELEVATION

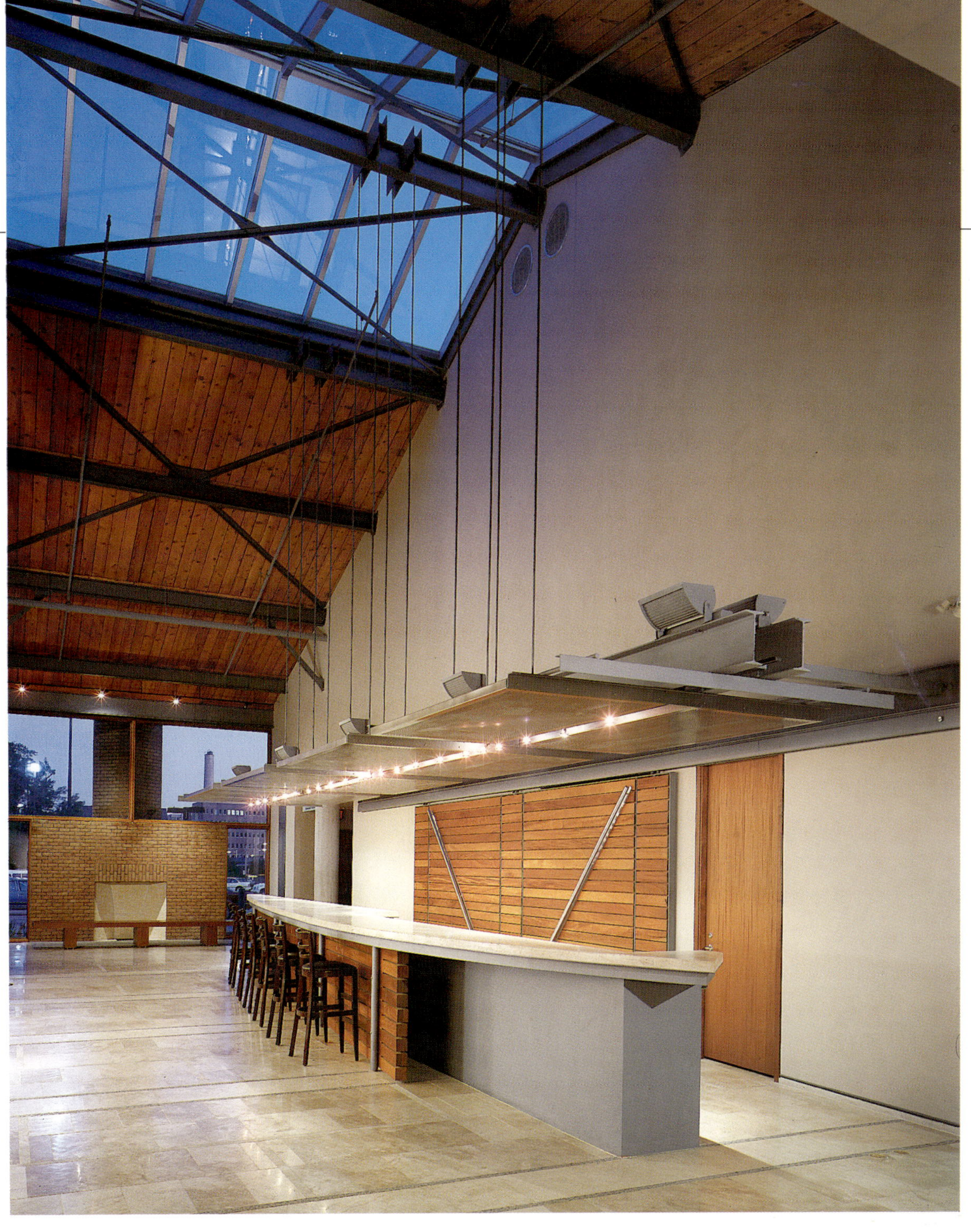

Fields Institute, University of Toronto

The Fields Institute was founded in 1991 as an advanced institute for research in the mathematical sciences. The design for the Institute's new home, located at the downtown campus of the University of Toronto, explores the creativity of mathematics in its juxtaposition of consistent proportions, rhythm, and order with serendipitous forms and spontaneous events.

A masonry wall of red brick and rusticated limestone forms a discreet public facade, while the back of the building, facing the interior of the street block, is framed by two circulation towers clad in purple stucco. Inside, a four-story structure of exposed concrete defines a central atrium with open corridor-balconies around its perimeter. Because the Fields Institute sought a supportive environment for both collaborative and independent working modes, these ambulatory spaces along with slate blackboards throughout the building are designed to accommodate informal, peripatetic mathematical research. Three dynamic elements organized along the building's central axis animate the atrium space: a large wood-burning fireplace finished with Italian stucco, a wood-paneled helical stair, and an elliptical reception desk.

The roof, a single plane of Douglas-fir decking suspended from a system of exposed metal trusses creates clerestory windows on all four sides. The interior material palette combines plaster walls, carpet, and tinted concrete for simplicity, economy, and warmth, whereas the selective use of wood, metal, and stone makes reference to the tradition of collegiate architecture at the University of Toronto.

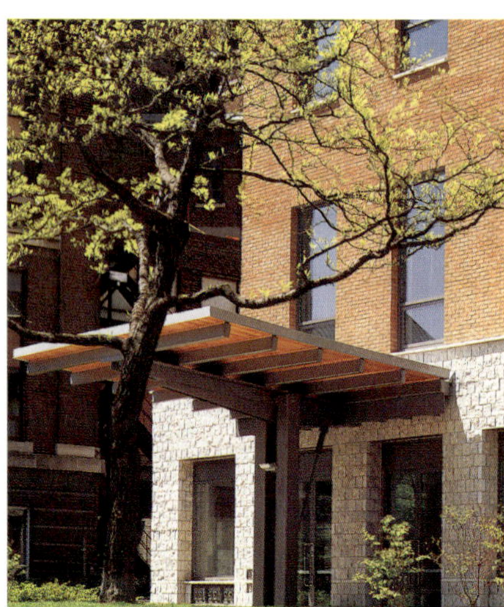

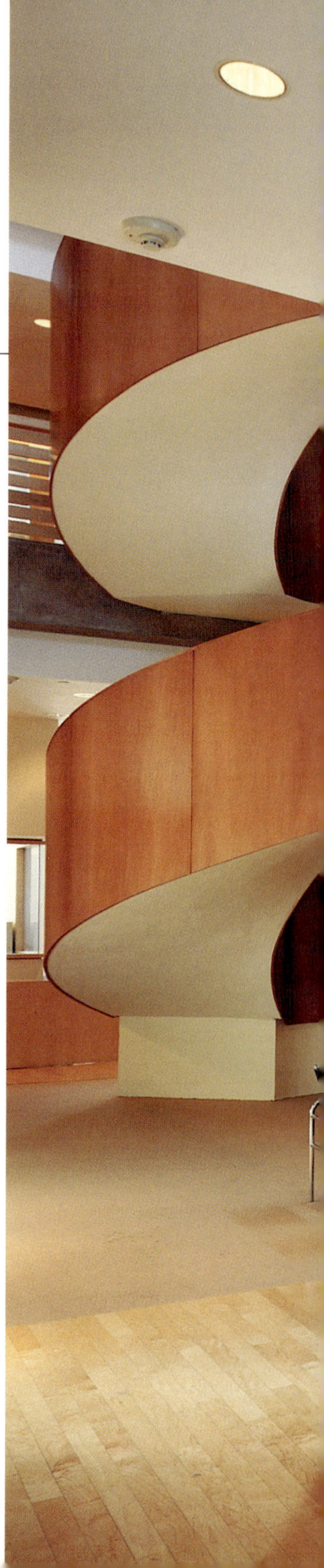

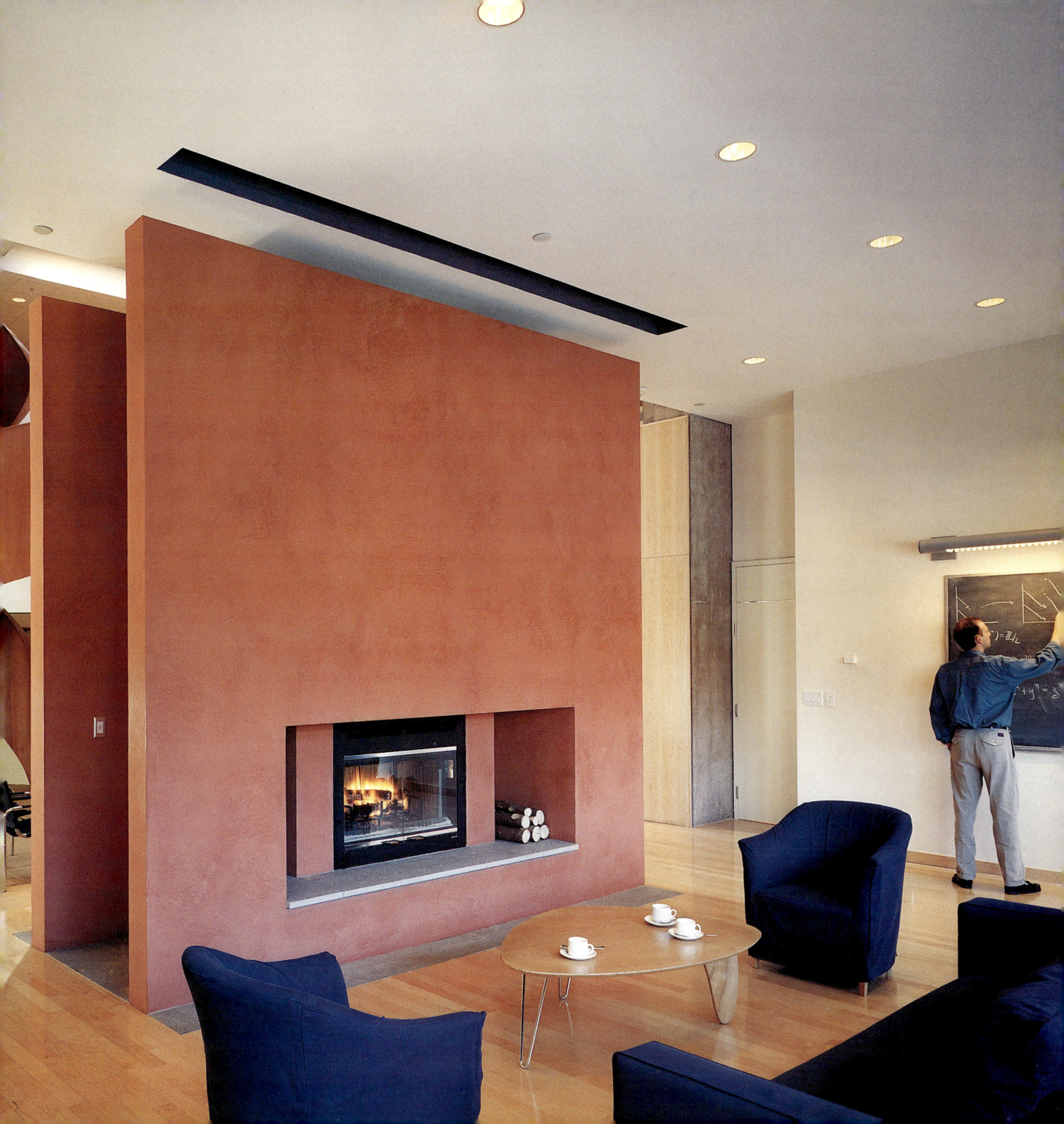

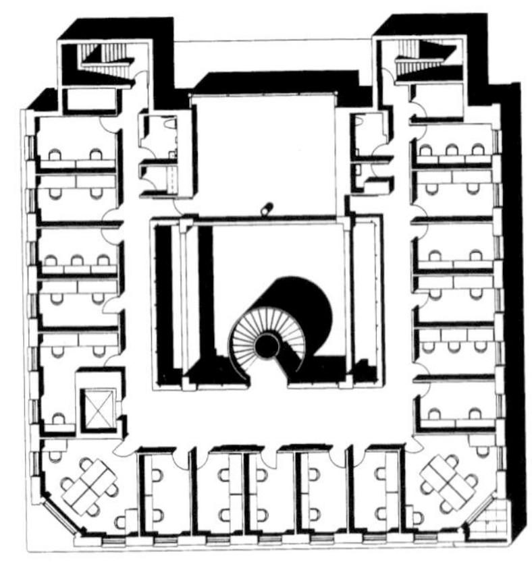

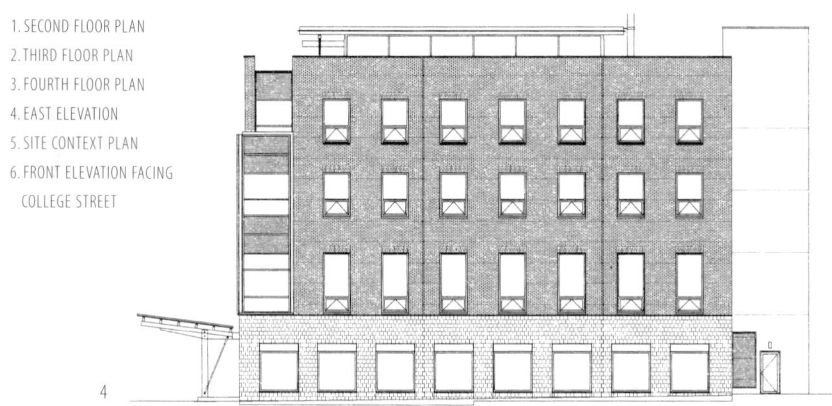

1. SECOND FLOOR PLAN
2. THIRD FLOOR PLAN
3. FOURTH FLOOR PLAN
4. EAST ELEVATION
5. SITE CONTEXT PLAN
6. FRONT ELEVATION FACING
   COLLEGE STREET

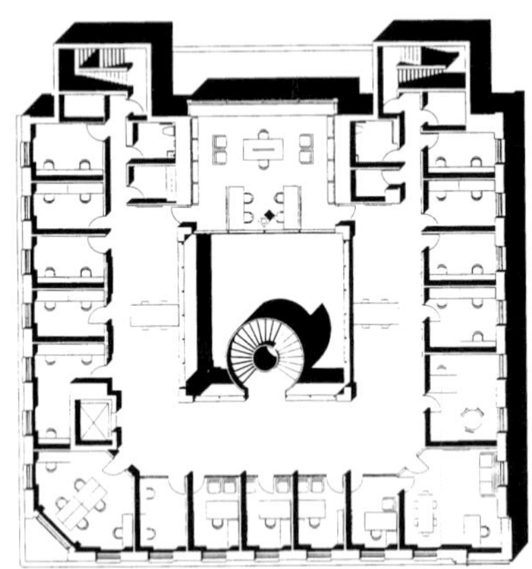

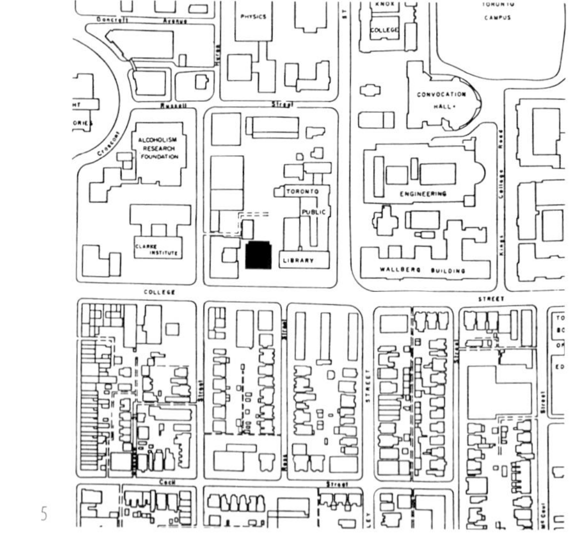

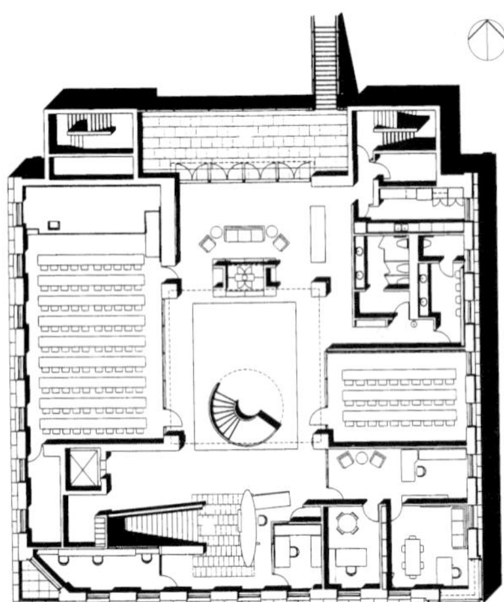

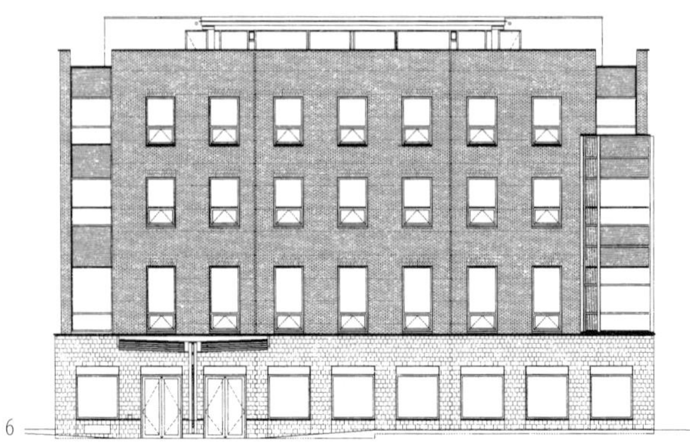

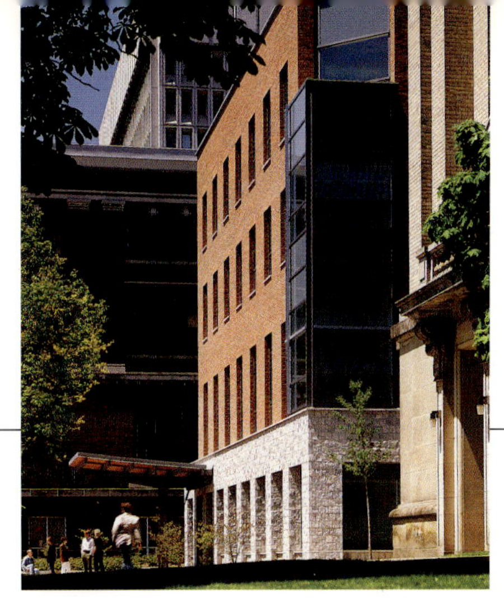

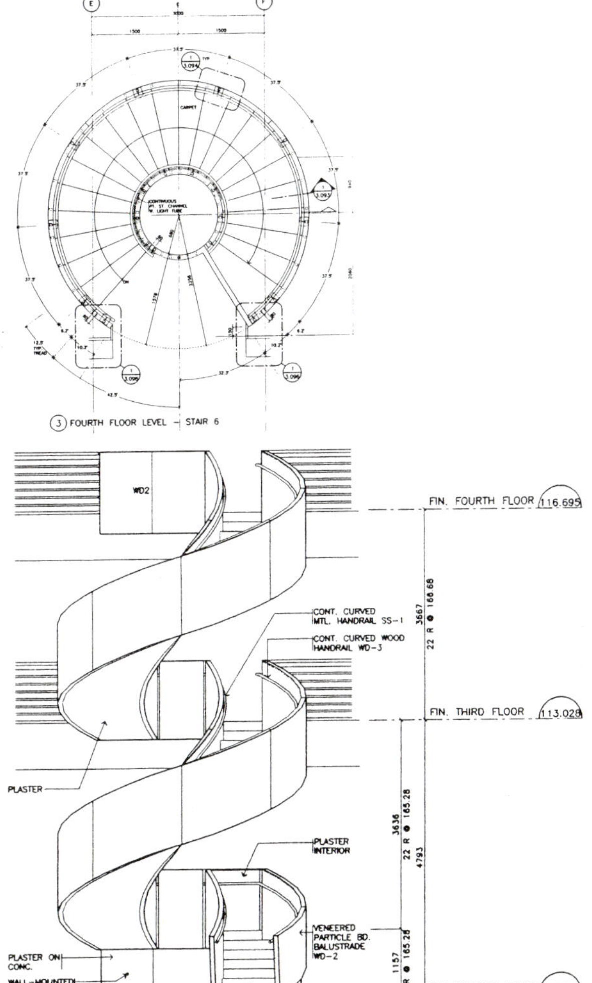

3 FOURTH FLOOR LEVEL — STAIR 6

WD2

CONT. CURVED MTL. HANDRAIL SS-1

CONT. CURVED WOOD HANDRAIL WD-3

FIN. FOURTH FLOOR 116.695

PLASTER

FIN. THIRD FLOOR 113.028

PLASTER INTERIOR

VENEERED PARTICLE BD. BALUSTRADE WD-2

PLASTER ON CONC.

WALL-MOUNTED SPRINKLER

FIN. SECOND FLOOR 108.235

CARPET

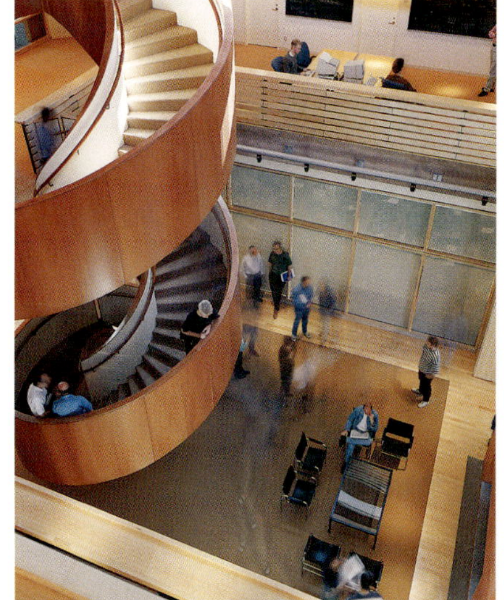

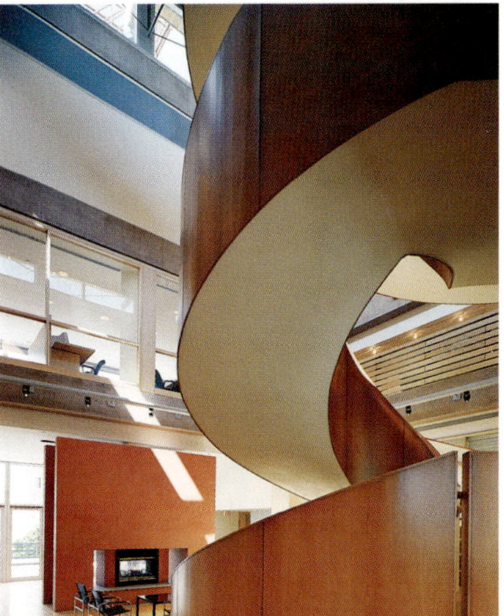

The facade of the Fields Institute mediates between two Beaux-Arts landmarks on either side of the building (top). Inside, a dramatic helical stair rises through an atrium lined with open corridors for informal meetings and brain-storming sessions (middle). A fireplace with twin openings lies on axis with the helical stair (bottom).

Walter Carsen Centre for the National Ballet of Canada

Named after its donor, Walter Carsen, the project is nestled between the Gardiner Expressway and Lake Ontario, in the base of the King's Landing Condominium designed by Arthur Erickson in 1982. The new Carsen Centre consolidates the National Ballet of Canada (NBC) organization under one roof for the first time in its history. Reconfigured existing spaces offer views of Toronto's skyline to the north and the waterfront to the south, while dancers' lounges and terraces on the lower two floors open to expansive views of the Lake Ontario. Corridors terminate with glazed screens that glow with daylight and frame views to the urban landscape.

Structural and spatial features of the design reinterpret elements associated with performance: the curtain, stage, and scenic backdrop. Thus, in the double-height reception hall, two concrete piers define the space as a type of stage; a mesh screen hangs on a light metal frame suspended from the ceiling; and a folded steel-plate stair, veiled by the screen, rises like a backdrop to the activity taking place before it. Circulation systems, studios, and administrative spaces are seen as design opportunities to choreograph the body's movement through space. Cadence, rhythm, expansion, contraction, and variation inspire the forms and expression of ceiling, wall, and floor surfaces. To meet the requirements for an economic but durable environment, the project employs tough, cost-effective materials such as bush-hammered concrete, thick rubber floor tiles, and painted steel. Translucent, metal-framed screens layered over punched wall openings recall the strong yet ephemeral gestures formed by the dancer's body in motion.

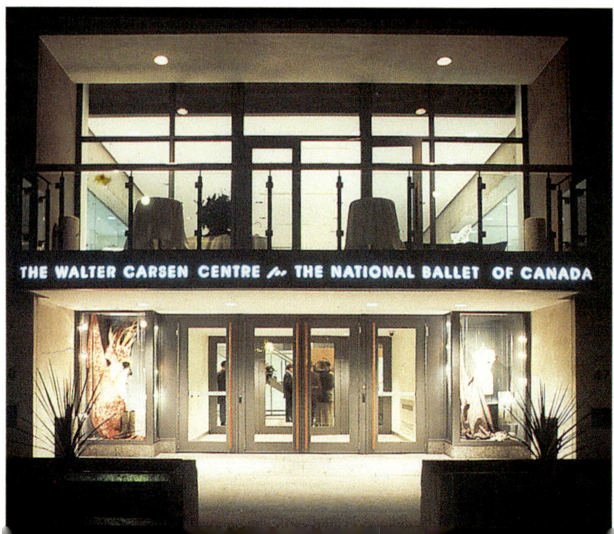

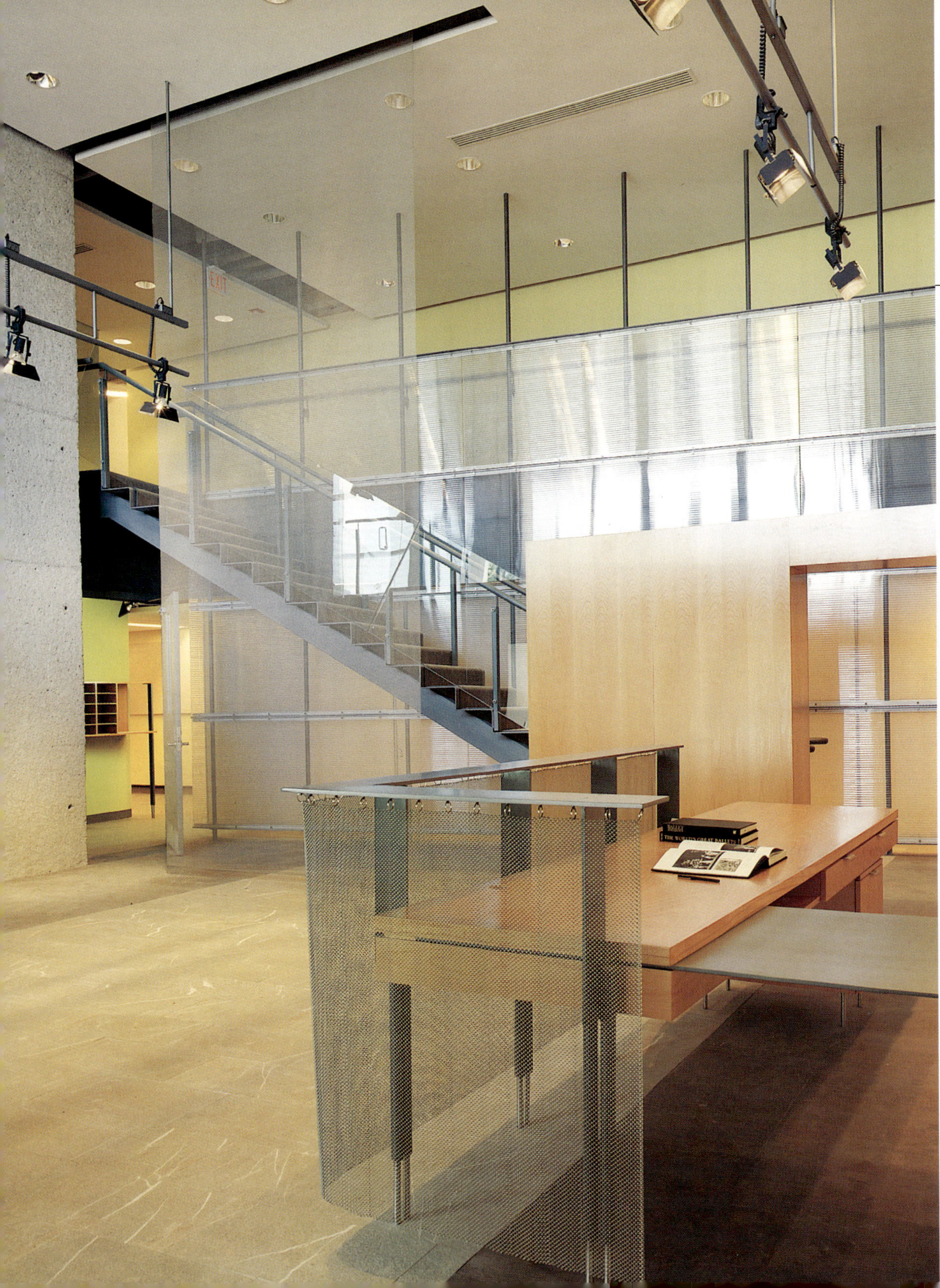

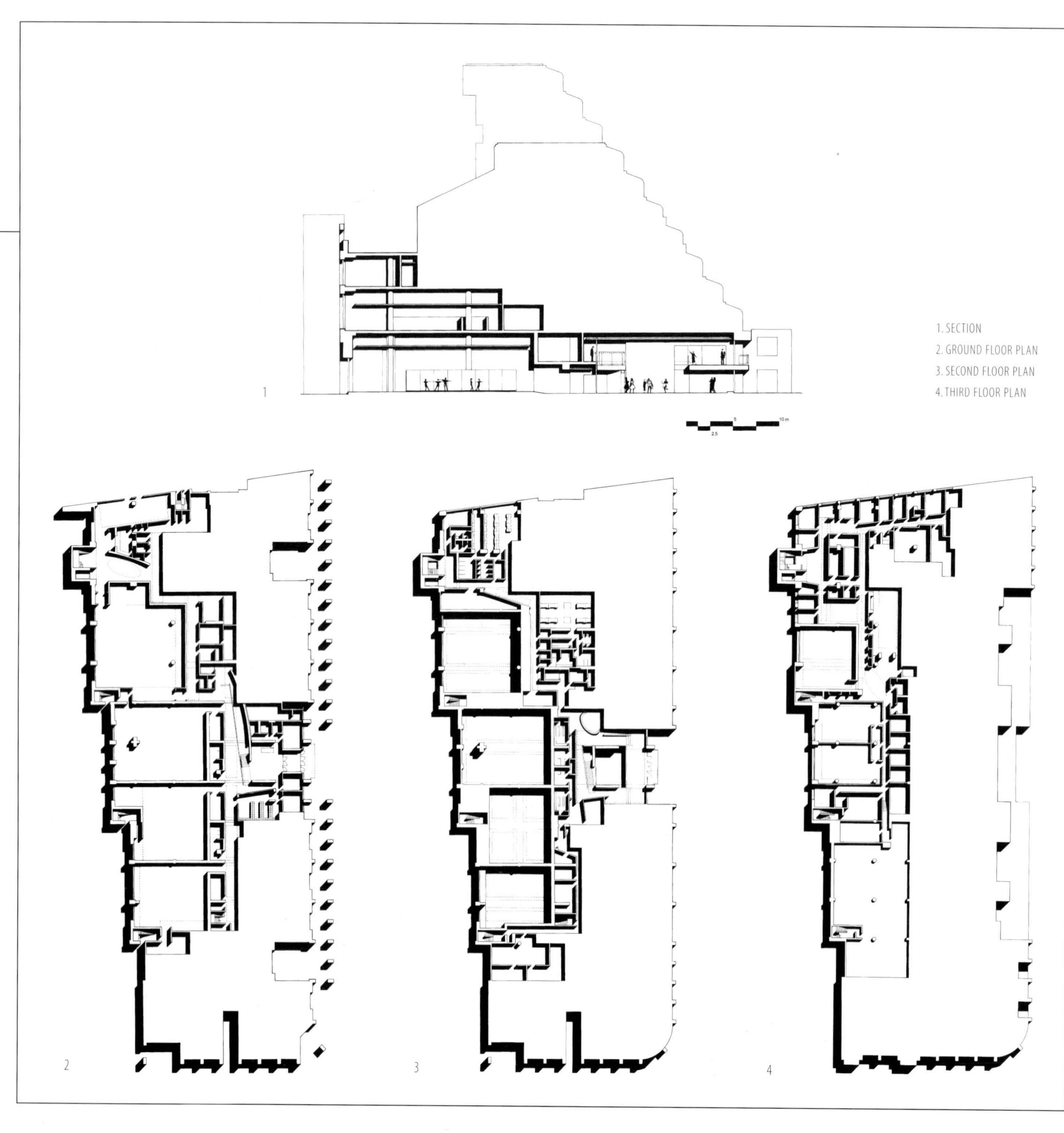

1. SECTION
2. GROUND FLOOR PLAN
3. SECOND FLOOR PLAN
4. THIRD FLOOR PLAN
2.5
5
10 m
1
2
3
4

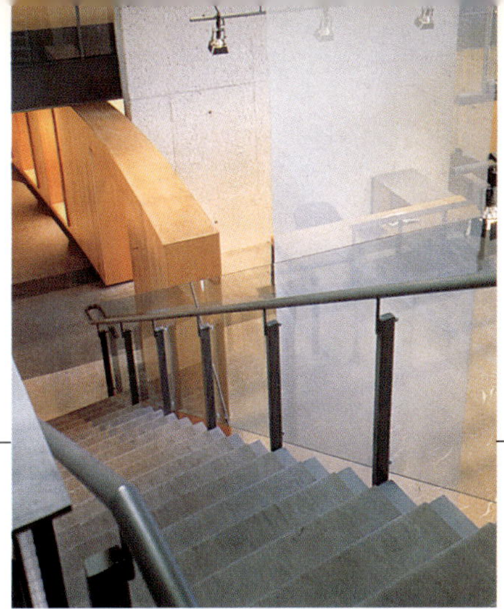

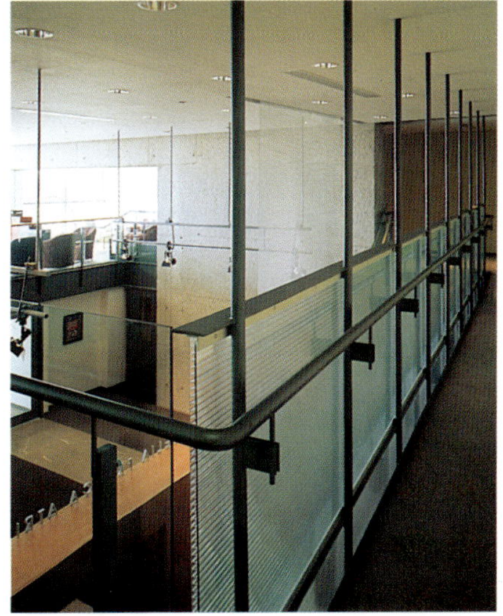

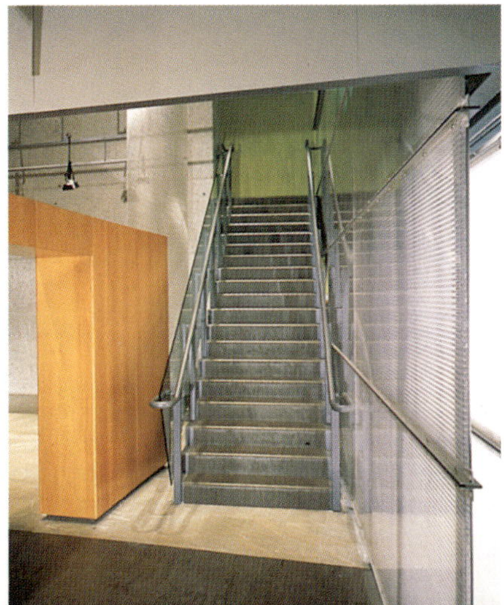

The public atrium, named in honor of National Ballet Company founder Celia Franca, includes elements associated with stage performance such as mesh screens (top), metal railings, incandescent spotlights, and steel stairs (center, bottom).

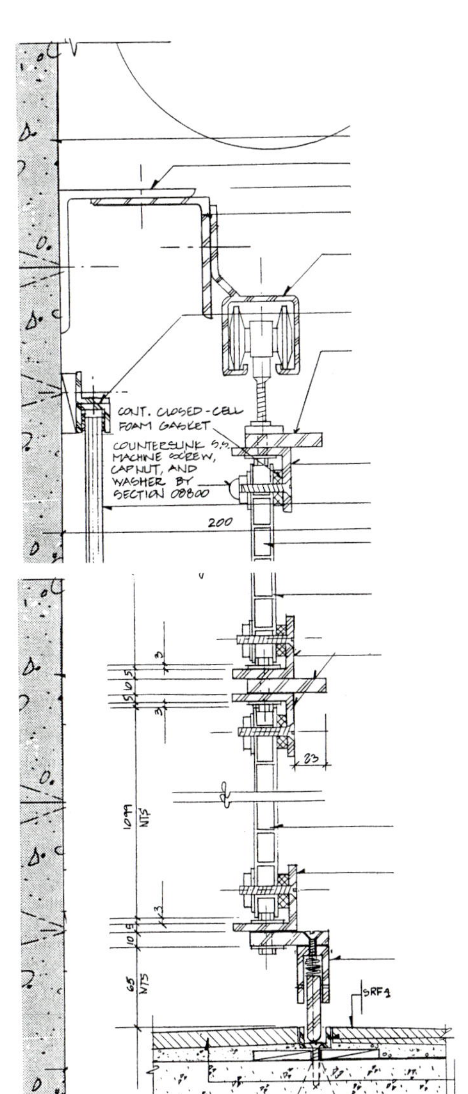

DETAIL OF TYPICAL SLIDING SCREEN WITH HEAD, MID-RAIL, AND BOTTOM RAIL

The Design Exchange

The Design Exchange (D/X) is a new institution dedicated to the economic and cultural promotion of design in Canada and internationally. Located in the heart of Toronto's financial district, the D/X inhabits the former Art Deco Stock Exchange Building at the base of the Ernst Young Tower, the fifth tower in the expansion of Mies van der Rohe's 1967 Toronto Dominion Centre. The design seeks to transform and clarify the layout of the existing art moderne and modernist spaces, and to accommodate a diverse program of exhibitions and events.

A scheme of bold linear elements such as walls, ceiling planes, and stairs define the public circulation route, create a distinct architectural presence for the D/X, and reappear in various forms to provide continuity through the existing structures.

The historic trading hall of the Stock Exchange Building is restored as a multipurpose space with retractable auditorium seating for 450 people. It is also used for exhibits, trade shows, fashion shows, special events, and banquets. From the trading floor, a new bridge/stair acts as a dramatic platform to view murals by Charles Comfort, and leads up to the third-floor gallery and resource center with its catwalk/stair to a library balcony.

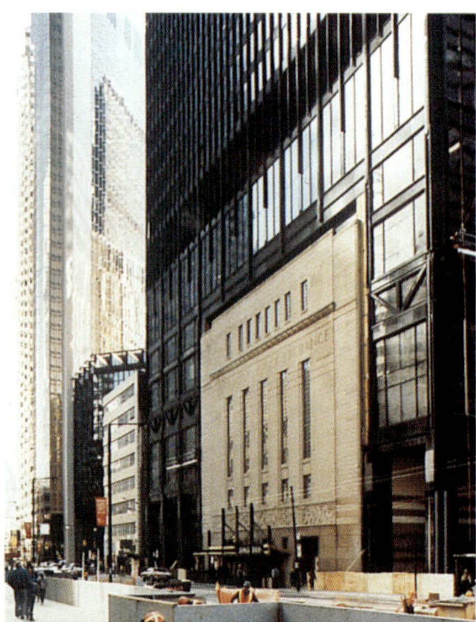

The material palette, which refers to both the historic and contemporary structures, comprises stone, sandblasted crystal glass, and stainless steel. The color scheme of chartreuse, ochre, and azure is inspired by the restored Charles Comfort murals on the trading floor and featured in each space of the D/X.

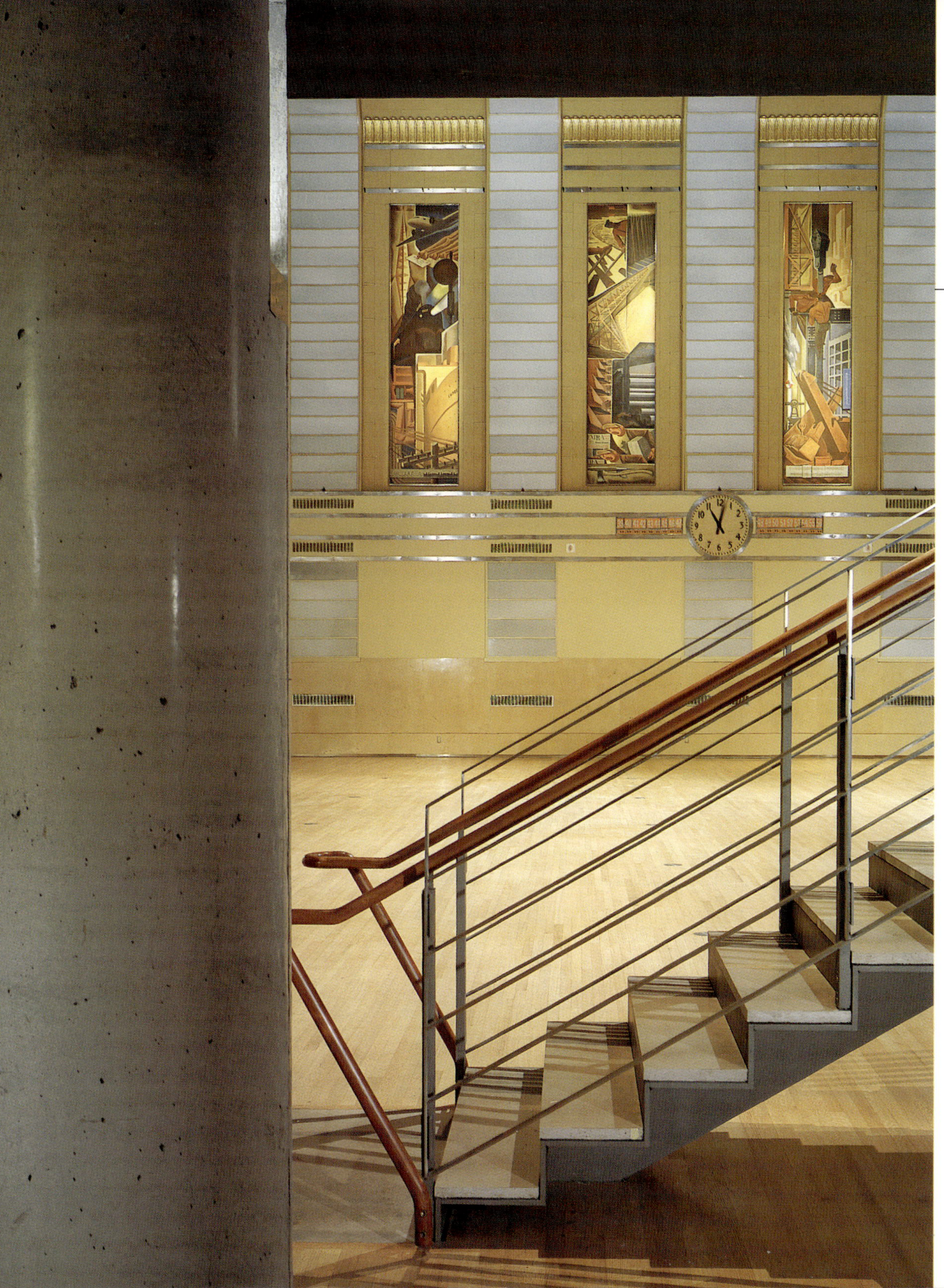

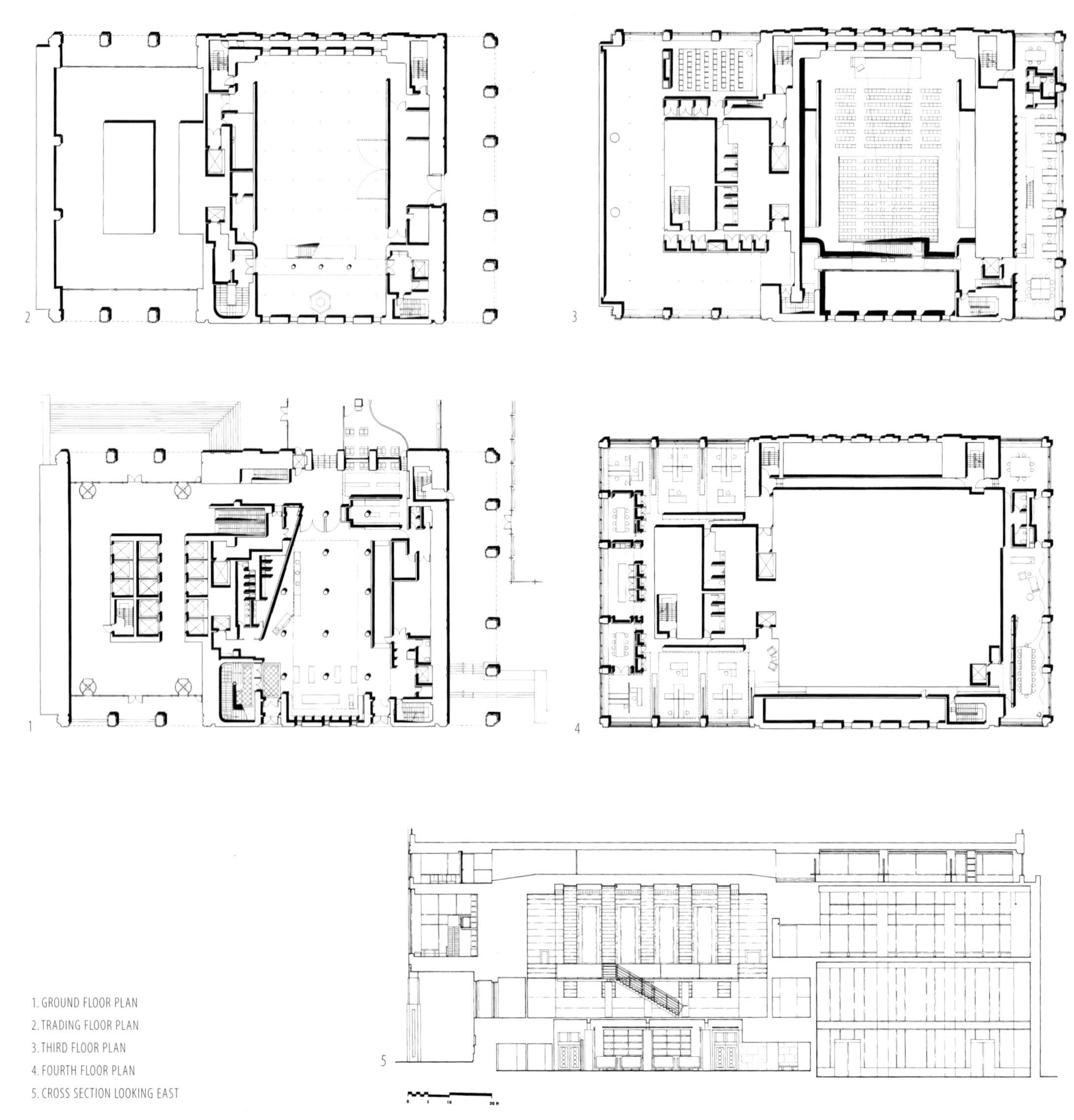

2
3
1
4
5
1. GROUND FLOOR PLAN
2. TRADING FLOOR PLAN
3. THIRD FLOOR PLAN
4. FOURTH FLOOR PLAN
5. CROSS SECTION LOOKING EAST
0   5   10   30 ft

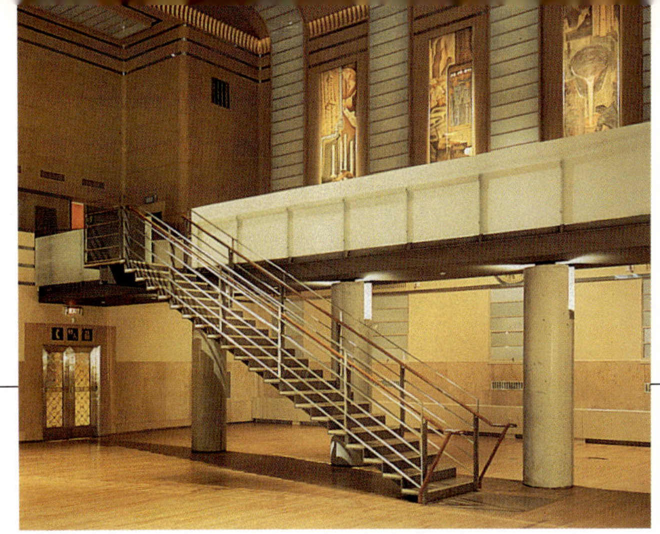

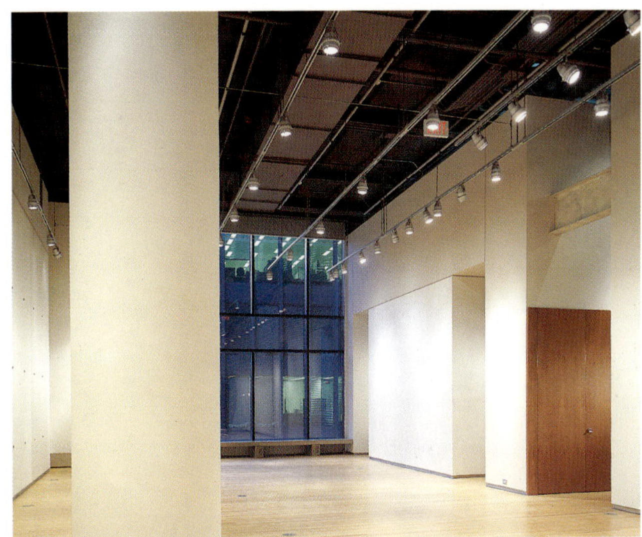

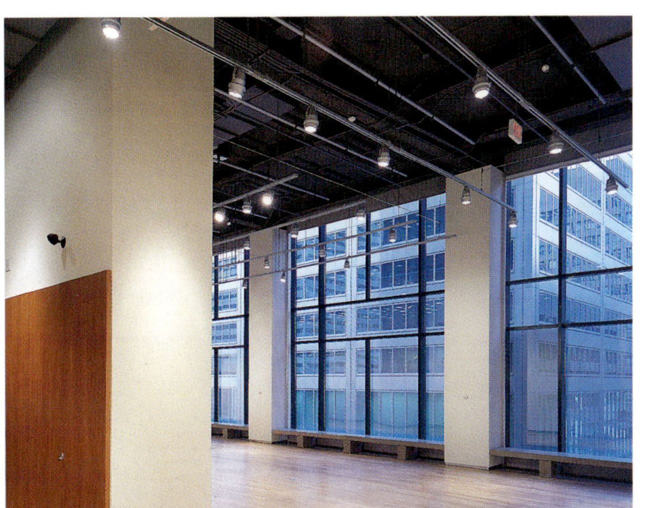

The new bridge/stair in the restored trading floor links the third floor north and south wings (top). Exhibit halls provide lofty, flexible spaces lit by natural daylight or banks of spotlights (center, bottom). The library and resource center overlooks the Toronto Dominion Plaza designed by Mies van der Rohe (overleaf).

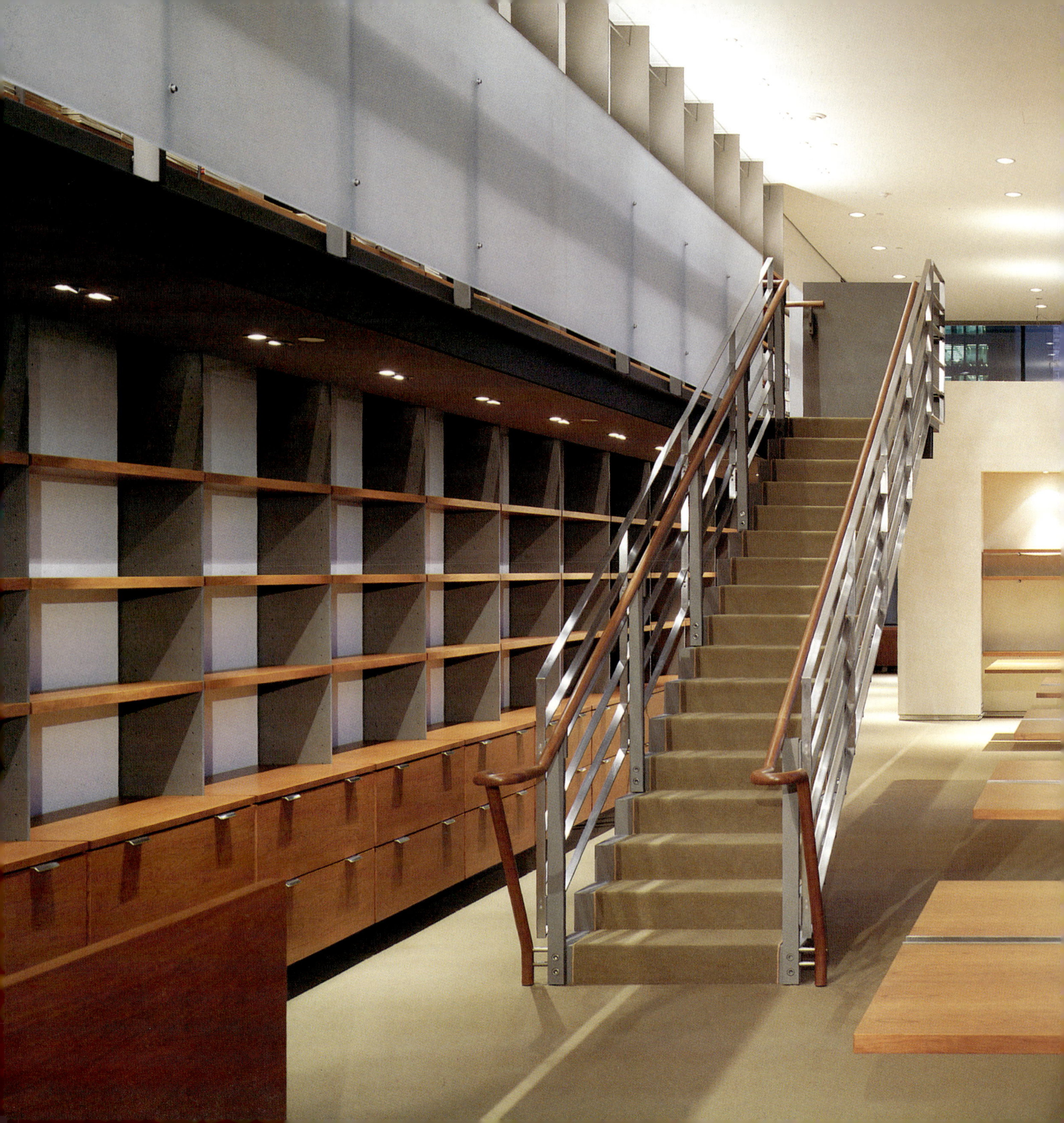

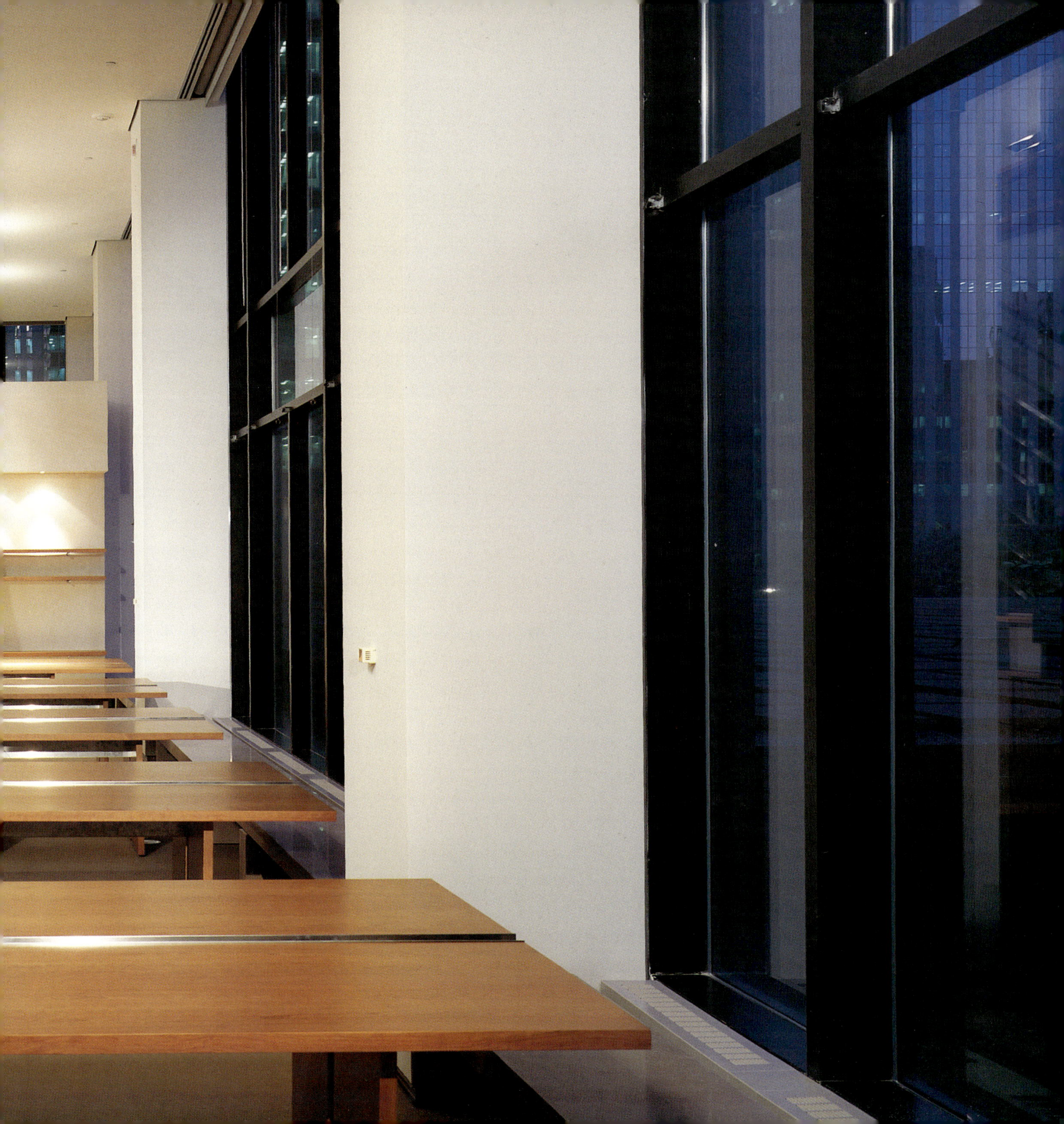

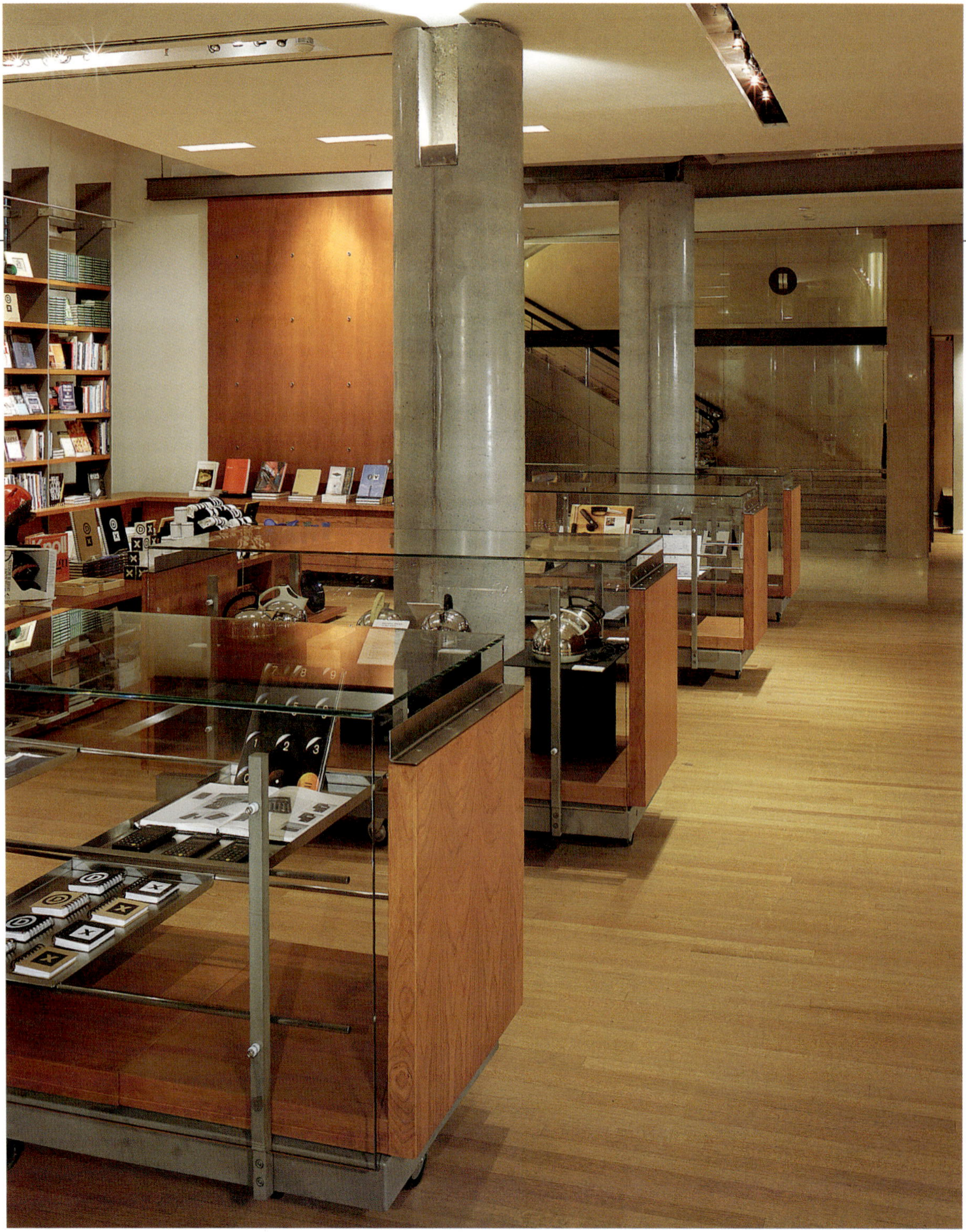

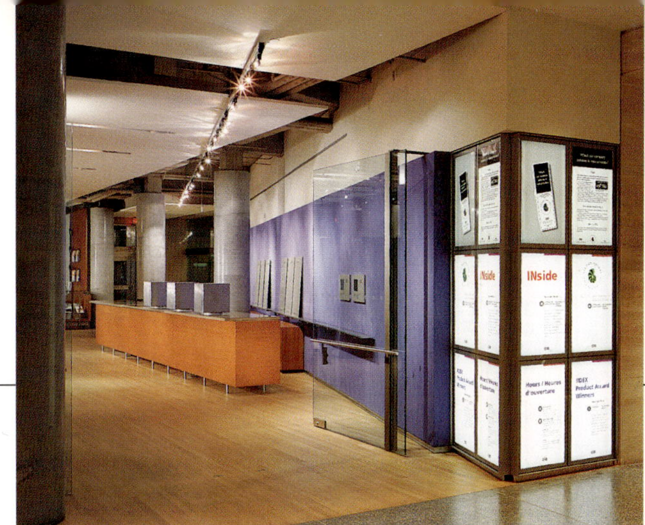

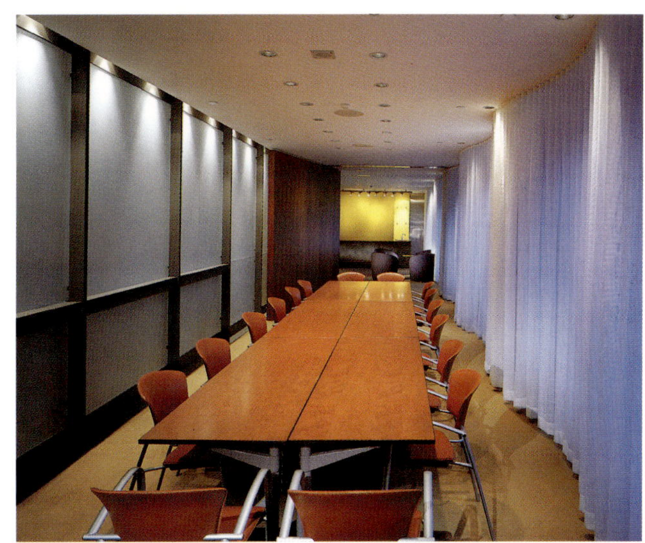

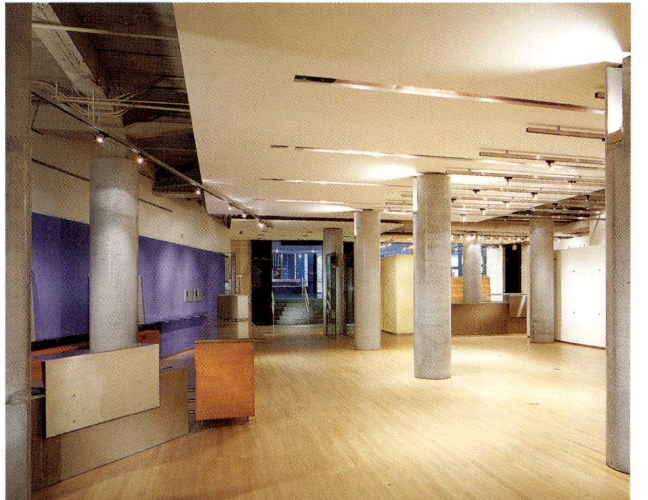

The information desk (top, bottom) and bookstore (opposite page) at the main entrance of the historic Stock Exchange Building serve to orient visitors. This lobby area doubles as a venue for changing exhibitions and product displays. The fourth-floor members' lounge also accommodates meetings and seminars (center).

King James Place

One of the firm's earliest commissions, King James Place benefited from extended study and collaboration among the architects on issues of architecture in an urban context.

A rich mix of historic buildings surrounds the site, which is adjacent to St. Lawrence Town Hall and faces St. James Cathedral and Park on King Street East. Strict city guidelines mandated that the new commercial building incorporates an existing historic facade, and the project addresses the ambiguity created by recomposing the existing streetscape while adding a contemporary structure.

The main entrance to the building, planned to hold the Canadian headquarters of Saatchi and Saatchi, is marked by the existing facade and leads to a three-story-high lobby. Multicentered, dense, and textural, the new facade balances local symmetries with formal shifts that establish alignments, registrations, and material and tectonic relationships with the adjacent buildings. A rhythm of paired bays reiterates the double-bay expression of the York Belting Building to the west. A stone octagon anchors the east corner, and alludes to the town hall cupola and the cathedral steeple across the street.

Depth and texture created by the detailing of channel reveals, windows, and cornices expresses the relationship of this new street wall to the historic facade. Predominantly limestone and brick, the building terraces back at the upper levels to preserve an important view of St. Lawrence Town Hall.

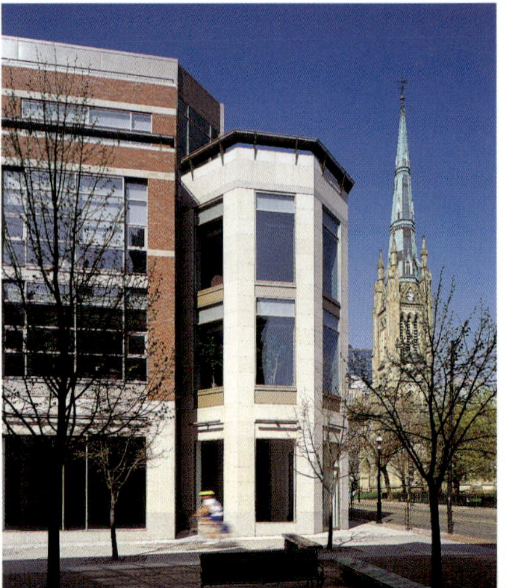

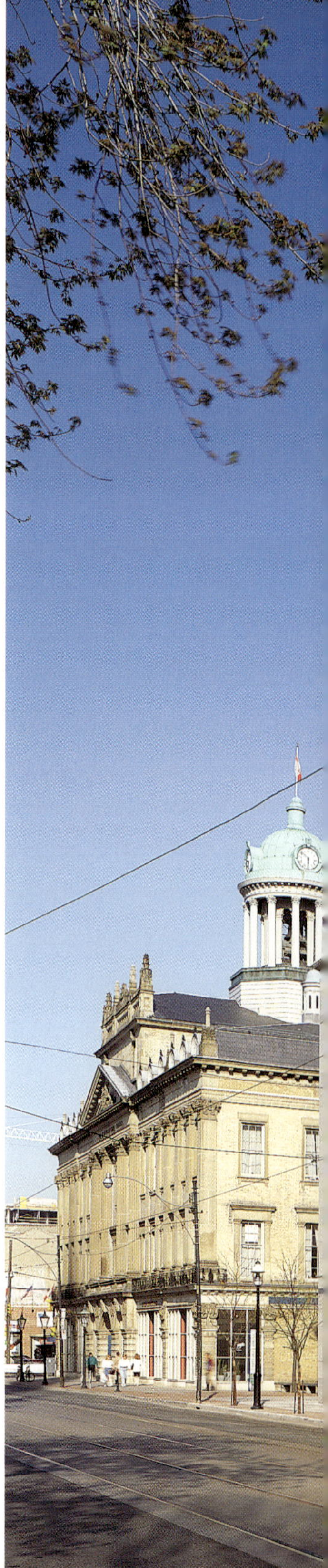

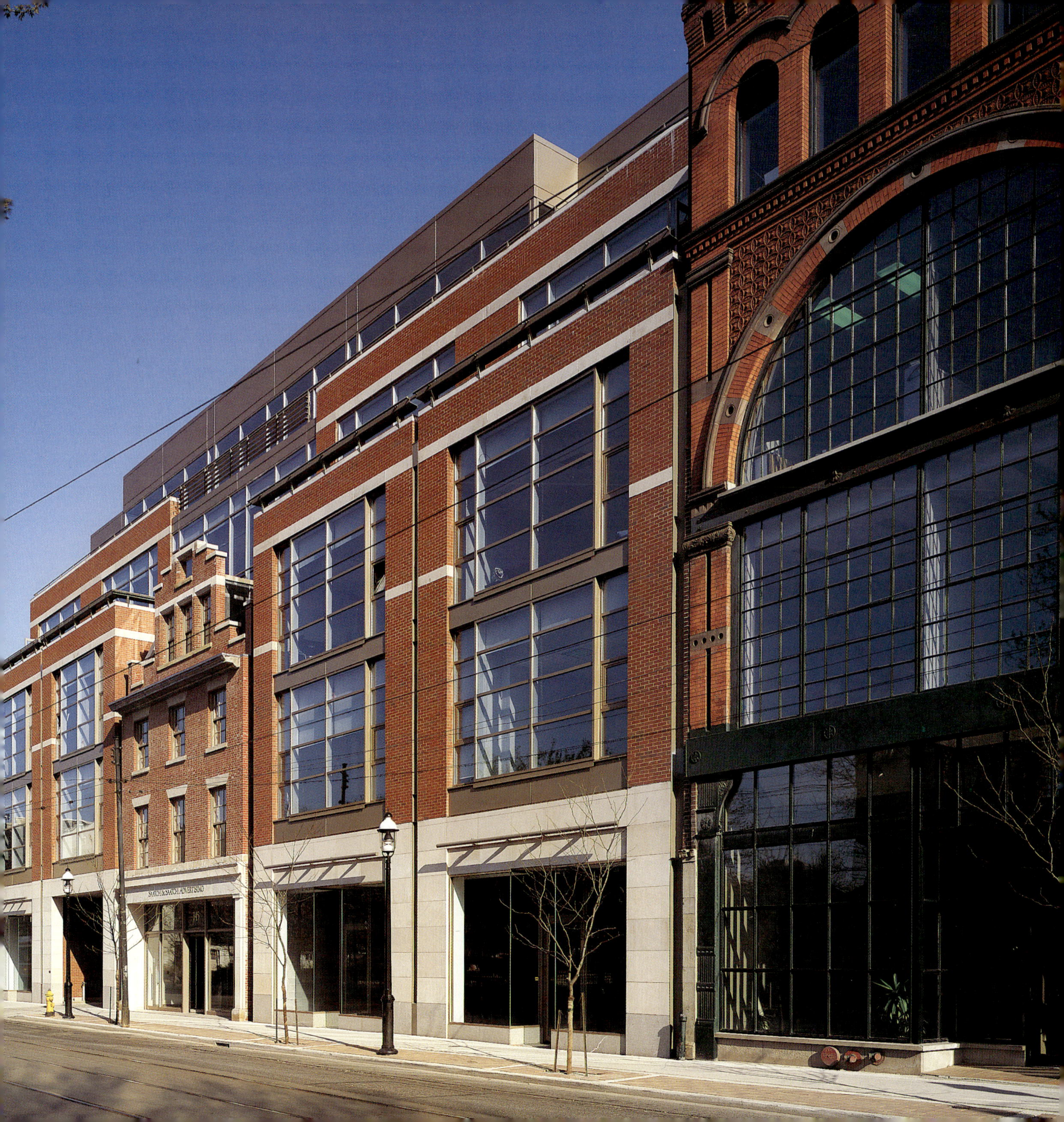

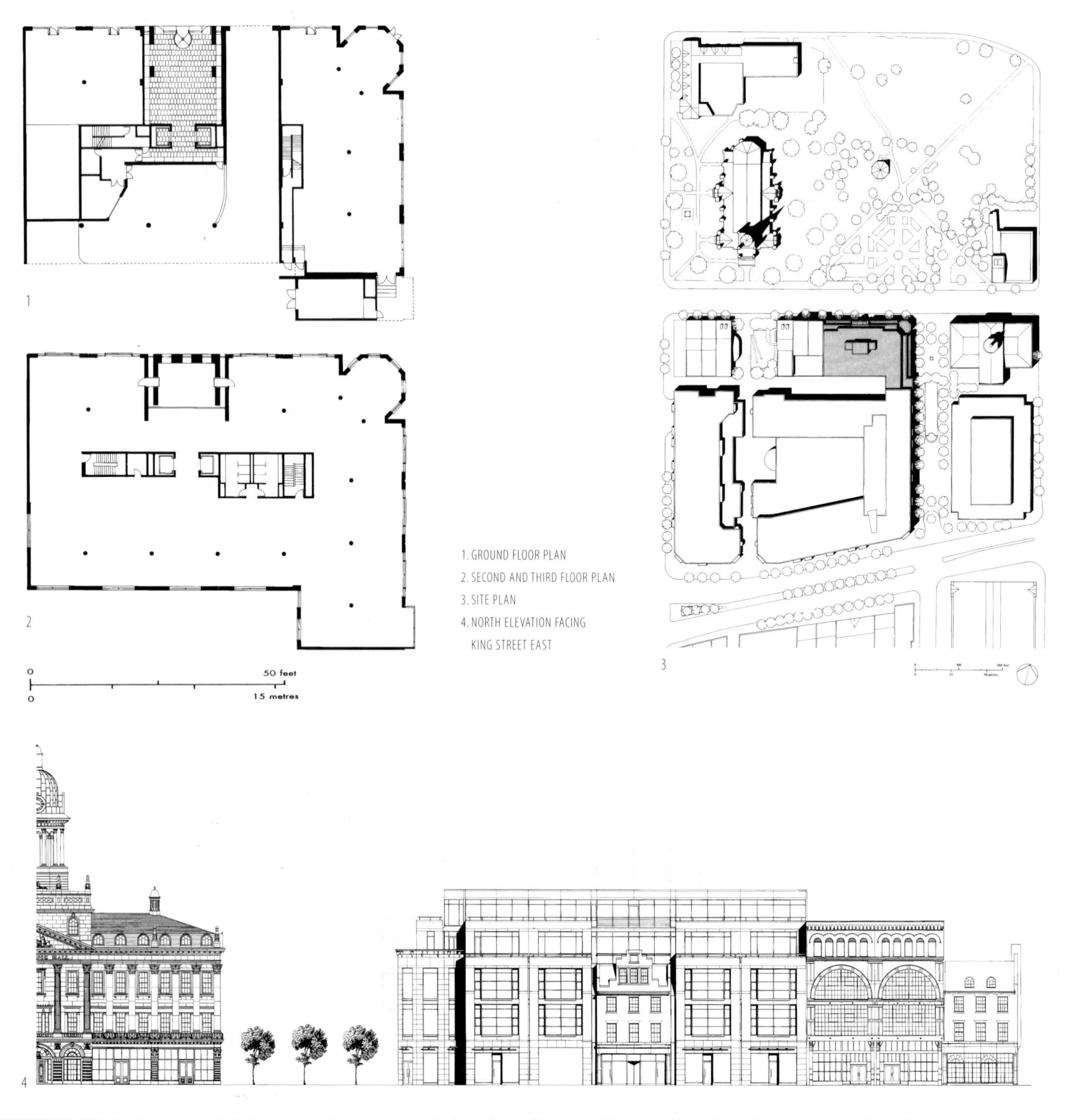

1
2
3
4
1. GROUND FLOOR PLAN
2. SECOND AND THIRD FLOOR PLAN
3. SITE PLAN
4. NORTH ELEVATION FACING
   KING STREET EAST
50 feet
15 metres

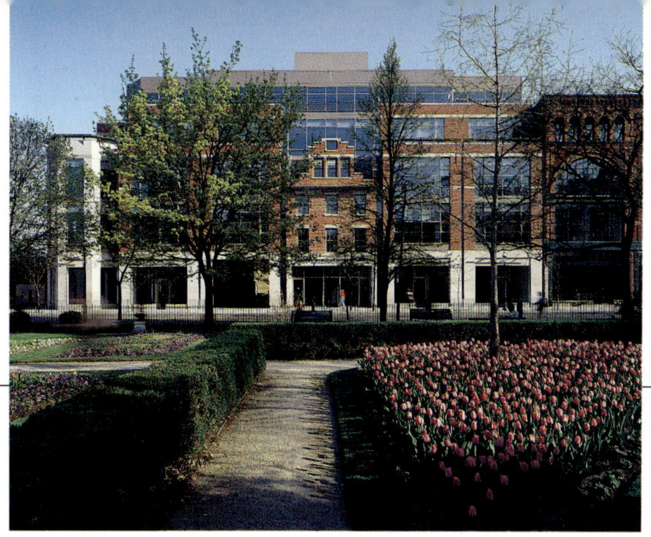

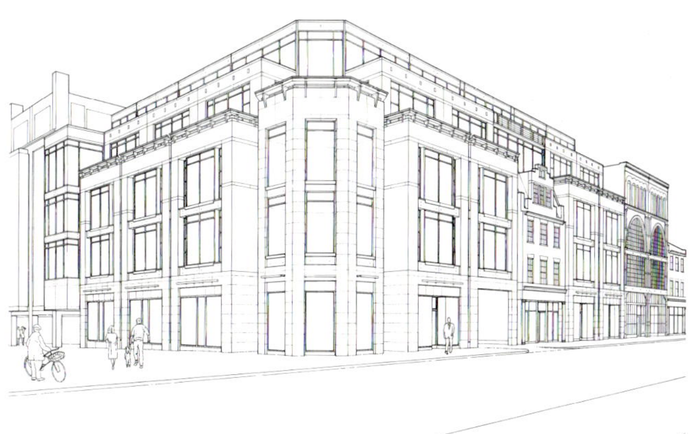

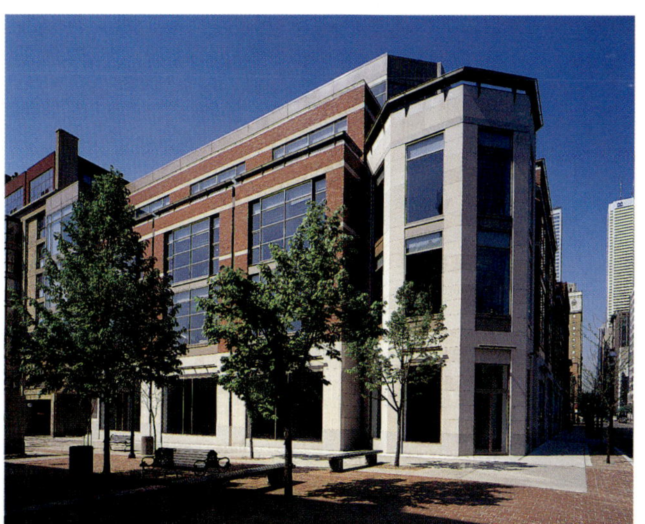

View from St. James Park reveals the extremely tight spatial envelope in which the developer was allowed to erect the new structure (top). The stone-clad octagonal form echoes the shape of the 1851 St. Lawrence Town Hall cupola (bottom).

Marc Laurent

The project for the Marc Laurent retail interiors began as a collaboration between Bruce Kuwabara, Thomas Payne, and the client and owner, Harry Bendayan. The initial project established basic design principles and architectural language to be extended and transformed for subsequent phases. The overall design demonstrates how a retail business can expand while maintaining the quality of design and service in a dynamic market.

The Marc Laurent concept balances design with retail marketability, permanence with flexibility, and high-tech materials such as steel, aluminum, rubber, and glass with natural materials such as wood and stone. The interior planning maximizes the role of sales staff in the retail environment. Based on two types of vertical supports, the steel racking system was custom designed to allow for a range of combinations of shelves, hanging bars, and face-out displays. As merchandise is sold through each season, the system can be transformed to allow regrouping of the various collections.

Movement is based on a series of loops, bringing customers in contact with all areas of the store while allowing choice and diversity. An interconnecting stair acts as a pivotal connection between the street-level spaces and lower-level retail spaces. Cash desks, display panels, display tables, screens, and aluminum canopies mark identifiable points in the circulation sequence through the store. Areas of special retailing identity include a section for women's fashions as well as separate sections for individual designers.

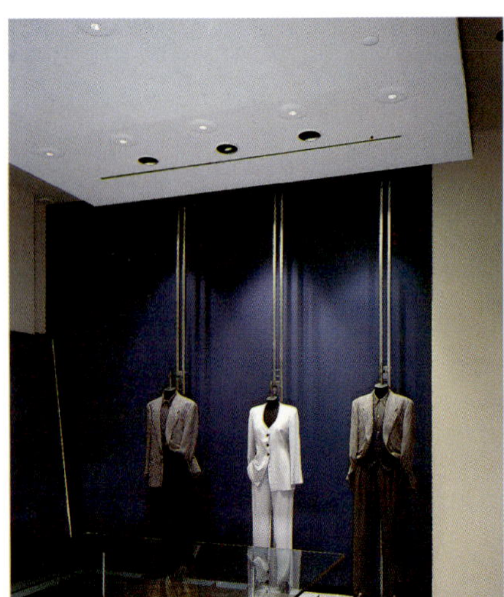

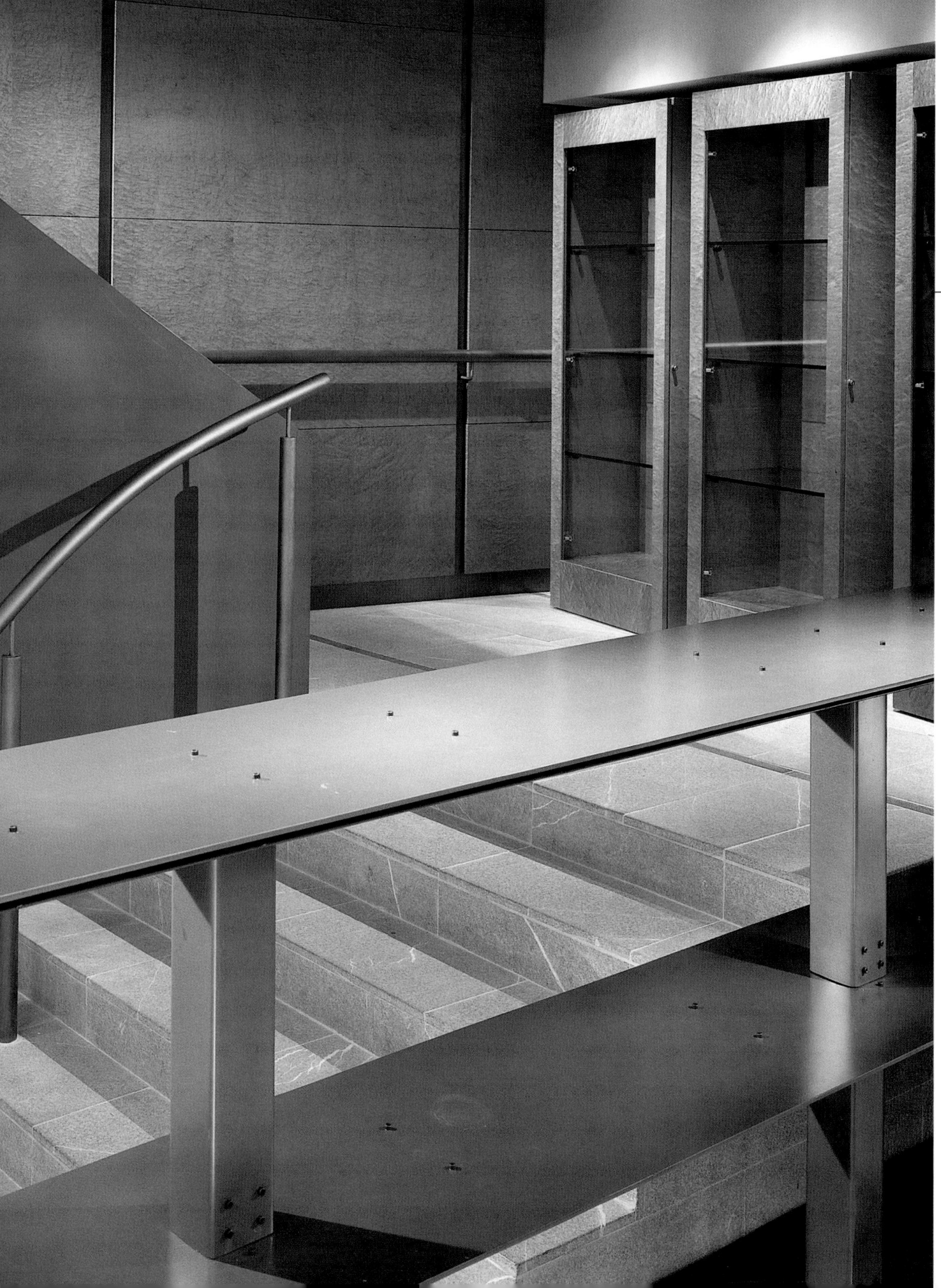

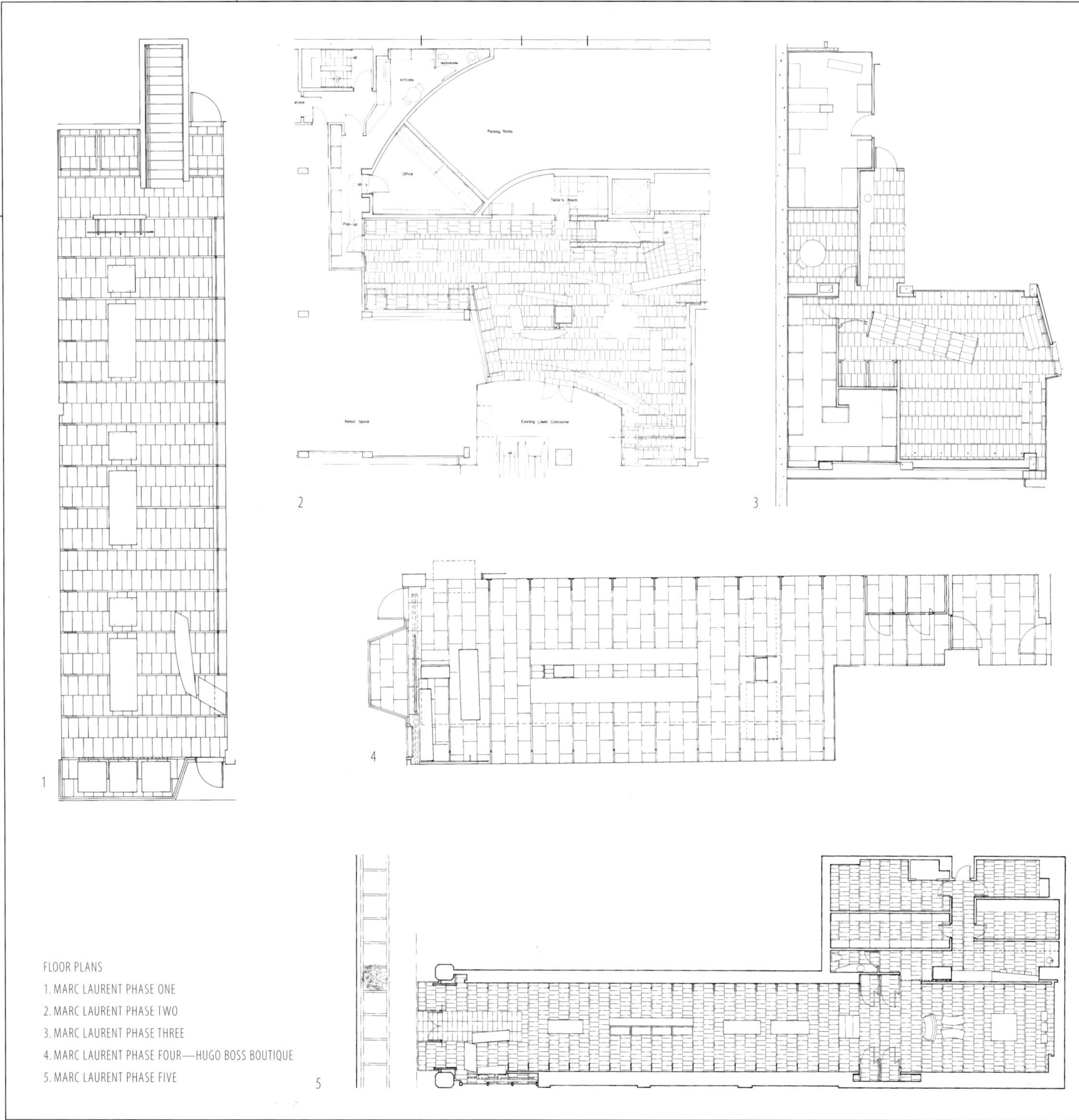

FLOOR PLANS
1. MARC LAURENT PHASE ONE
2. MARC LAURENT PHASE TWO
3. MARC LAURENT PHASE THREE
4. MARC LAURENT PHASE FOUR—HUGO BOSS BOUTIQUE
5. MARC LAURENT PHASE FIVE

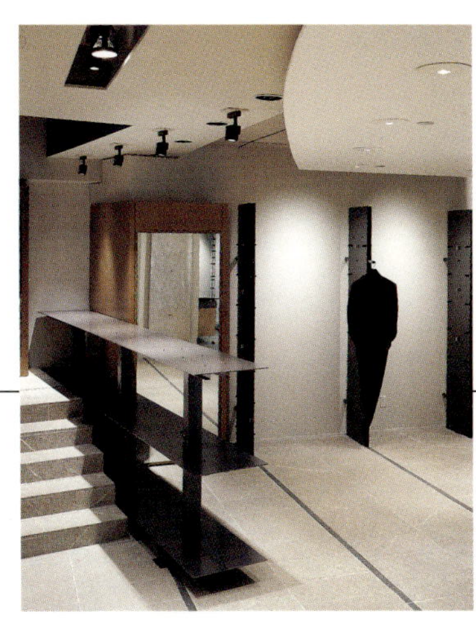
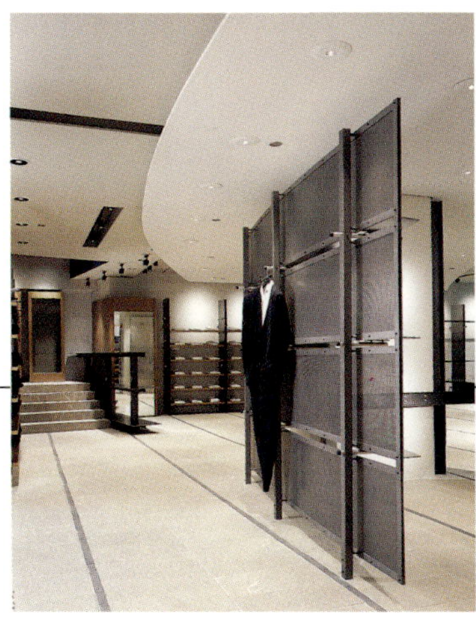
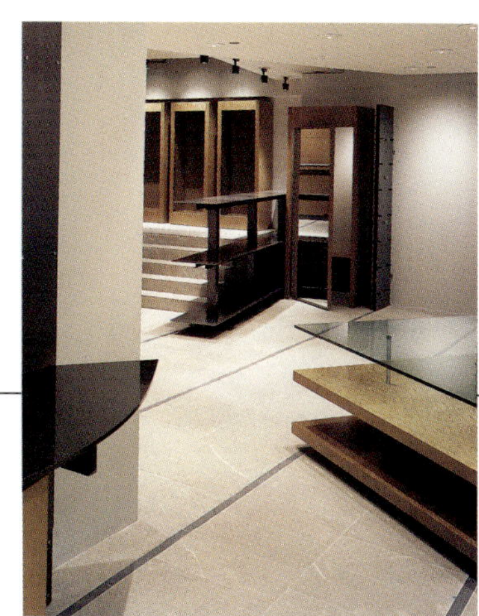

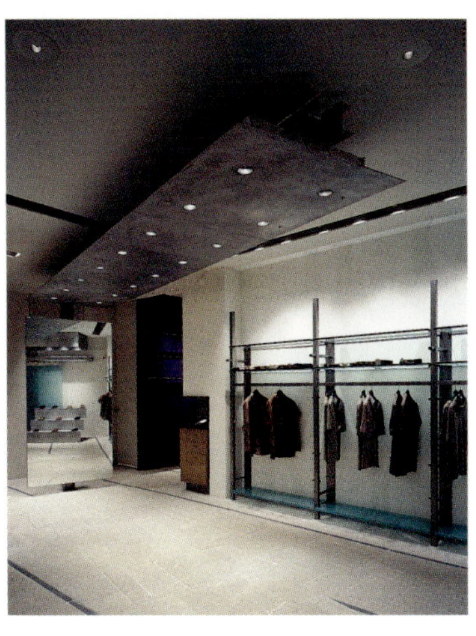
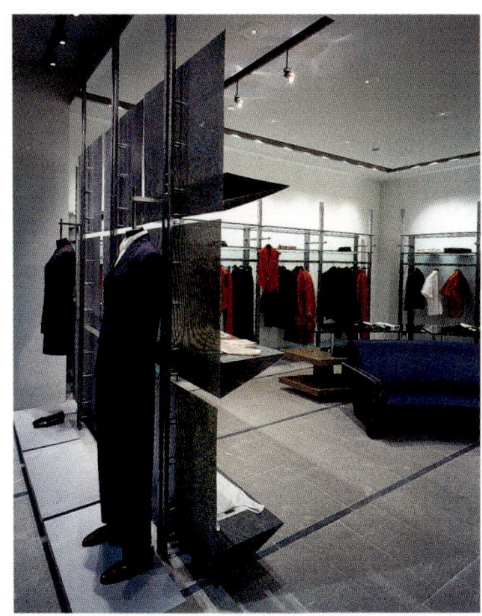
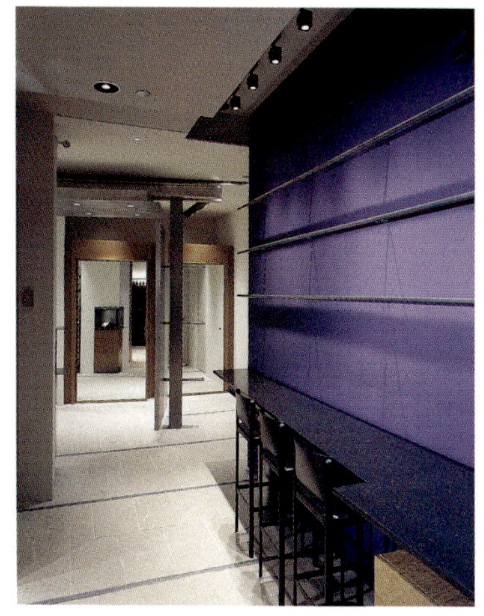

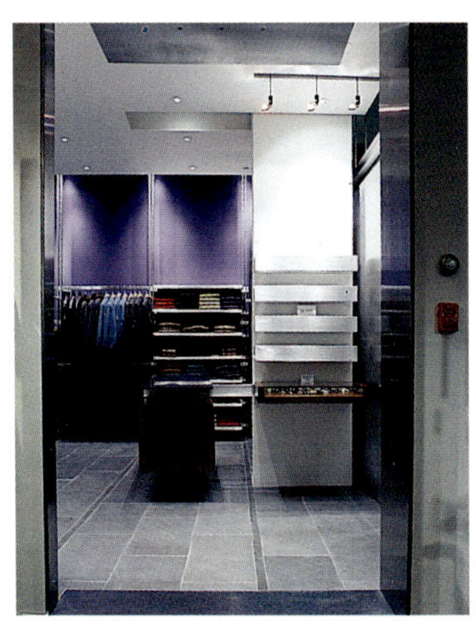
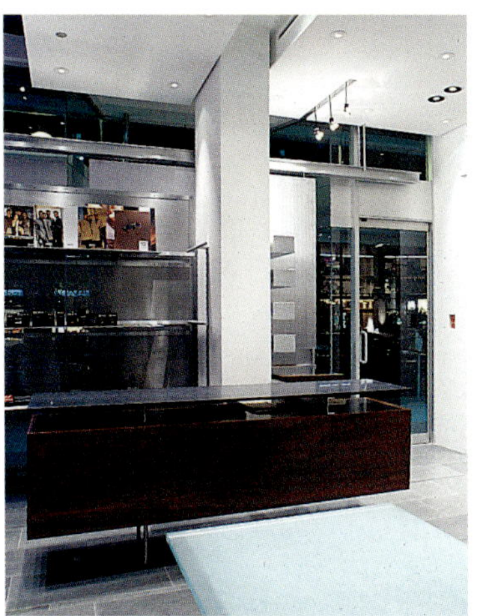
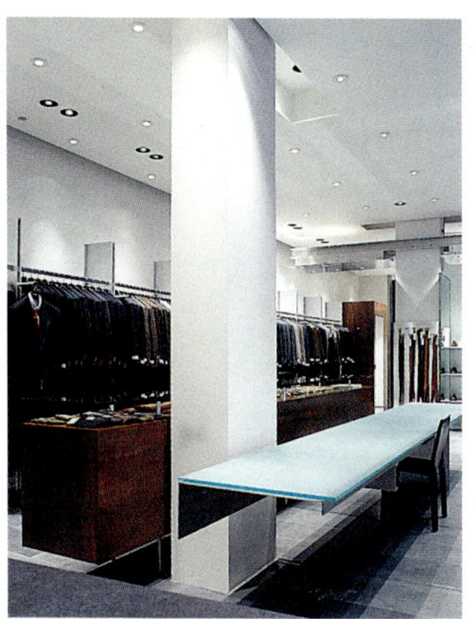

Phases two and three on the lower concourse level develop the basic design vocabulary established for phase one in 1986 (top, center rows). The street-level boutique for Hugo Boss represents Phase four (bottom row). Curved planes and rectilinear objects are set at oblique angles upon the regular floor grid (overleaf).

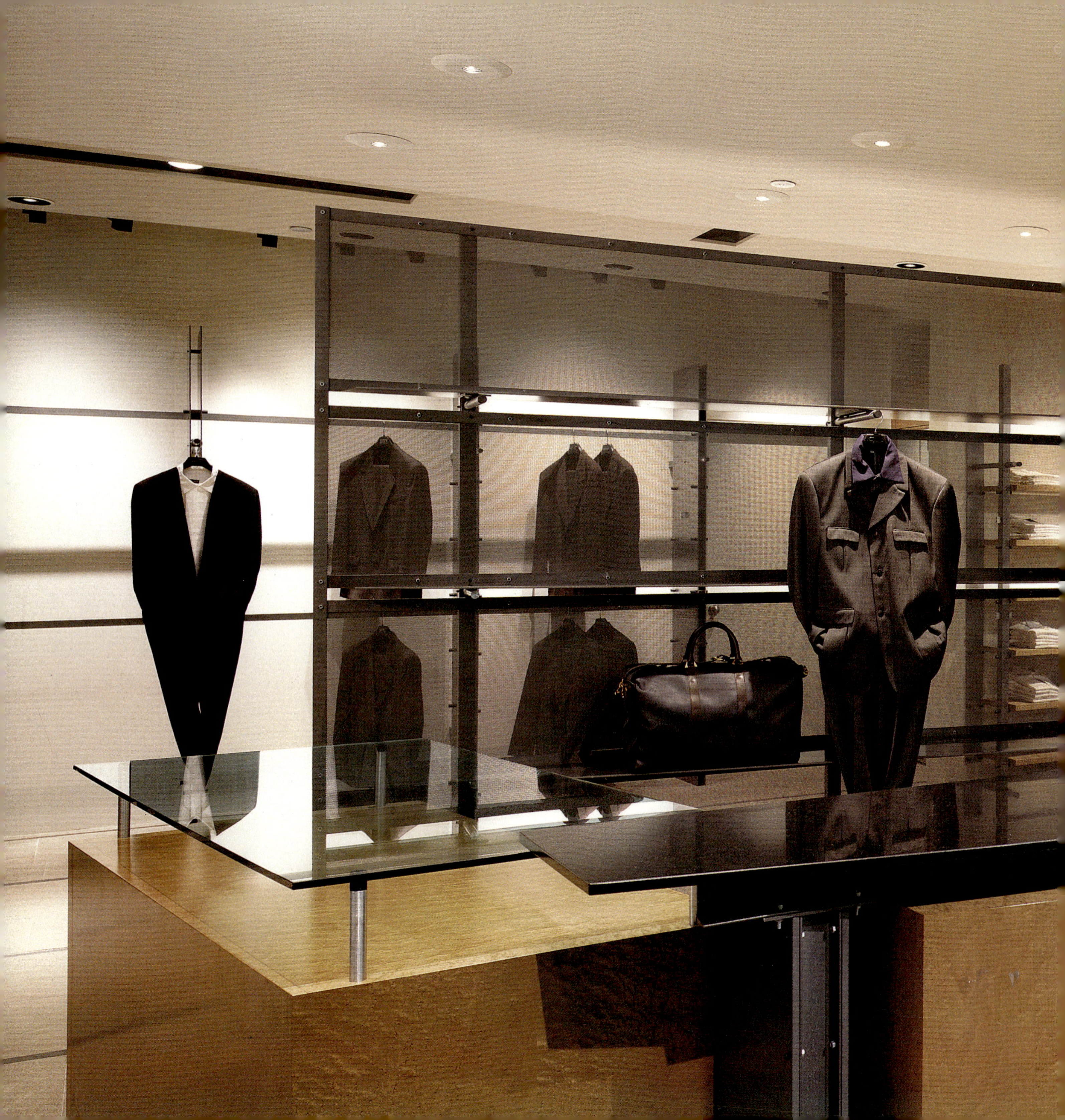

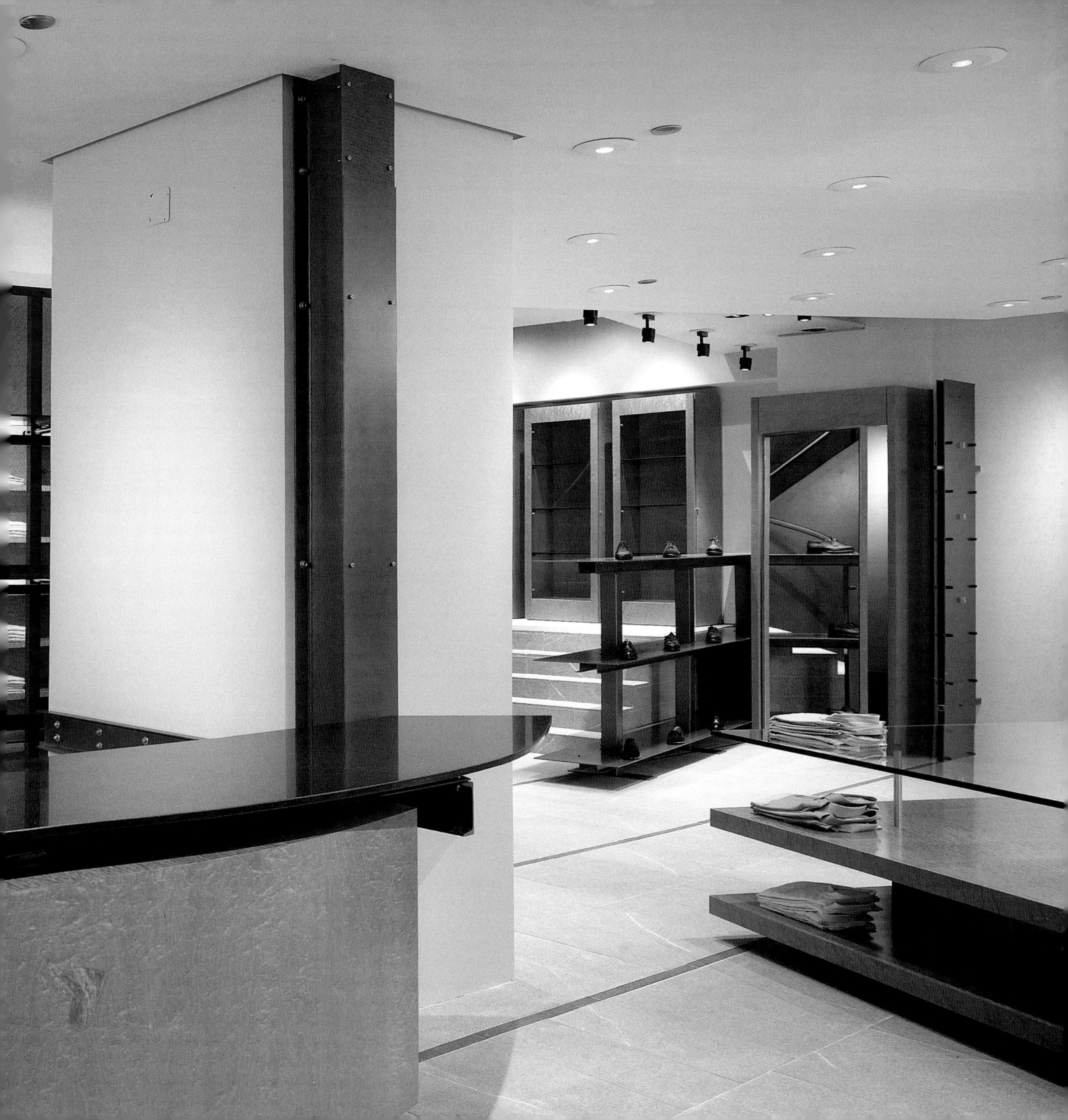

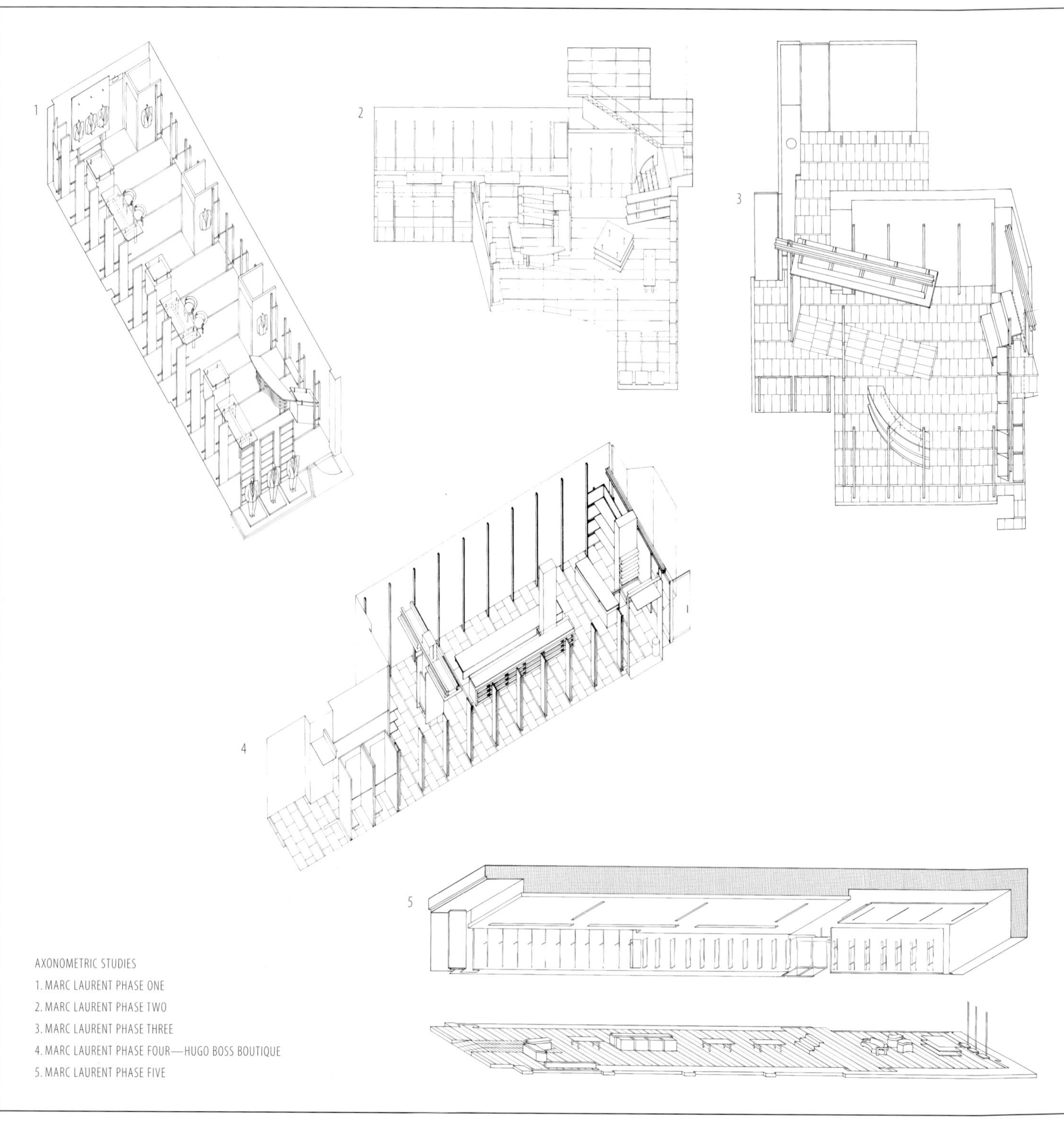

AXONOMETRIC STUDIES
1. MARC LAURENT PHASE ONE
2. MARC LAURENT PHASE TWO
3. MARC LAURENT PHASE THREE
4. MARC LAURENT PHASE FOUR—HUGO BOSS BOUTIQUE
5. MARC LAURENT PHASE FIVE

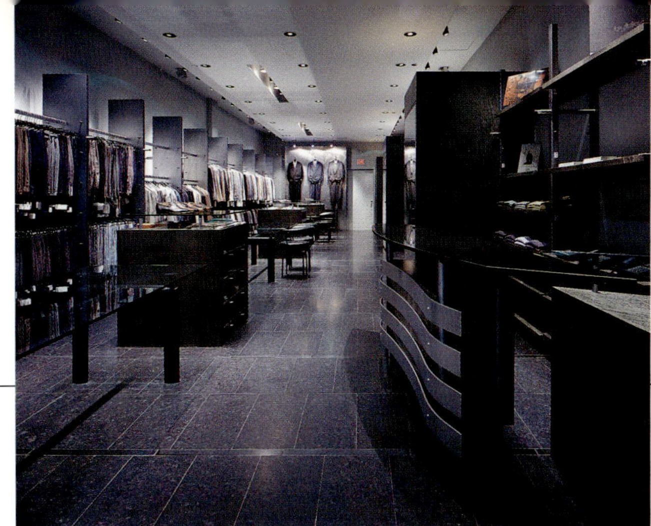

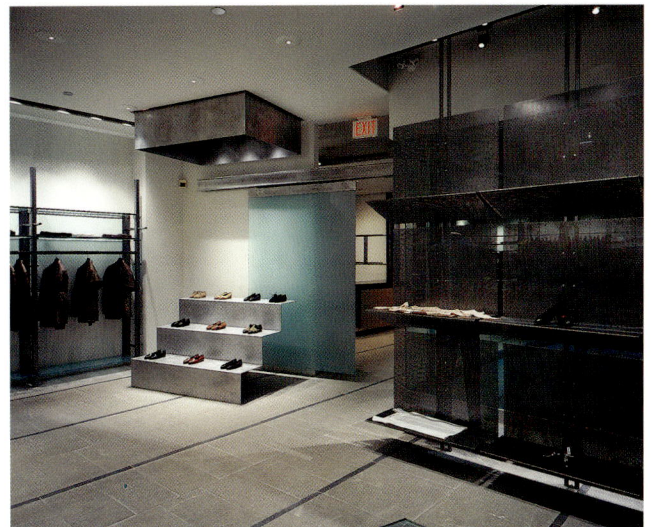

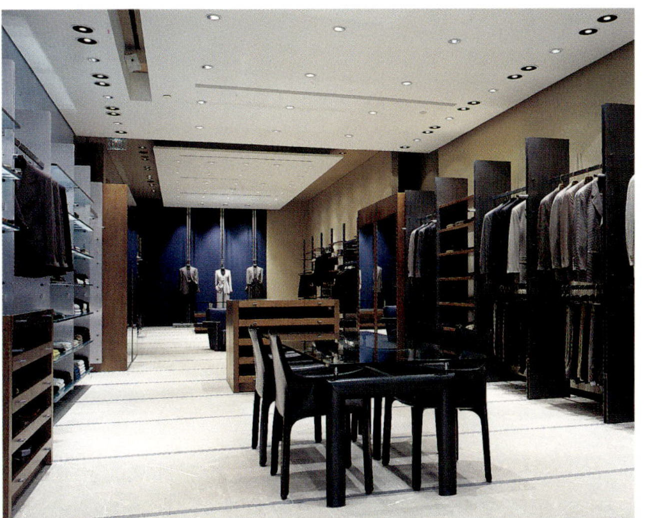

The ingenious steel rack system developed by the architects for the original store (top) proves its versatility in the new location opened in 1996 (bottom). The palette of materials contrasts aluminum and glass with natural stone and wood (center).

Creed's Interiors

Part of the expansion and internal reorganization of an exclusive Toronto women's fashion store, the new multifunctional retail court, and a linear boutique are linked together and to the rest of the store by two new staircases.

The new court space provides a flexible venue for retailing and a wide variety of events, including presentations, fashion shows, special seasonal displays, and social and fund-raising efforts. A circular ceiling fixture provides an armature of theatrical lighting. Display cases between stone-clad piers on all four sides of the court create a series of boutiques facing the new space.

A system of vertical, sandblasted steel pilasters and horizontal baseboards, chair rails, and slots supports brackets for a variety of hanging rods and display shelves. The merchandising system itself is based on a standard module using panels of stained cherry. The material palette of cherry paneling and sanded, lacquered, and sandblasted steel is carried into the changing area, where three-way mirrors are designed to open into a special cabinet within each fitting room. Flamed granite and black lace slate form the patterned floor for the court. The floors in the linear boutique, which connects to an existing retail mall, are etched concrete inlaid with ribbons of black and silver glass tile.

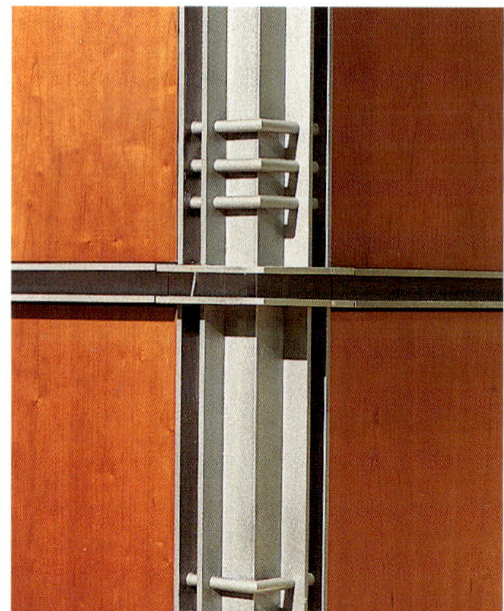

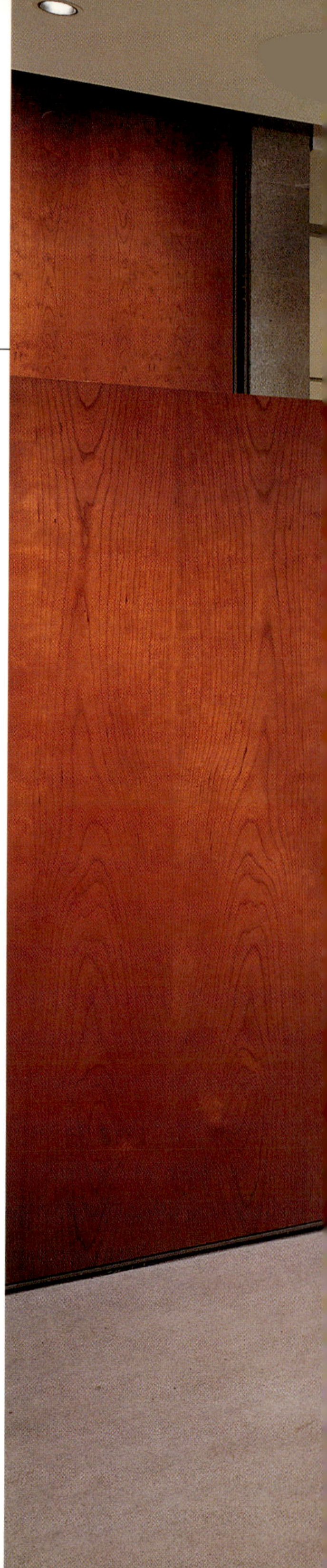

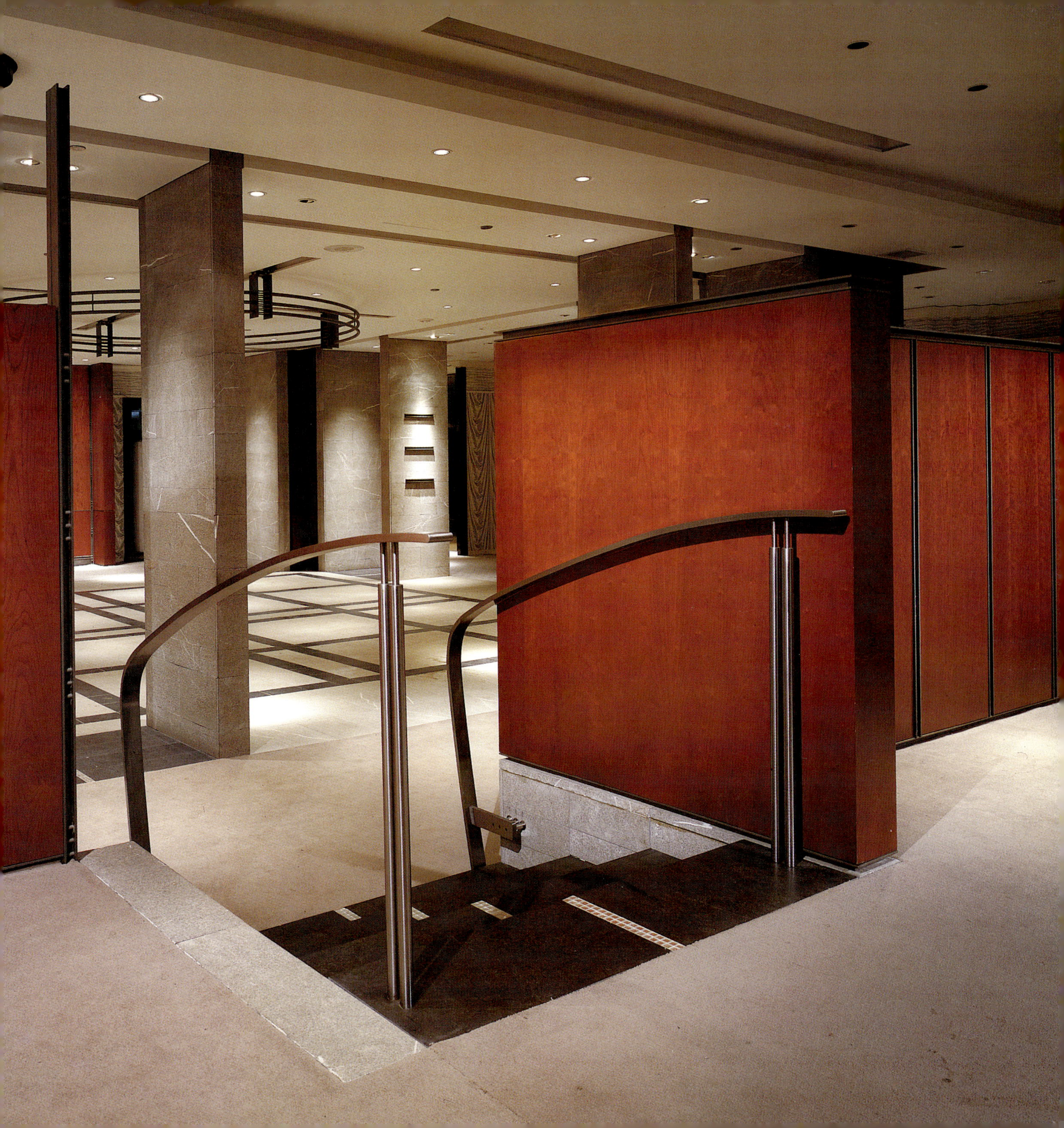

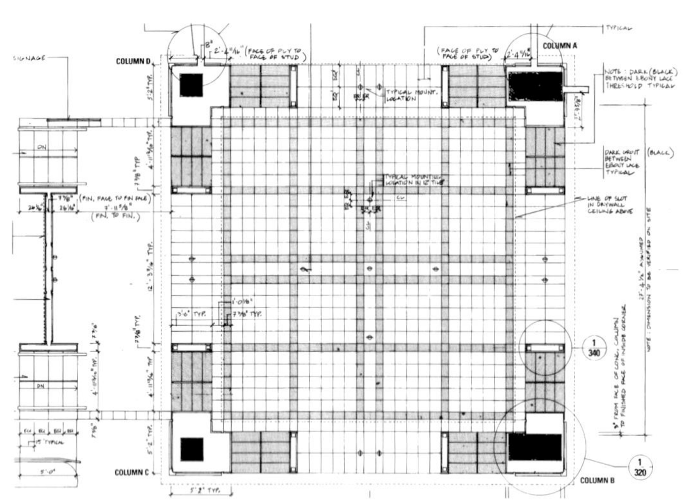

SIGNAGE
COLUMN D
COLUMN A
8"
2'-4 11/16" (FACE OF PLY TO FACE OF STUD)
(FACE OF PLY TO FACE OF STUD)
2'-4 11/16"
TYPICAL
COLUMN A
NOTE: DARK (BLACK) BETWEEN EBONY LACE THRESHOLD TYPICAL
DARK GROUT BETWEEN EBONY LACE TYPICAL
TYPICAL MOUNT. LOCATION
TYPICAL MOUNTING LOCATION IN 12" TILE
LINE OF SLOT IN DRYWALL CEILING ABOVE
DN
(FIN. FACE TO FIN FACE)
7'-11 5/8" (FIN. TO FIN.)
DN
COLUMN C
COLUMN B
5'-2" TYP.
1 / 340
1 / 320

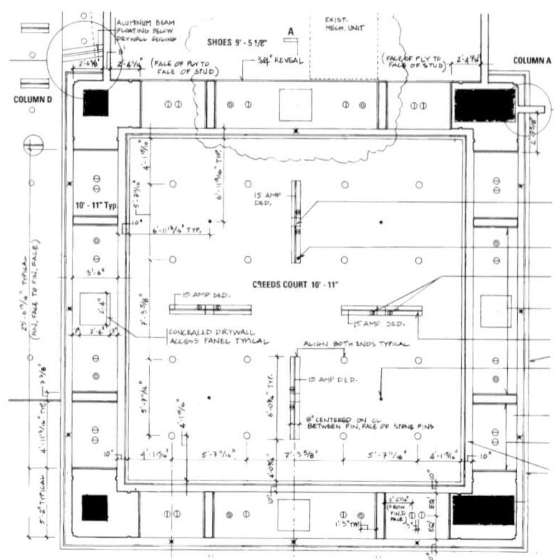

COLUMN D
COLUMN A
ALUMINUM BEAM FLOATING BELOW DRYWALL CEILING
SHOES 9'-5 1/8"
EXIST. MECH. UNIT
A
3/4" REVEAL
2'-6 7/8"
2'-4 11/16" (FACE OF PLY TO FACE OF STUD)
(FACE OF PLY TO FACE OF STUD)
2'-4 11/16"
10'-11" Typ.
15 AMP DED.
15 AMP DED.
CONCEALED DRYWALL ACCESS PANEL TYPICAL
15 AMP DED.
ALIGN BOTH ENDS TYPICAL
CREEDS COURT 10'-11"
15 AMP DED.
8" CENTERED ON CL BETWEEN FIN. FACE OF STONE FINS

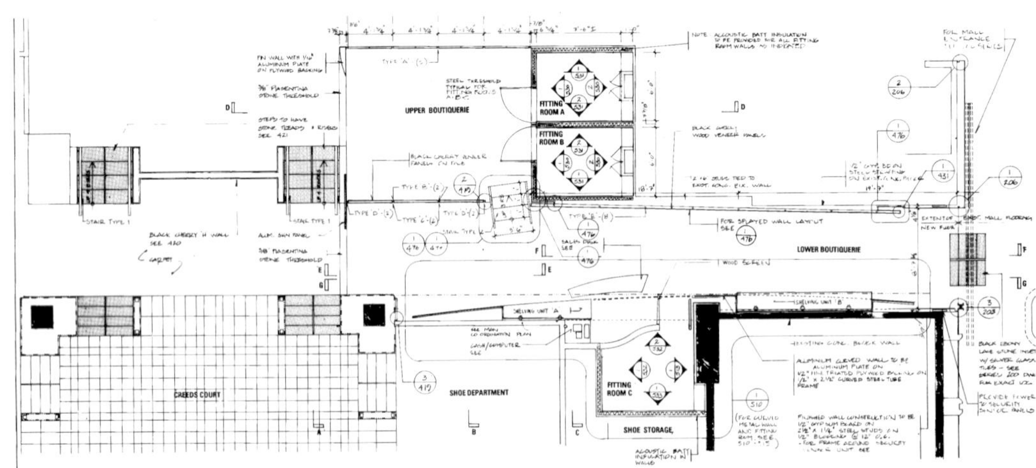

FIN WALL WITH 1/8" ALUMINUM PLATE ON PLYWOOD BACKING
3/8" FLORENTINA SPINE THRESHOLD
STEPS TO HAVE STONE TREADS + RISERS SEE 421
UPPER BOUTIQUERIE
STEEL THRESHOLD TYPICAL FOR FITTING ROOMS A-B-C
FITTING ROOM A
FITTING ROOM B
NOTE ACOUSTIC BATT INSULATION TO BE PROVIDED FOR ALL FITTING ROOM WALLS AS INDICATED
BLACK CHERRY WOOD VENEER PANELS
FOR MALL ENTRANCE
STAIR TYPE 1
BLACK CHERRY H WALL SEE 420 (CARPET)
3/8" FLORENTINA SPINE THRESHOLD
BLACK GROUT ANGLE FABRIC ON TILE
ALUM. SKIN PANEL
STAIR TYPE 1
TYPE B (2)
TYPE C (2)
TYPE D (3)
STAIR TYPE 1
SALON PROM SEE
1/2" GYP. BD. ON STEEL MOUNTING
2 x 10 JOISTS TIED TO EXIST. BLDG. BLK. WALL
FOR SPLAYED WALL LAYOUT SEE 476
LOWER BOUTIQUERIE
EXTENT OF WOOD WALL FLOORING NEW PWR.
WOOD SCREEN
CREEDS COURT
SHOE DEPARTMENT
SELLING UNIT A
SELLING UNIT B
SEE MAIN LIGHTING PLAN
SHOE/COMPUTER SEE
FITTING ROOM C
SHOE STORAGE
ACOUSTIC BATT INSULATION IN WALL
EXISTING CONC. BLOCK WALL
ALUMINUM CURVED WALL TO BE ALUMINUM PLATE ON 1/2" FIRE TREATED PLYWOOD BKG. ON 1/2" x 2 1/2" CURVED STEEL TUBE FRAME
FOR CURVED METAL WALL ADJ. FITTING RM. SEE 510
FINISHED WALL CONSTRUCTION TO BE 1/2" GYP. BD. BOARD ON 2 5/8" x 1 5/8" STEEL STUDS @ 16" O.C.
BLACK LACQUER LUXE WOVEN INSET W/ CENTER GLASS TILES - SEE PANELS, SEE DWG.
FLEXED TOWER W/ SECURITY SINGLE PANELS

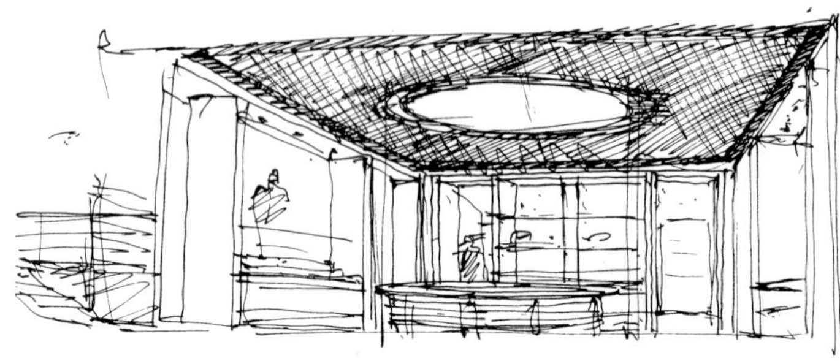

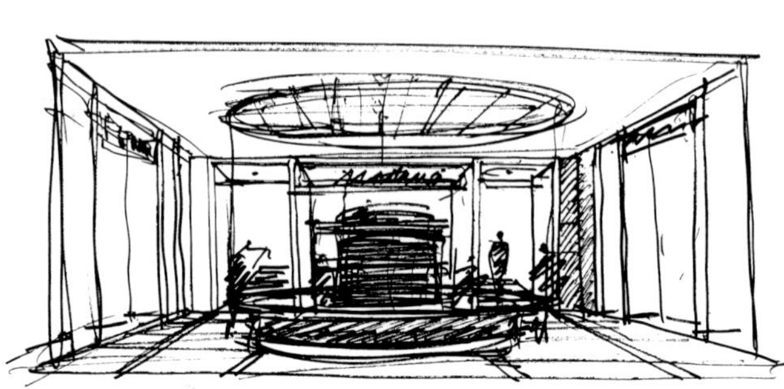

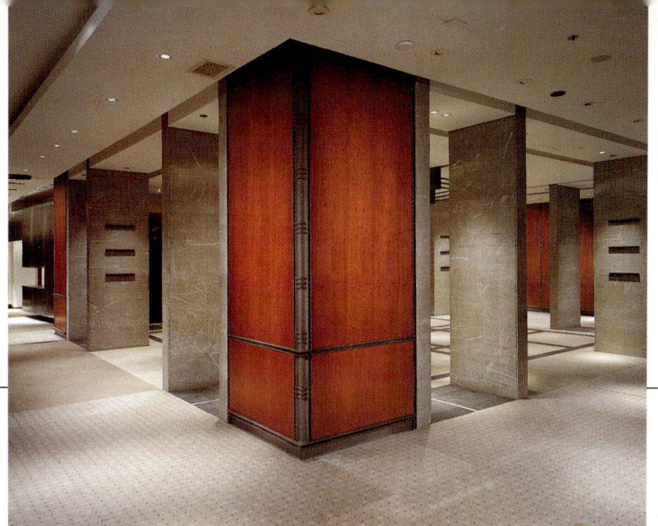

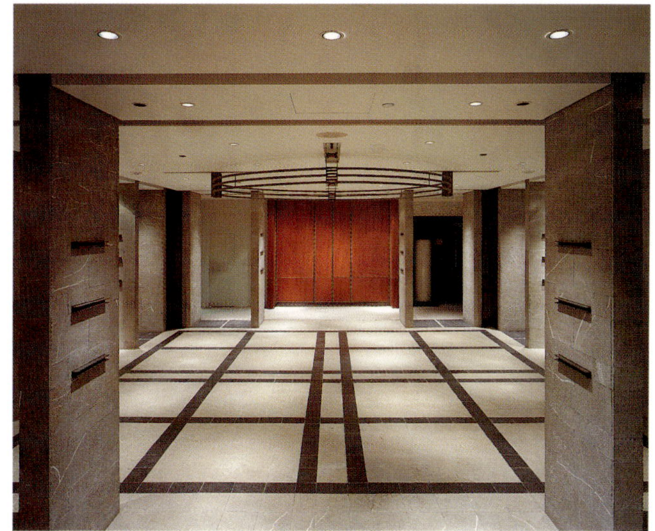

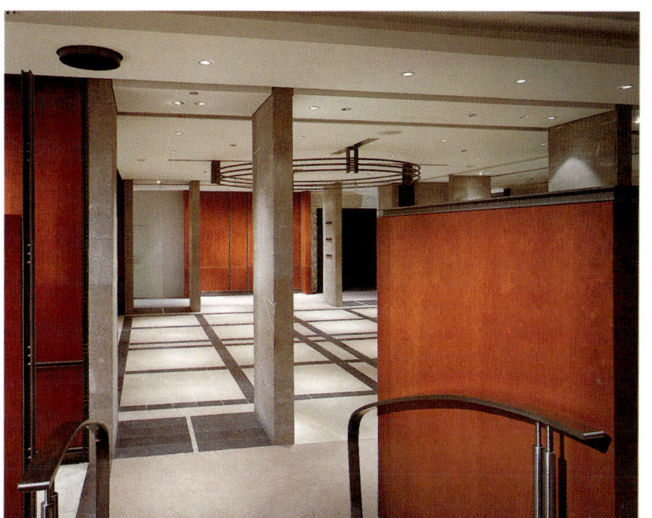

The new multifunctional court is perfectly suited for retail display and event presentation by leading fashion designers from Europe and North America. An elegant system of rails, slots, and brackets accommodates changing displays.

Nicolas

Nicolas, a menswear boutique, is located in Toronto's fashionable Bloor-Yorkville shopping district. The plan generates dynamic movement within the shop and provides maximum flexibility for the display of merchandise.

The storefront appears to slip through the rusticated base of the existing building, defined by a surrounding frame and fascia of steel finished with graphite paint. Stainless steel cladding conceals an existing structural pier. Nickel-plated letters and a sculptural stainless steel custom door-pull establish the store's initial image. A series of planes layer the retail floor from the street deep into the store, beginning with pivoting panels in the shop window, moving to a sliding aluminum screen that veils a private fitting area at the back of the store, and terminating with a wall of aluminum panels and doors.

The primary retail space is set beneath a large, circular aluminum disc with infill panels of Movingui wood veneer. The disc contains lighting and conceals the distribution and diffusion of air. Under the disc, an elliptical cash counter, a rectangular accessory unit, and a long parallelogram display table are positioned to balance and inflect the axis of layered planes centered on the shop window. Back-to-back suspended aluminum channels contain lighting and support the sliding aluminum screen. Sandblasted glass blades line the right side of the store, while a system of vertical aluminum channels form the racking system for the opposite wall. Two types of racking systems share interchangeable hanging rods and break-formed, perforated steel-plate shelves.

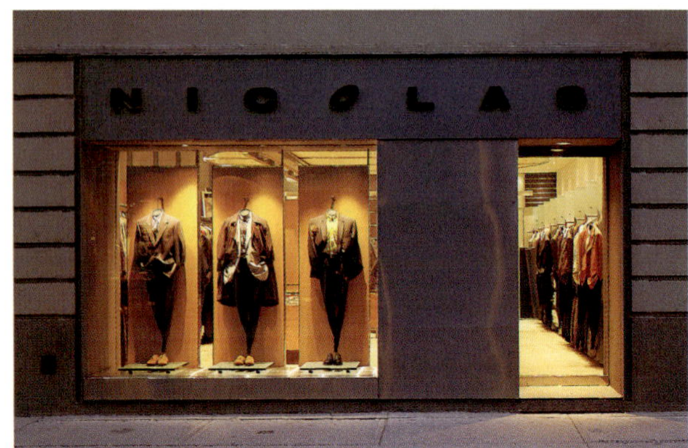

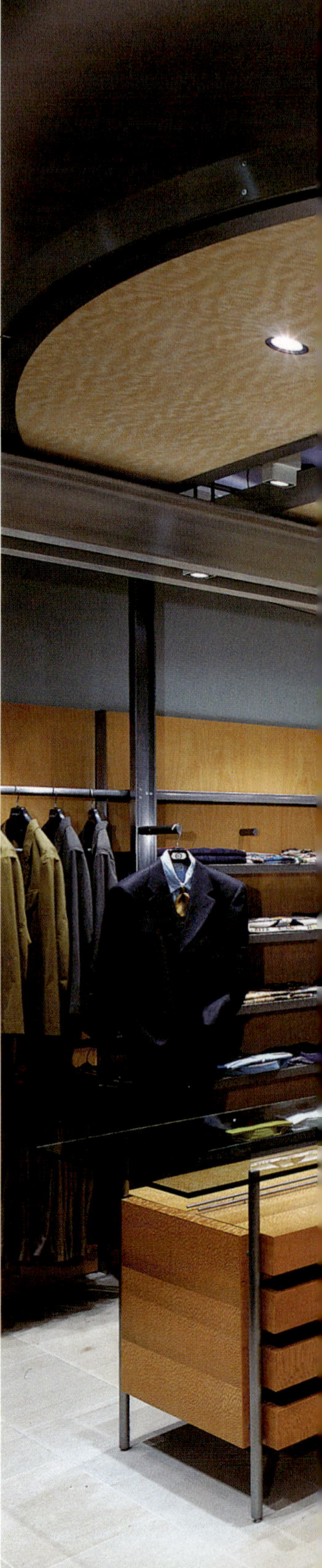

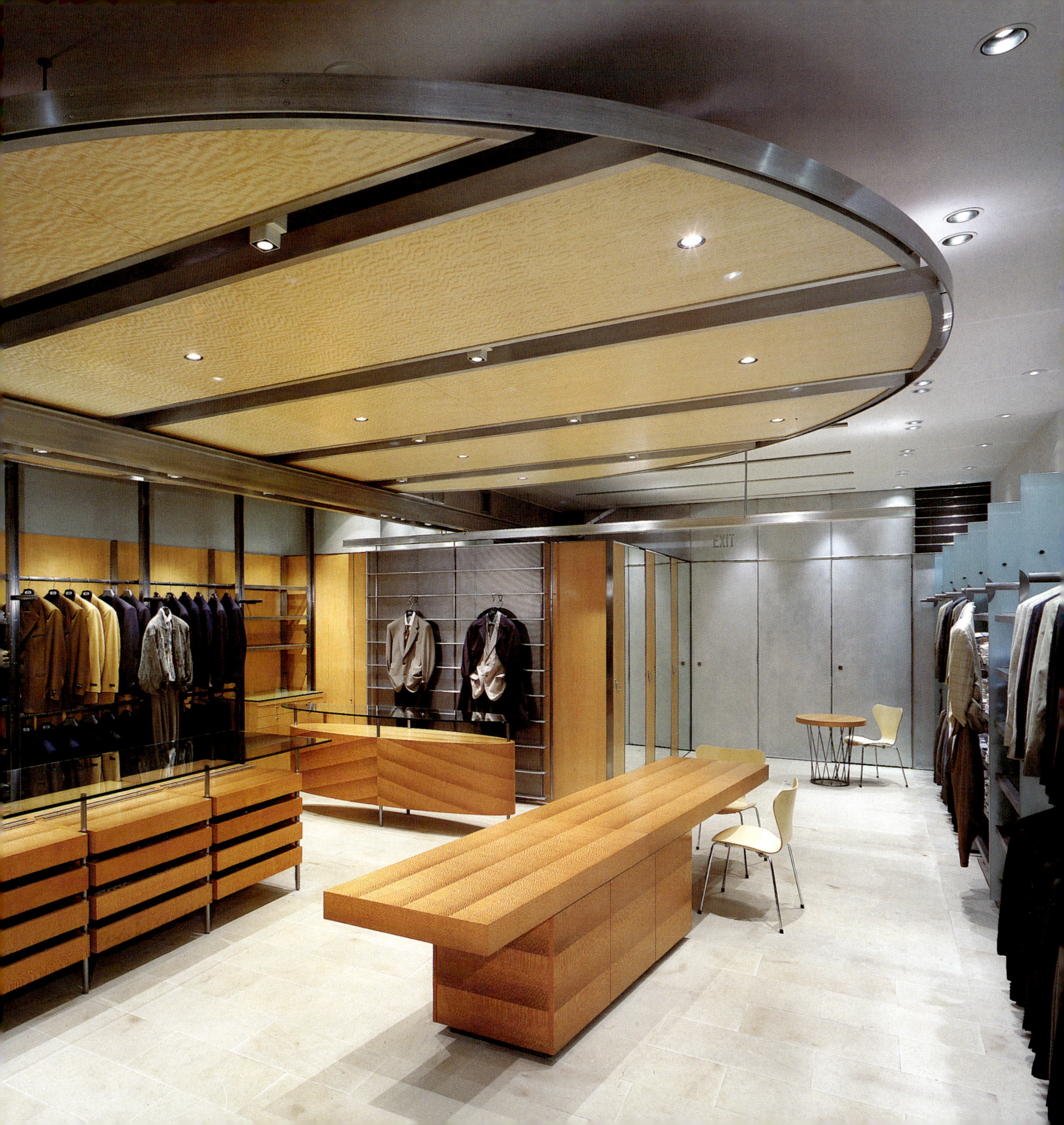

EXIT

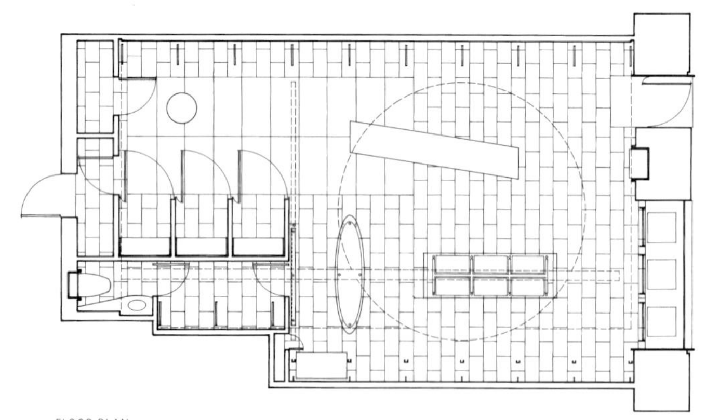

FLOOR PLAN

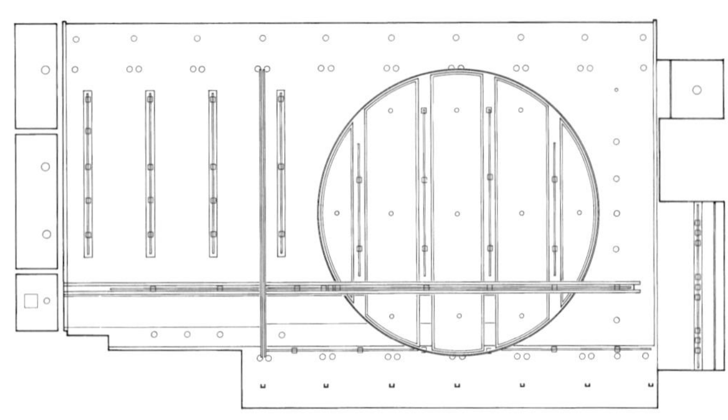

REFLECTED CEILING PLAN

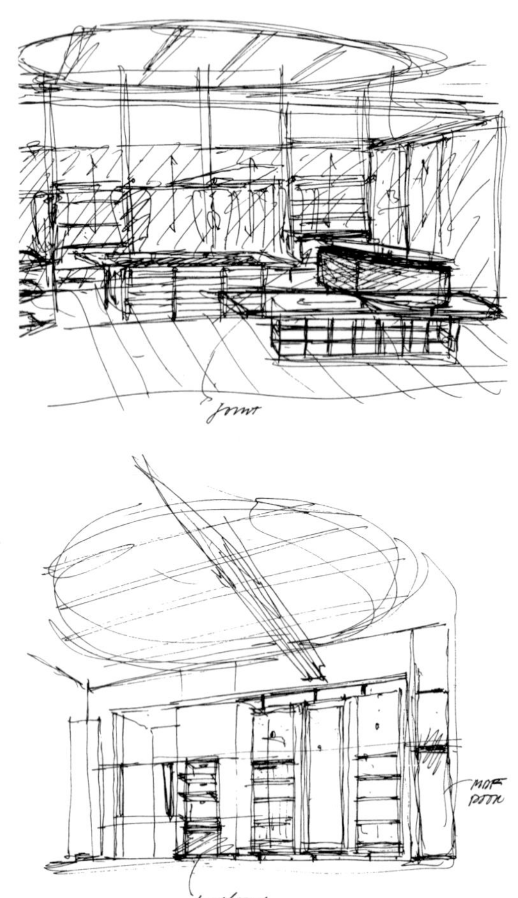

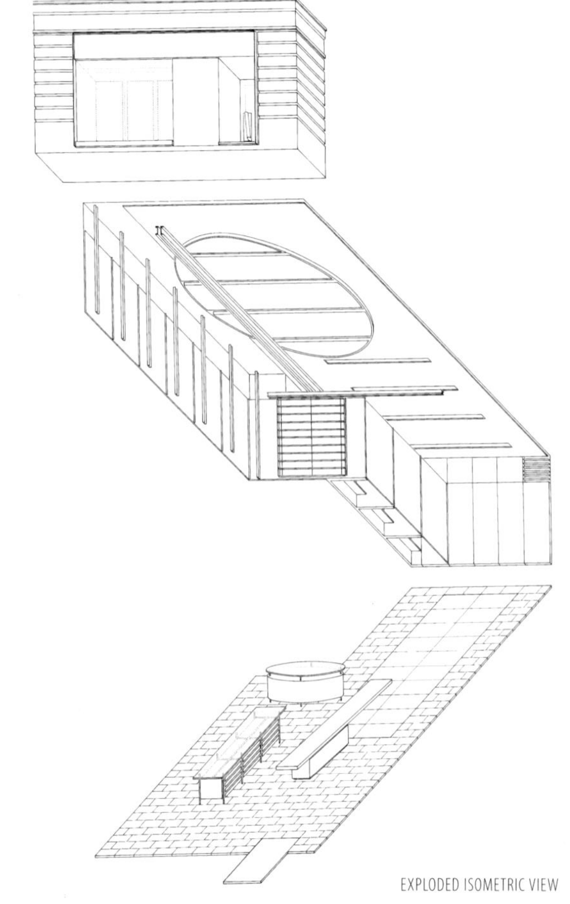

EXPLODED ISOMETRIC VIEW

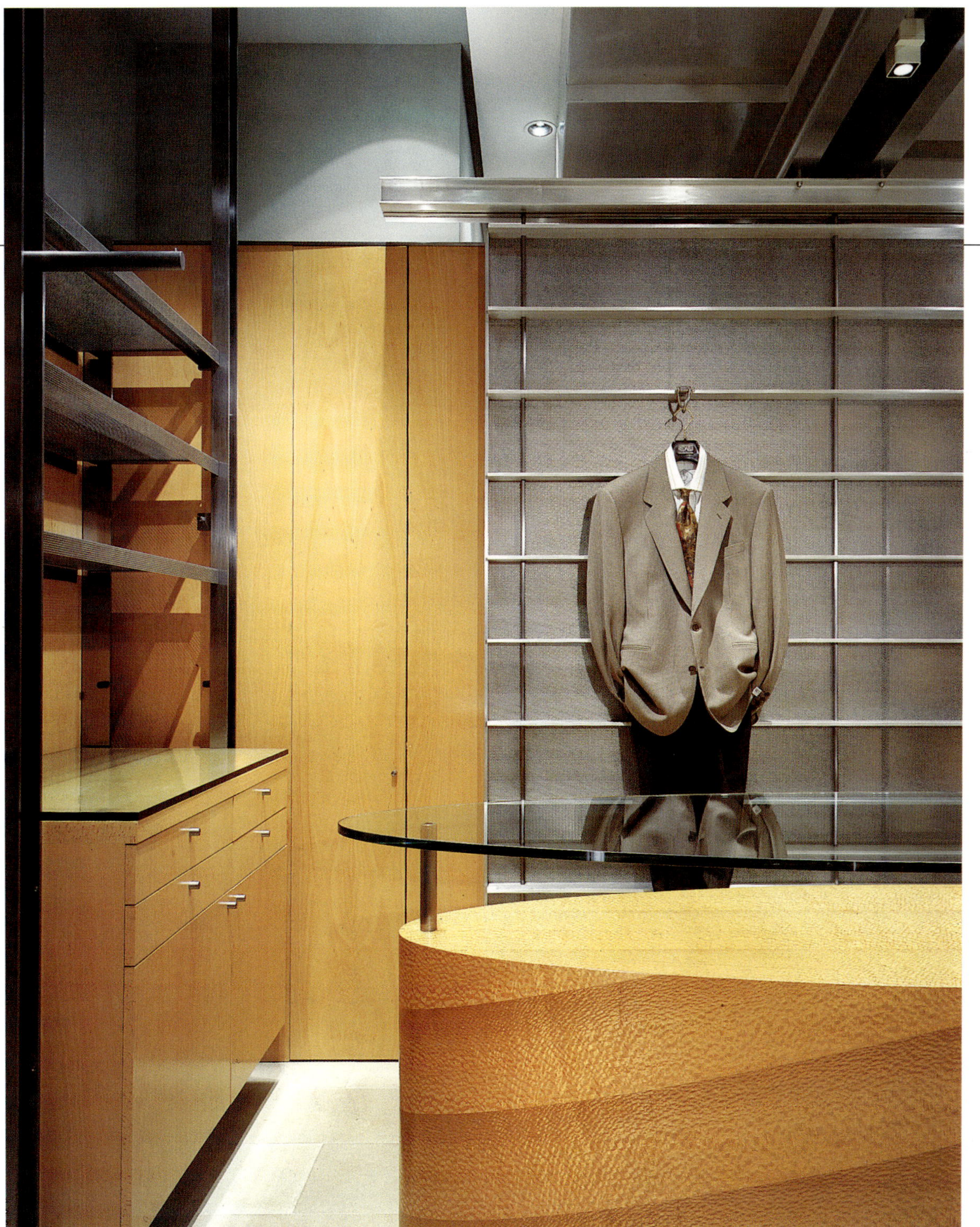

Tension and balance within the interior is created by juxtaposing circular, elliptical, and rectilinear elements with the pure geometry of the suspended disc containing lighting and mechanical elements.

Oasis Parfumerie

Oasis presents a new retailing concept for parfumerie products that features cosmetics, fragrances, accessories, environmental products, and spa services in one store. The interior offers an imaginative shift in the way cosmetics are merchandised in traditional department store settings, allowing the customer to touch, smell, and explore the merchandise. Fragrances for both men and women occupy a large area of the selling floor, which also features cosmetic lines by Lancôme, Christian Dior, Clarins, and Clinique.

The design balances a sense of warmth and permanence with maximum flexibility in merchandising and displays. The ambiance is serene; yet areas of intimate focus within the store offer animation and surprise. Sensuous curvilinear forms juxtaposed with rigorously ordered wall display units create a feeling of movement and informality within a clearly defined, unified spatial concept.

Natural materials, including maple hardwood flooring, Piacentina granite floor slabs, and European beech and figured maple veneers for custom-designed display units are used throughout the store. The lighting concept combines ambient, natural, and artificial light with dramatic highlighting of products, while ceiling and wall planes of painted drywall are accented with color and composed to create visual interest. All steel supports and accessory display elements are finished with powder-coated paint.

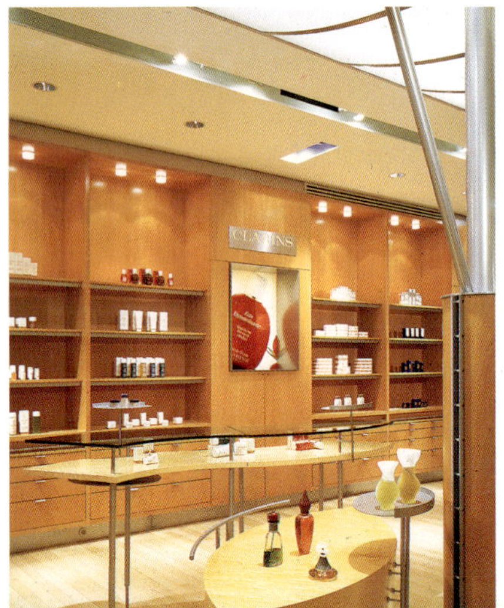

">

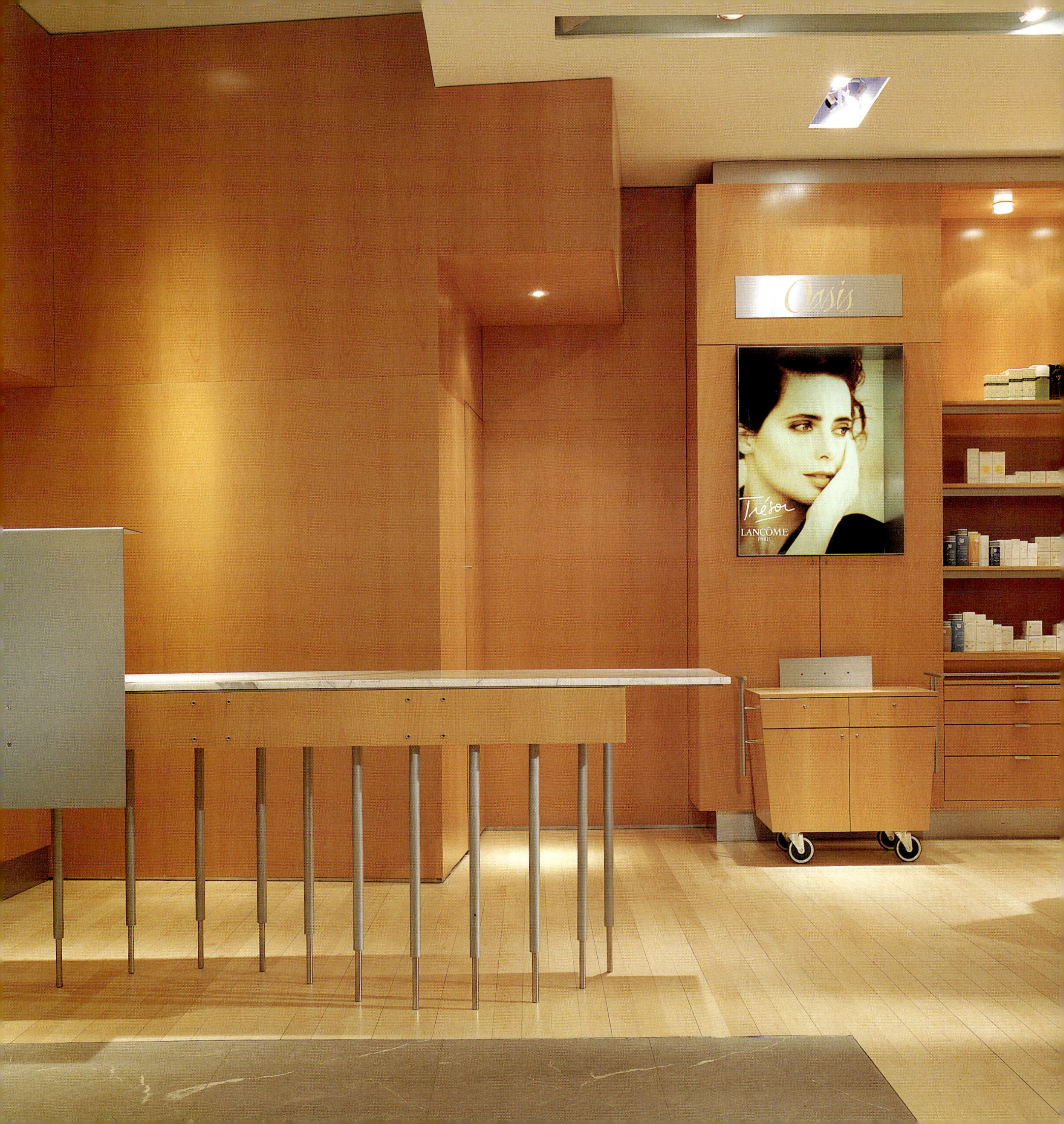
Oasis
Trésor
LANCÔME
PARIS

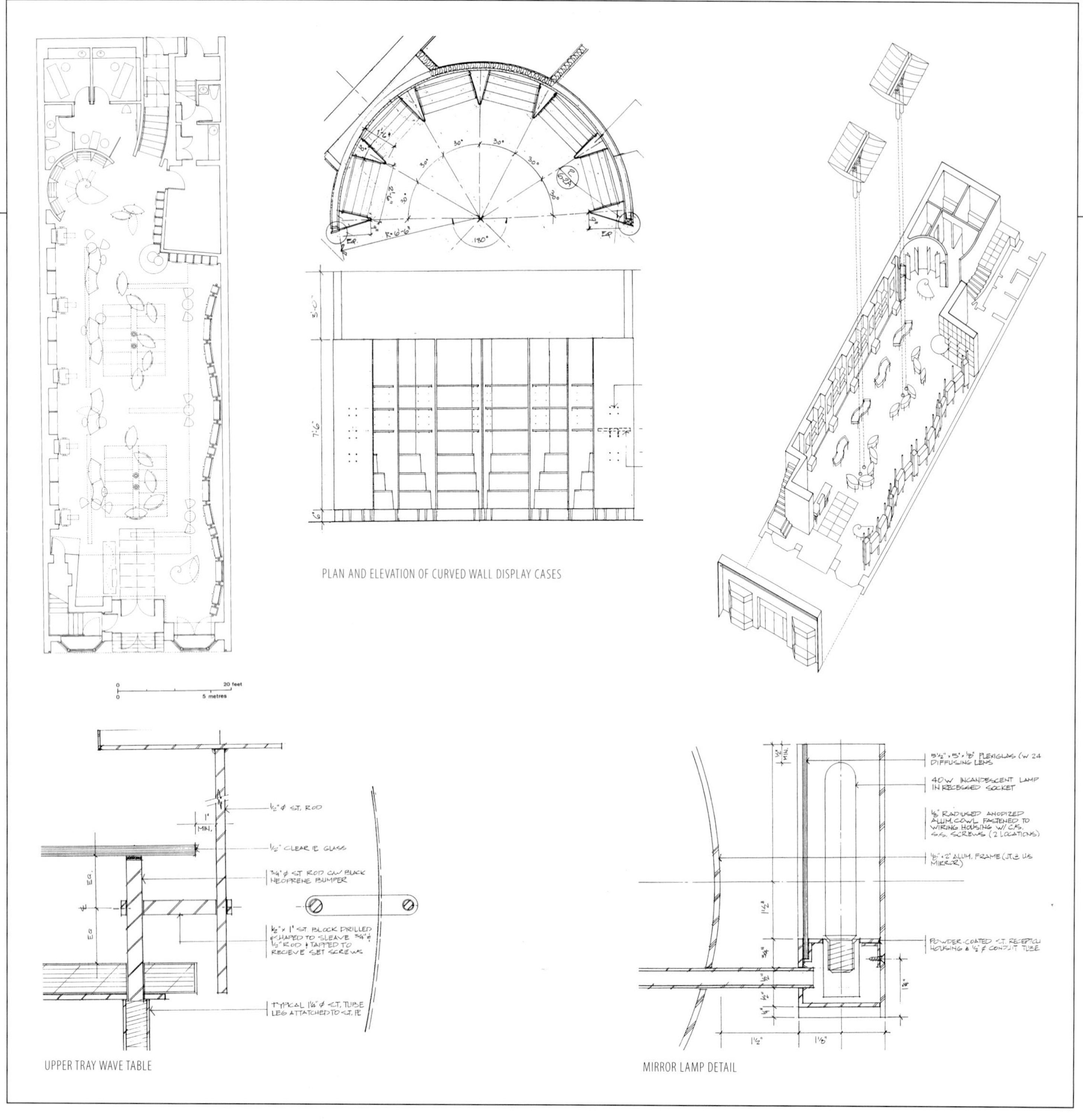

PLAN AND ELEVATION OF CURVED WALL DISPLAY CASES
30°
30°
30°
30°
180°
R·6'-6"
EQ
UPPER TRAY WAVE TABLE
1/2" ø ST. ROD
1/2" CLEAR P GLASS
3/4" ø ST. ROD C/W BLACK NEOPRENE BUMPER
1/2" x 1" ST. BLOCK DRILLED & SHAPED TO SLEAVE 3/4" ø & 1/2" ROD & TAPPED TO RECIEVE SET SCREWS
TYPICAL 1 1/4" ø ST. TUBE LEG ATTATCHED TO ST. P
MIRROR LAMP DETAIL
5 1/2" x 5" x 1/8" PLEXIGLAS (W 24 DIFFUSING LENS
40W INCANDESCENT LAMP IN RECESSED SOCKET
1/8" RADIUSED ANODIZED ALUM. COWL FASTENED TO WIRING HOUSING W/ C/S. S.S. SCREWS (2 LOCATIONS)
1/8" x 2" ALUM. FRAME (JT. @ U/S MIRROR)
POWDER-COATED ST. RECEPTICLE HOUSING & 1/2" ø CONDUIT TUBE
0   20 feet
0   5 metres

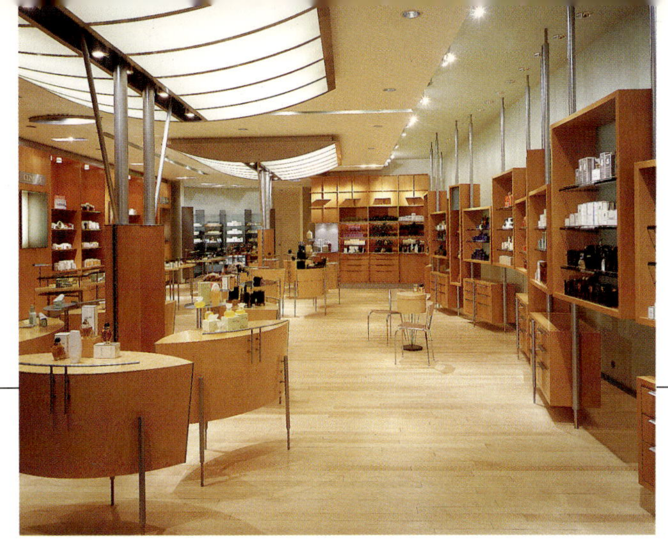

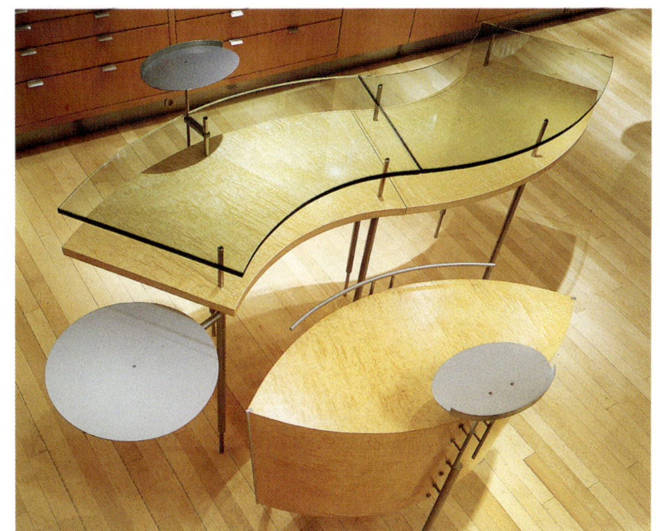

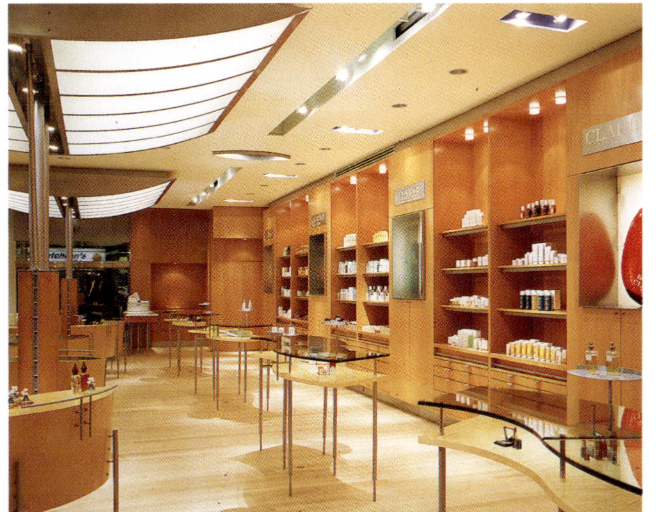

Oasis customers are encouraged to touch and feel cosmetic products on display, rather than in locked cabinets, in an informal and open setting (top). Forms and materials allude to earth, air, fire, and water, including "wave" tables and small "leaf" display cases (center). Sail-like overhead fixtures conceal ventilation and lighting (bottom).

Creative Copy & Design

The interior for Creative Copy & Design (CC&D), a graphic reproduction and design company, occupies two bays of retail frontage at King James Place, also designed by KPMB (page 58). Completed on a small budget, the project employs color, simple forms, and varied textures to create a successful workspace with a vivid image.

Inexpensive and recycled materials, such as reconstituted wood fiber panels, fiberglass, plastic laminate, and medium-density fiberboard are creatively used. A low wall, clad in corrugated wood fiber panels, divides the space into a front reception area and a rear staff work area. With boomerang-shaped counters for customer service in front, and an "open kitchen" of reproduction technology and computer imaging equipment in back, this low wall also offers glimpses into the production workspace through an aluminum window.

Bold forms and simple surfaces create a strong visual identity for CC&D. Stained fiberboard and painted wall planes are treated with colors familiar to the printing industry, such as cyan (deep blue), which is analogous to printer's ink, and pale yellow, which is similar to the color of manila envelopes. The two large glass bay windows are unified by a translucent elliptical canopy that is tilted and suspended from above. Deeper in the space, a "service box" clad in medium-density fiberboard contains the processing room, washrooms, and mechanical equipment. A large, low, blue wall defines the upper-level work area.

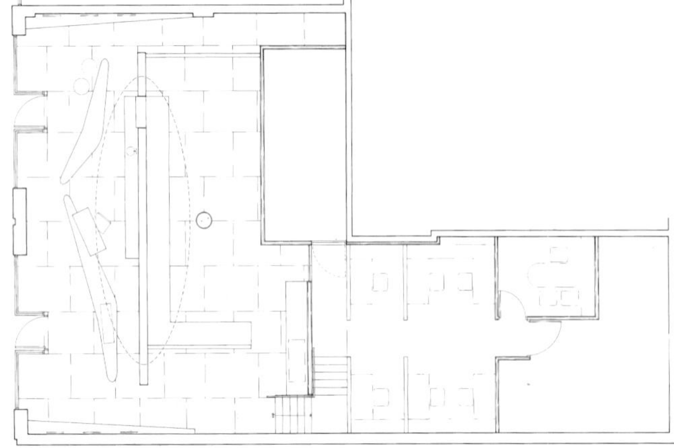

GROUND FLOOR PLAN

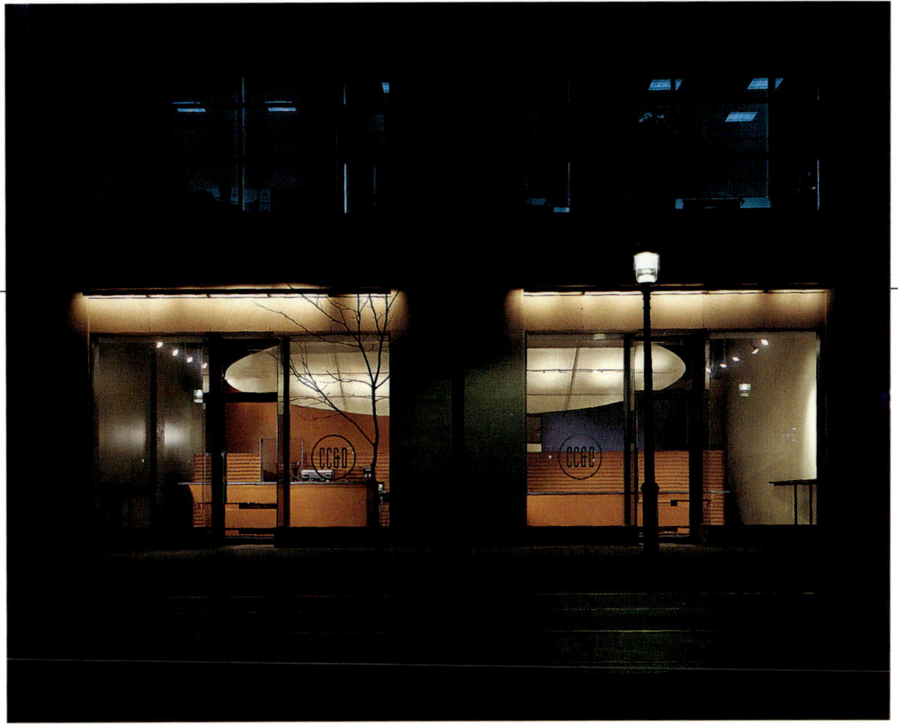

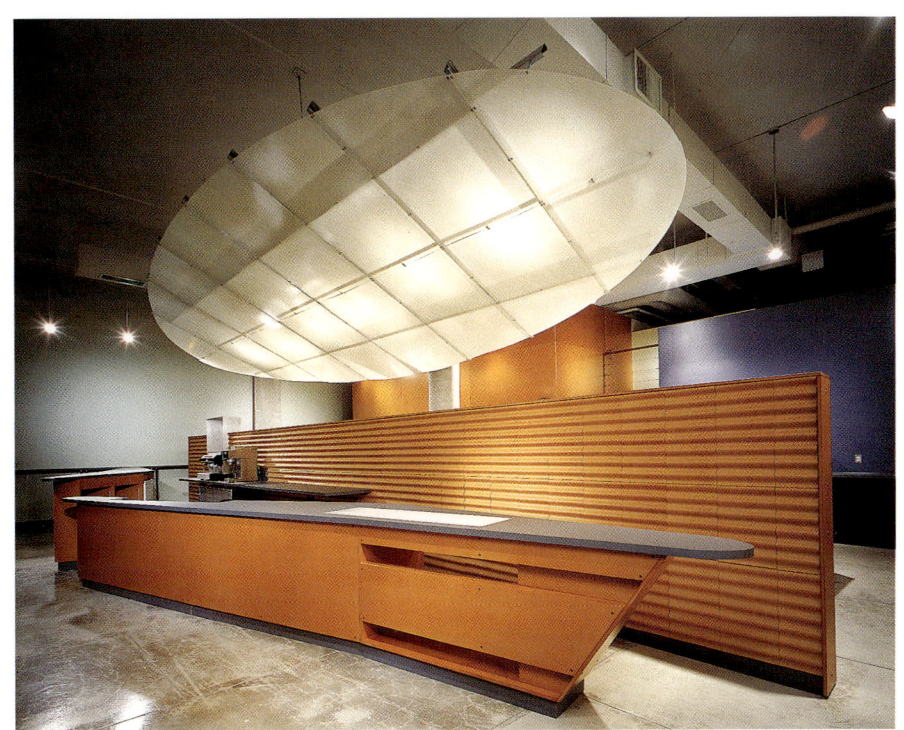

Sega City @ Playdium

Sega City @ Playdium, a location-based family entertainment center, is a light, steel-framed structure designed to merge technology, spectacle, and event on a developing urban site. A playful exterior characterizes the games inside: walls vibrate with painted patterns; the roof explodes with colorful trapezoidal projections; and large electronic, three-dimensional images animate surfaces. A glass pavilion under an oval disc marks the entrance to the Playdium, oriented toward a major intersection to the southwest.

From the entry pavilion, the visitor is drawn through a tunnel into the game area, its plan in the figure of a parallelogram. Thematic zones of discovery, defined by audiovisual technology, organize the games. As the visitor moves from zone to zone, soundscapes recreate the "whoosh" of an Indianapolis race car rushing by on a track, the "roar" of a baseball crowd, or the ritual mantra of a martial arts fighter.

The building, a glowing container of activity by night, is visible from all directions in the surrounding city, with clear routes, passenger drop-off zones, and ample parking to provide easy access. Large, angular, wood screen walls divide the site landscape into areas for outdoor activities such as go-cart racing, volleyball, basketball, baseball, and rock climbing.

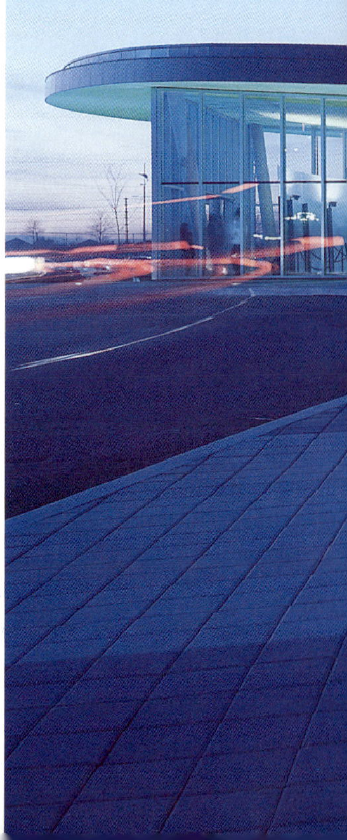

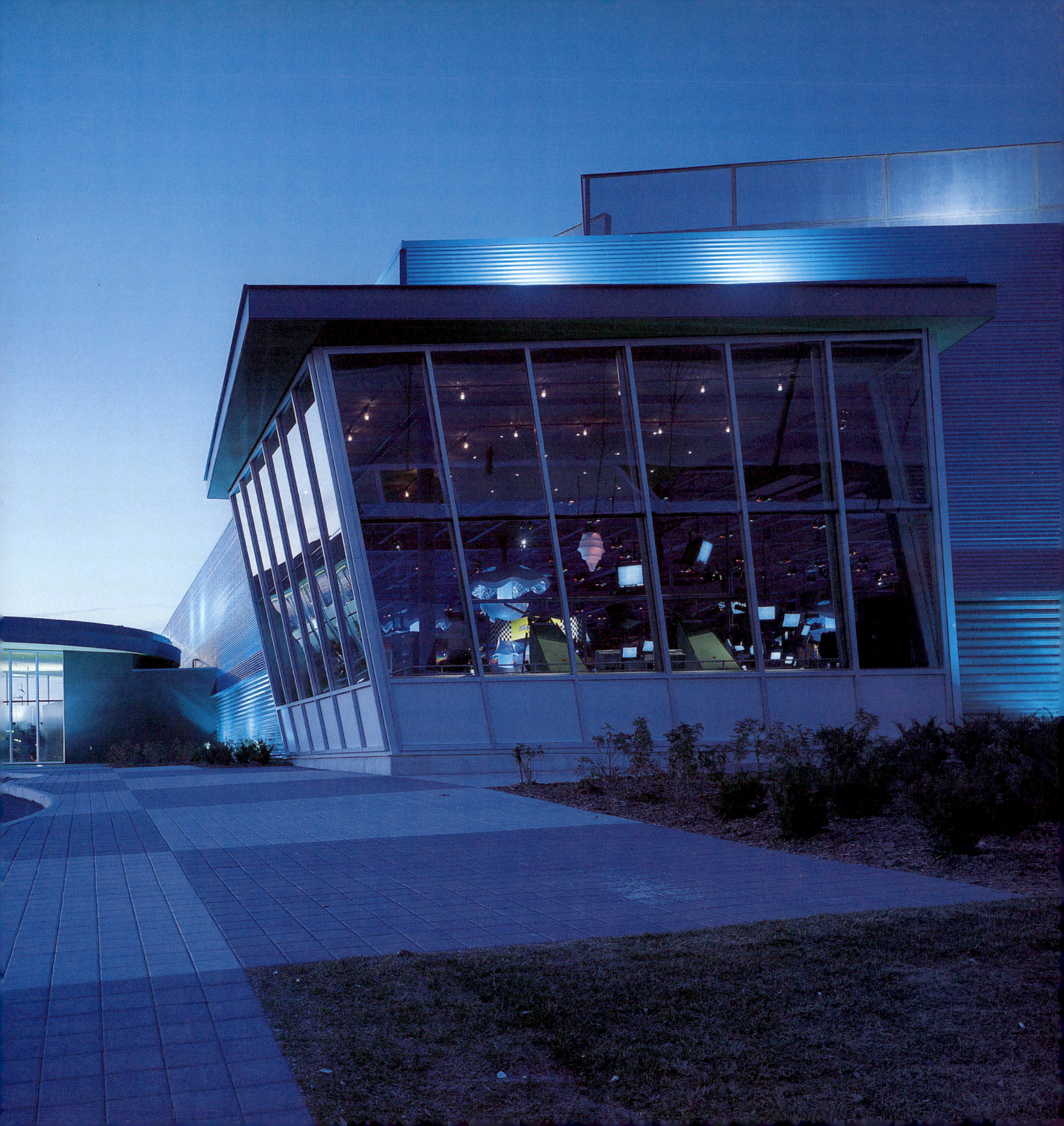

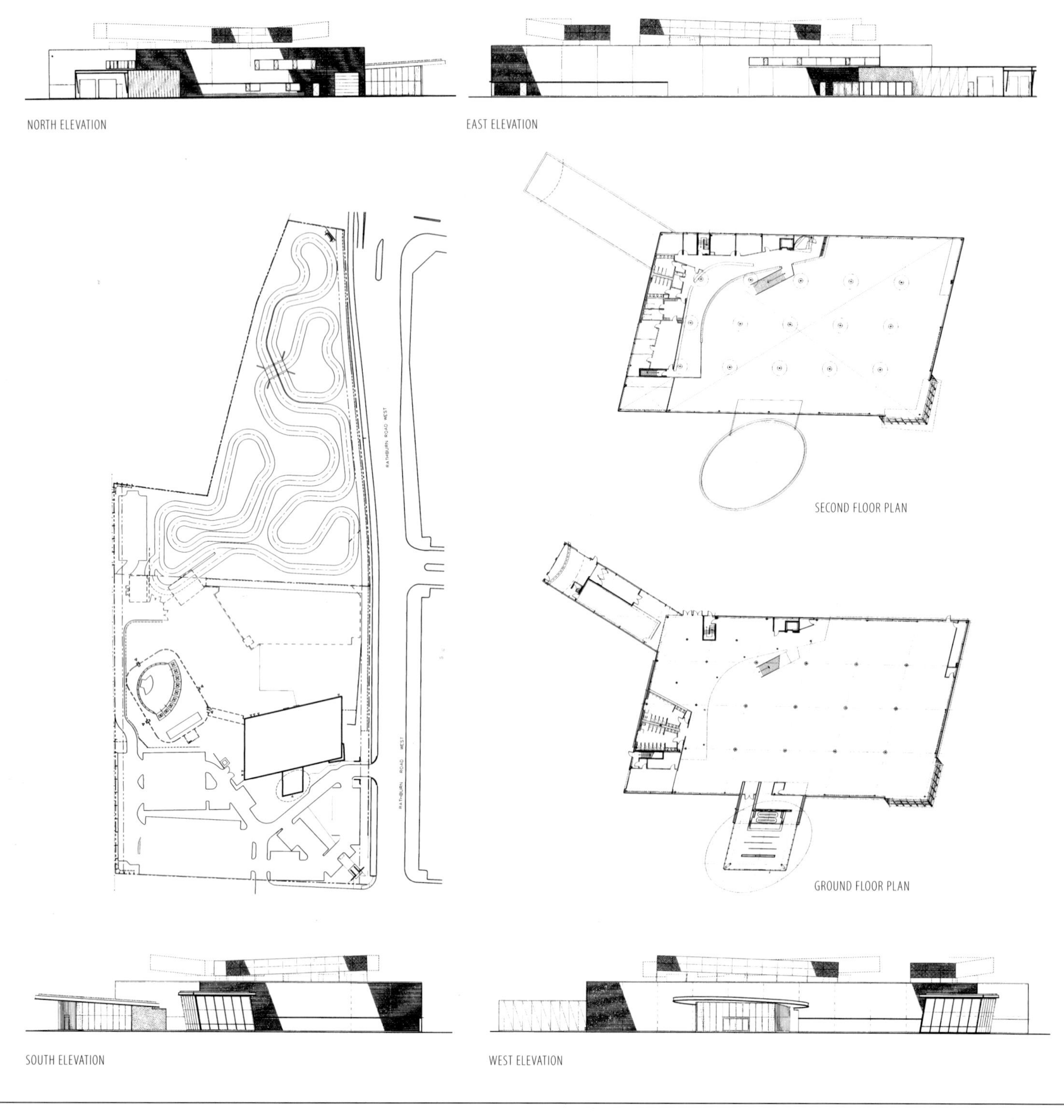

NORTH ELEVATION
EAST ELEVATION
SECOND FLOOR PLAN
GROUND FLOOR PLAN
SOUTH ELEVATION
WEST ELEVATION
RATHBURN ROAD WEST
RATHBURN ROAD WEST

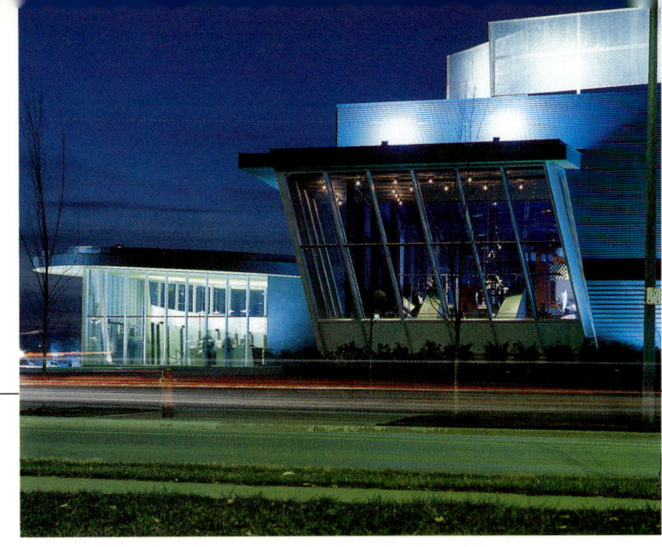

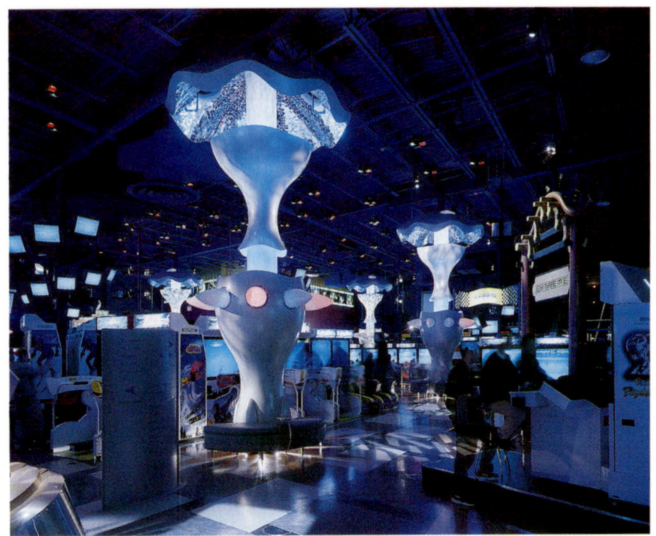

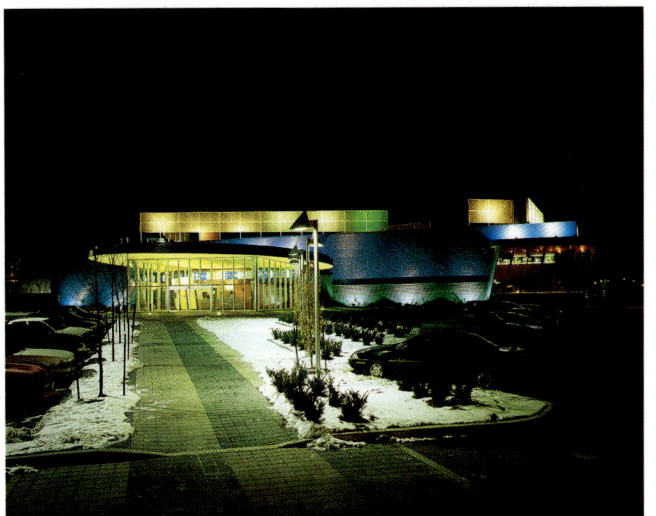

At night, pedestrians view activities inside the Playdium from adjacent streets and parking lots (top). The game area (by II BY IV Design) is organized into zones of play and discovery (center). A highly visible glass pavilion under a floating disc marks the entry (bottom).

Grand Valley Institution for Women

The Grand Valley Institution for Women represents a new direction in correctional services: the reintegration into society of women serving federal sentences. Architecturally, the challenge was to translate the recommendations of the Task Force on Federally-Sentenced Women into built form, and to transform the typical institutional atmosphere of womens' prisons into a more community-based, interactive environment.

Located on a rural site, the design is based on the model of a traditional village, and organized around a shared central green. Balancing communal and private spaces within a humanely-scaled complex, a series of interconnected buildings houses the individual program elements—administration, visiting areas, case work, the gymnasium, classrooms, and other services. A common circulation loggia, facing toward the green, unites the complex. An ecumenical space of worship and healing is expressed as a conical form that occupies a pivotal position in the plan of the complex. Internalized to ensure security and privacy, as well as to respect local community perceptions, the building complex presents intentionally modest and discreet facades to the public, with limited door and window openings.

Ten cottages, each housing eight women, are arranged around the green and linked to the complex through a series of pedestrian pathways and a circular drive. Deep porches, sloped roofs, and simple materials respond to the rural context and the community of Kitchener-Waterloo. The residential scale, natural light, color, and ventilation provide a healthy environment that fosters positive relationships between the women, staff, and visitors.

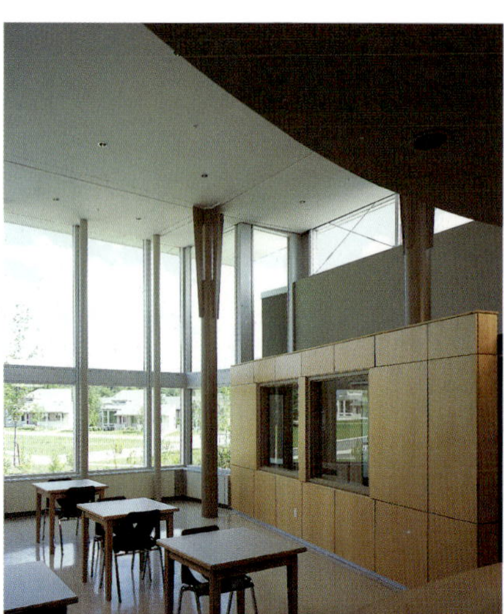

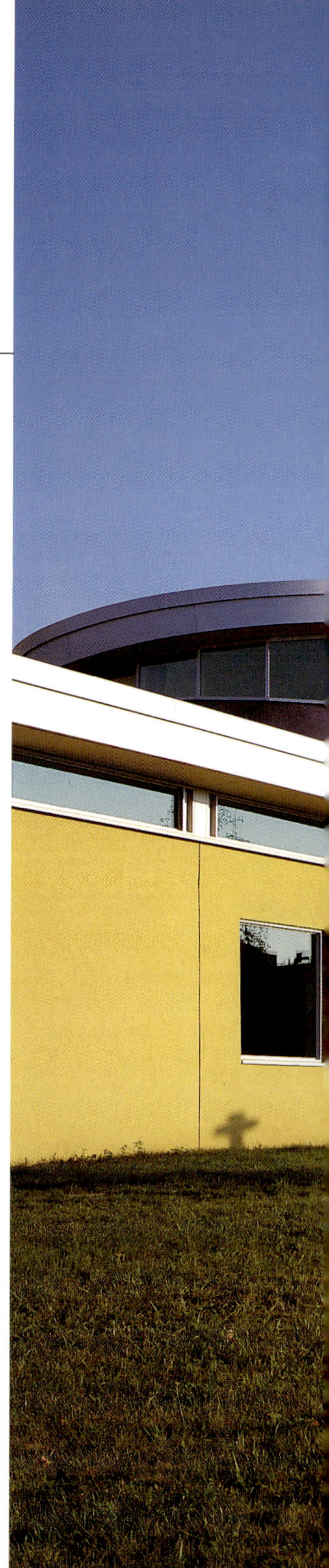

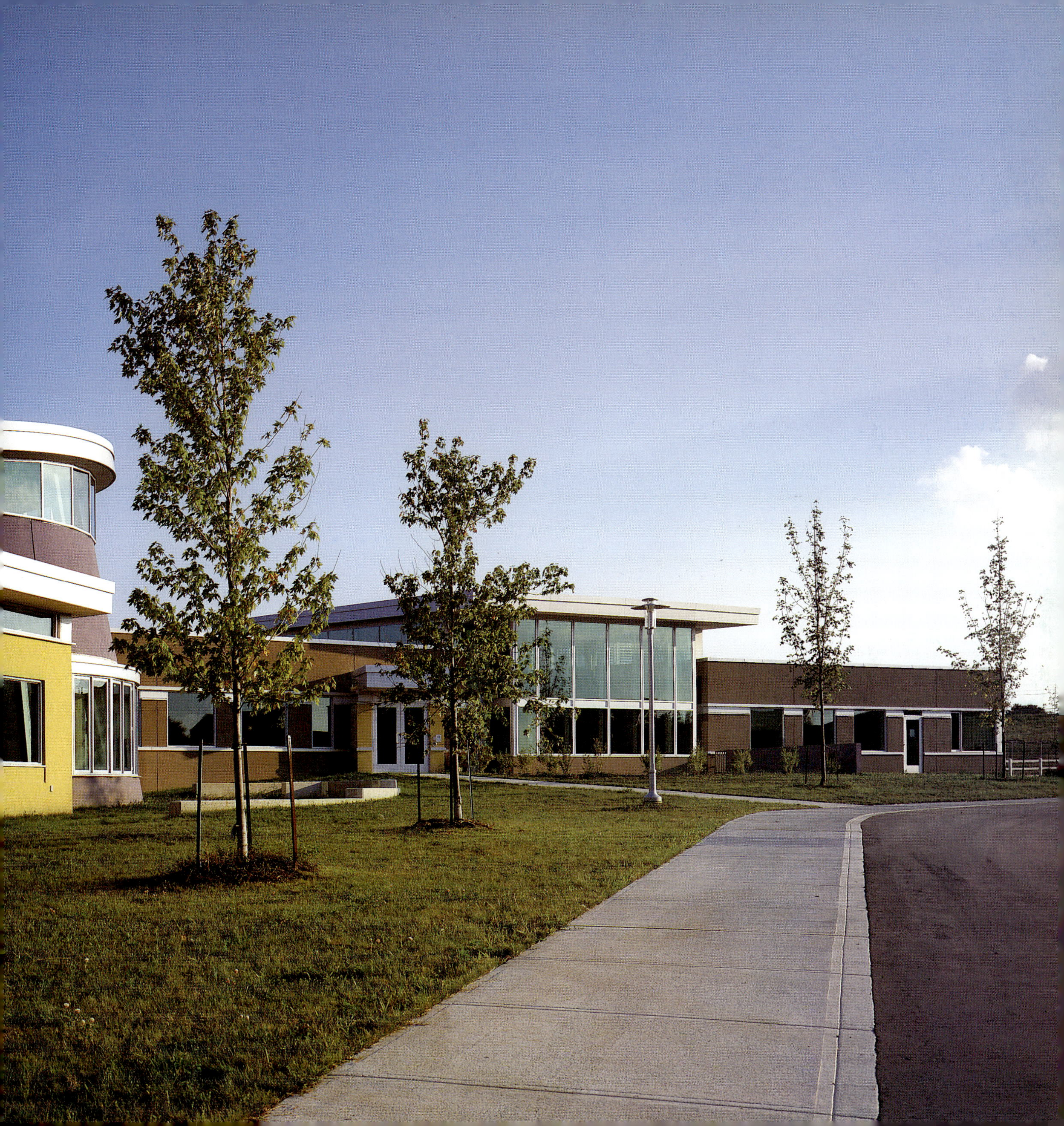

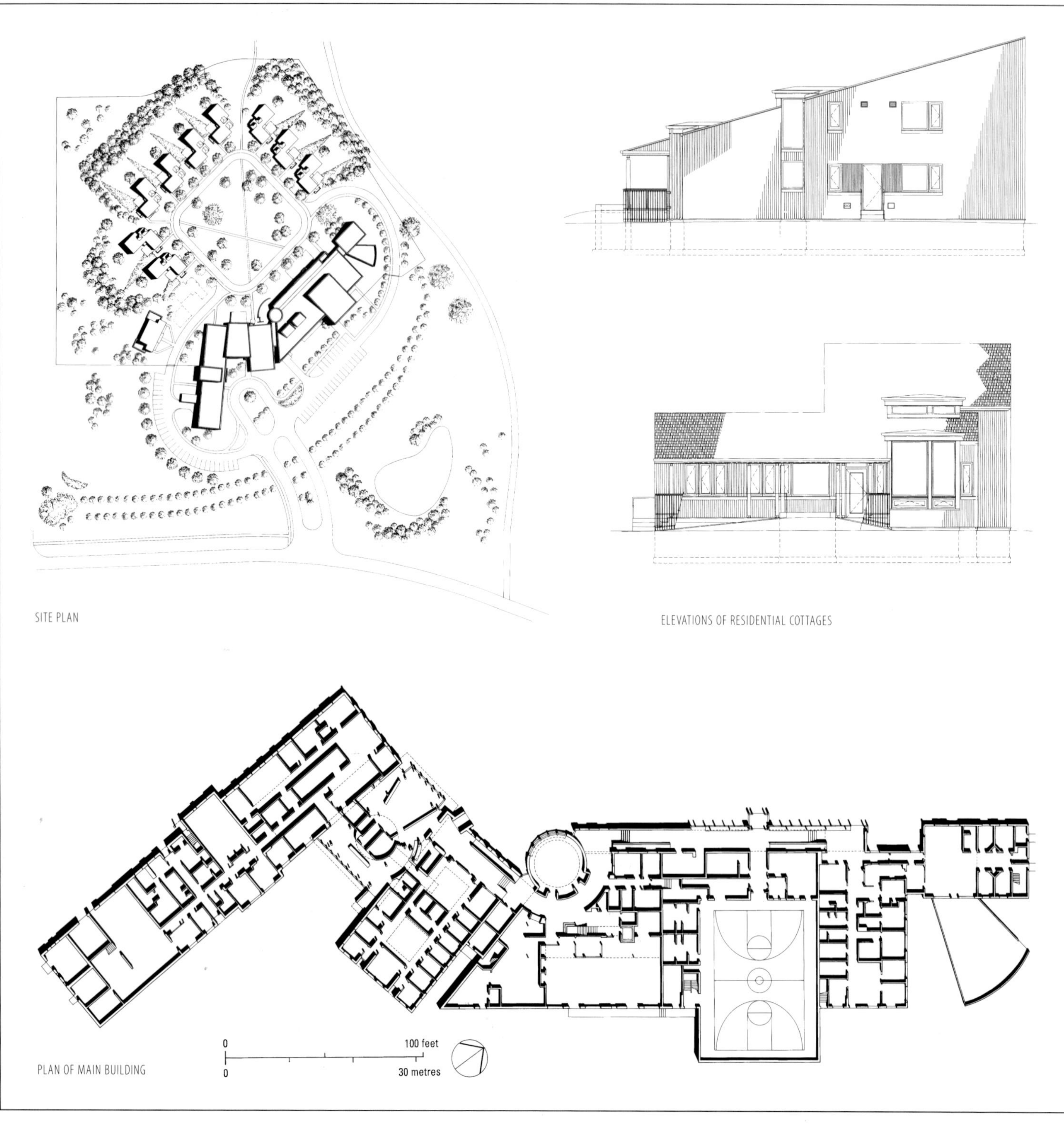

SITE PLAN

ELEVATIONS OF RESIDENTIAL COTTAGES

PLAN OF MAIN BUILDING

0   100 feet

0   30 metres

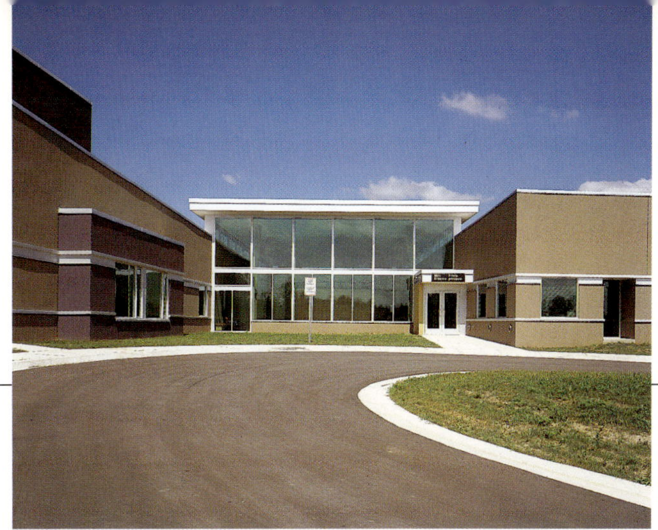

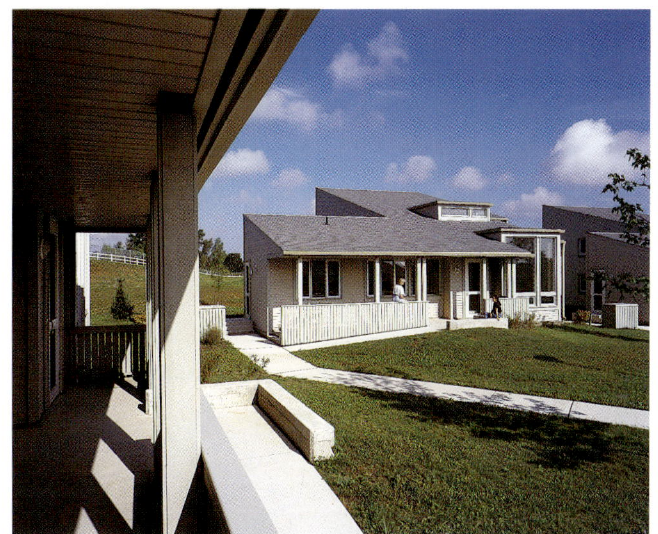

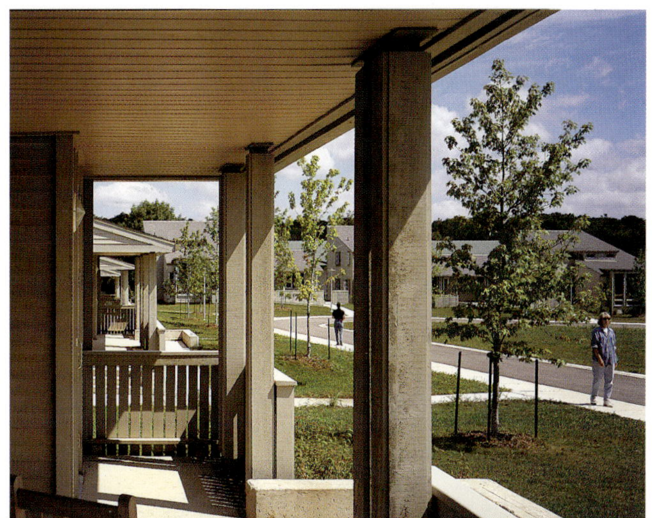

Street elevations of the complex are campus-like in character, and intentionally avoid institutional references (top). The internal village green is surrounded by residential cottage units for female inmates (center, bottom).

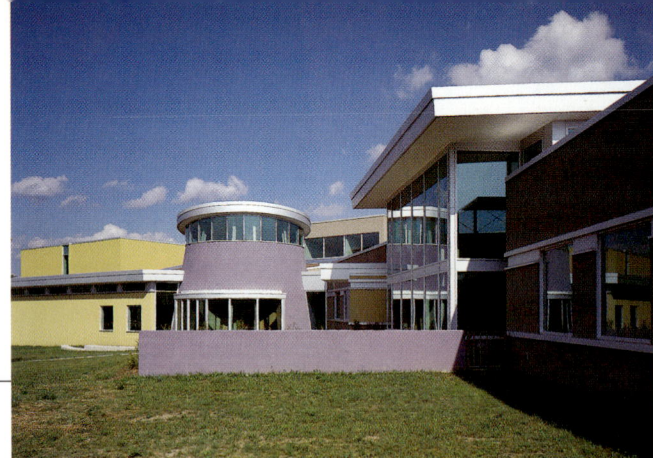

A pivotal element in the main complex is the conical-shaped spirituality room, an interdenominational space for worship and healing.

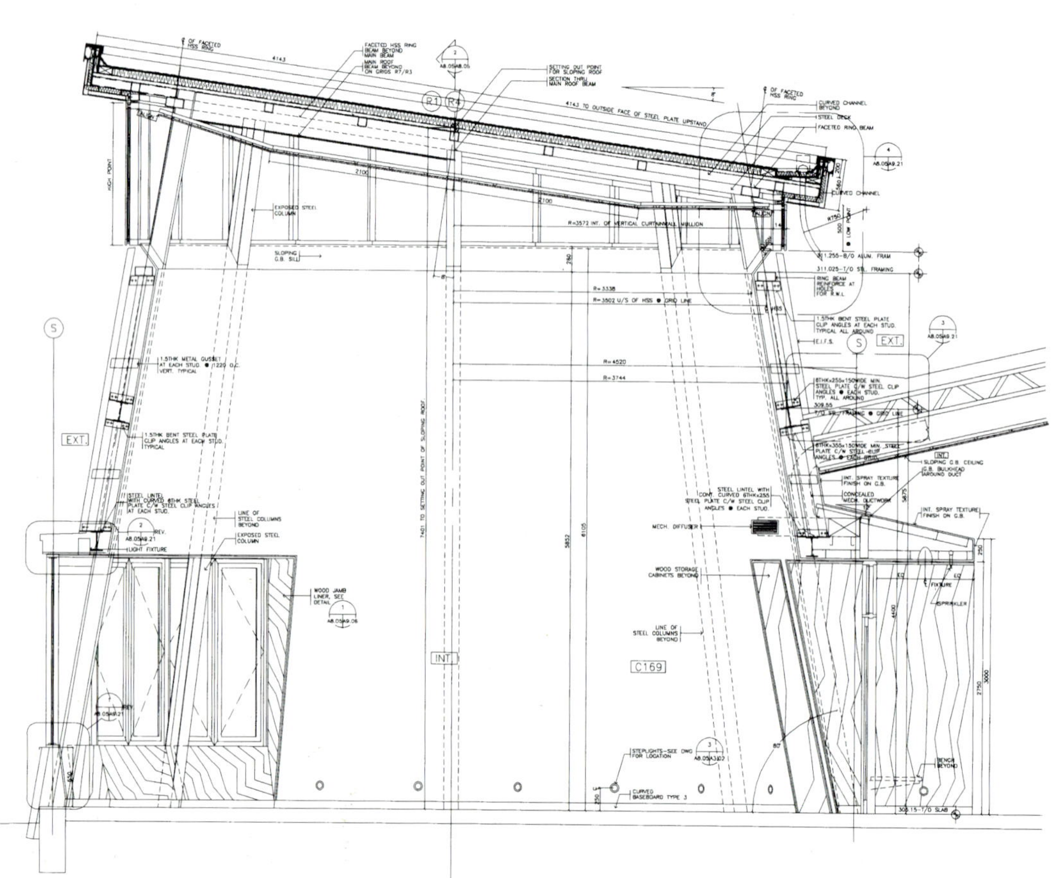

SECTION THROUGH SPIRITUALITY ROOM

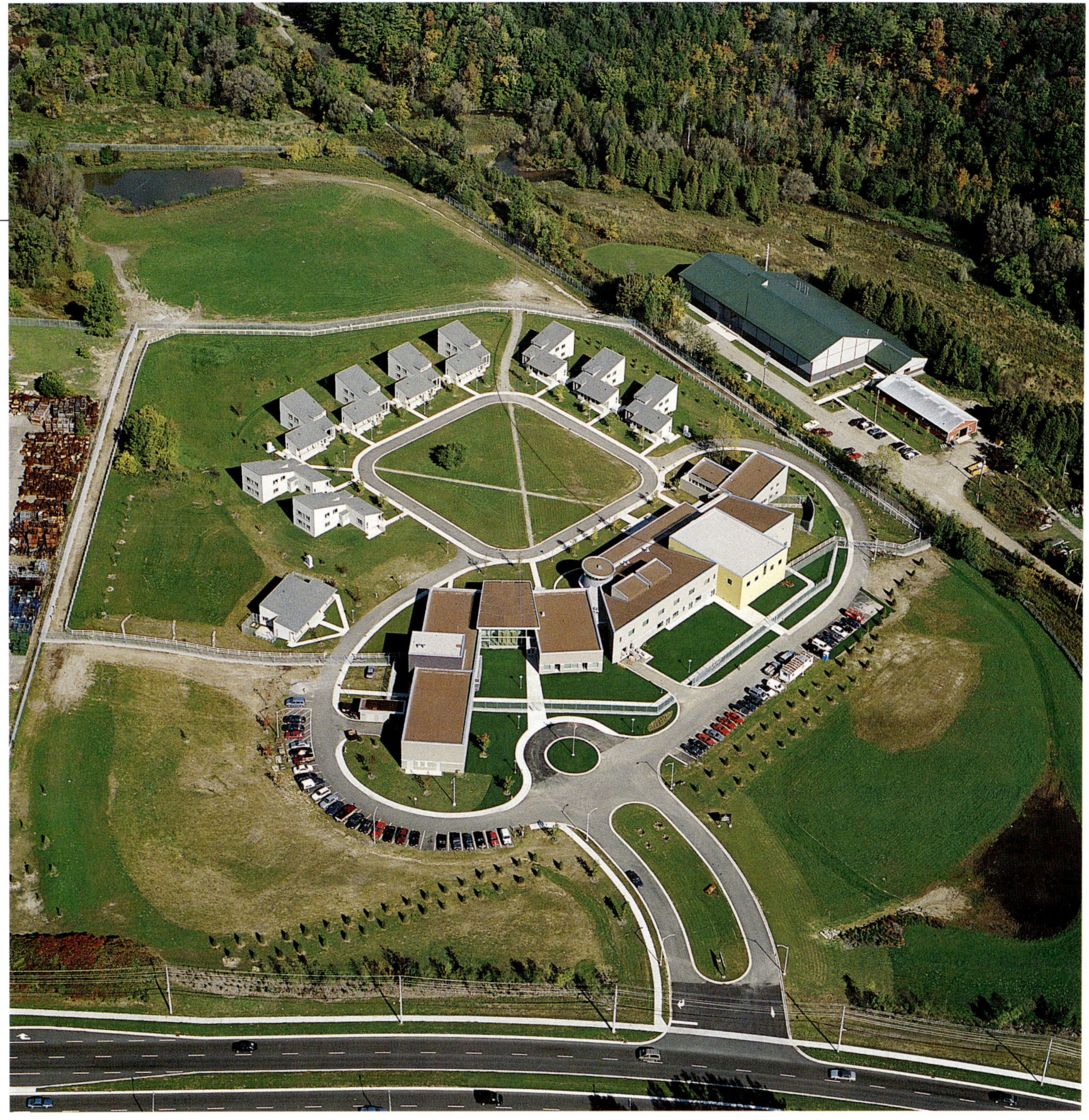

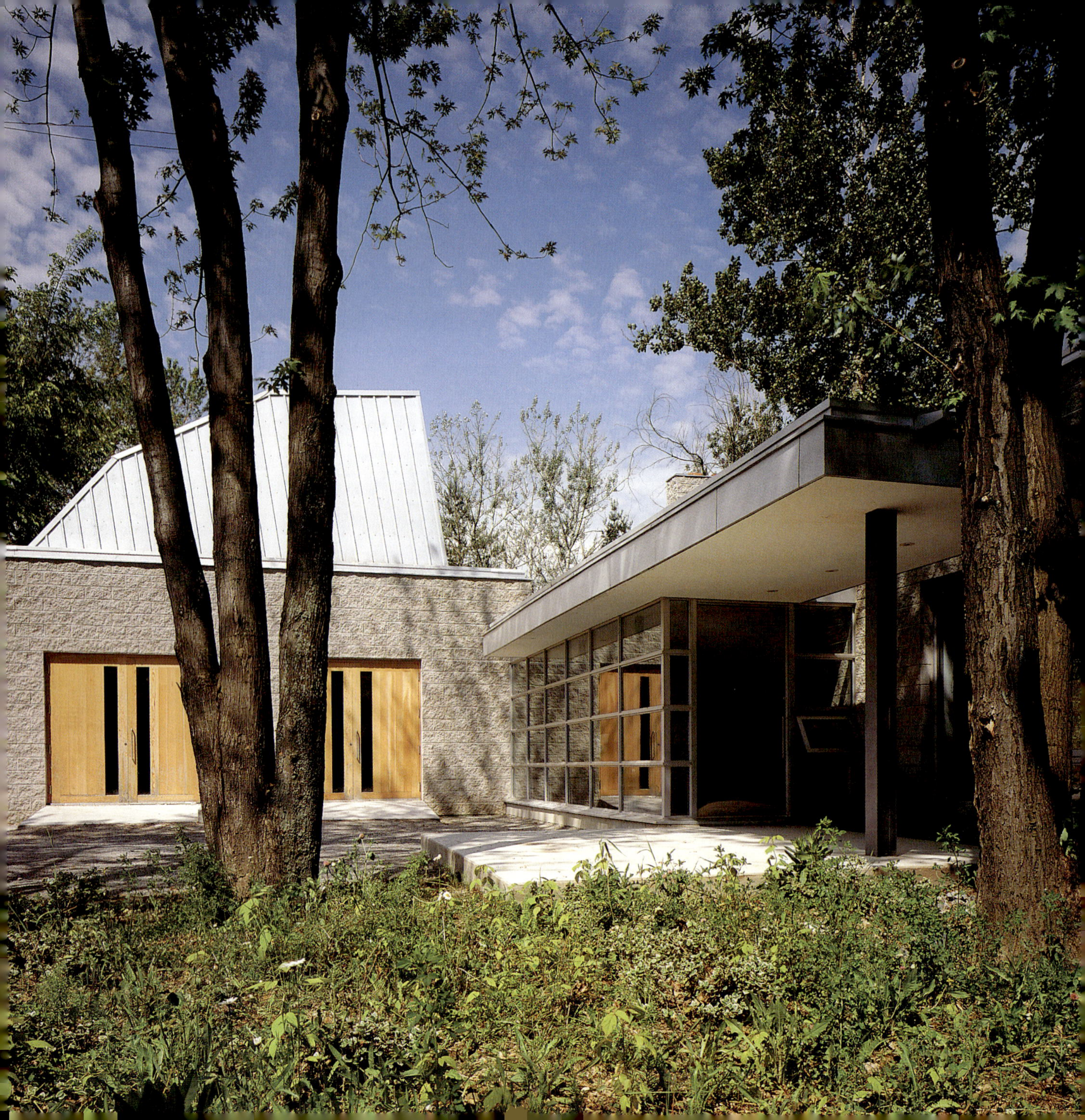

Private Realm ▶

Tudhope Studios

The design studios for Tudhope Associates are located in an existing brick warehouse building on King Street West. Two large-scale stucco panels transform the exterior of the building to create a dynamic image for the company; large, projecting aluminum mullions and sills reproportion the existing window openings; and an aluminum-sheathed, existing structural column and new entry canopy mark the entrance to the building.

Inside, a thick wall of plaster passes from the distinct volume of the entry stair into the primary space of the studios, locking the two elements together in plan and section. In the entry, this wall appears as a portal, and on the second and third floors, rises up to interconnect studio and reception areas. Graphic design studios occupy the north end of both floors. Enclosed boxes holding the conference room and production areas buffer the studios from the reception area, meeting rooms, and executive offices. Workstations constructed of steel and perforated-metal screen define the circulation through the studio. Three rotating screens create a meeting area beyond the third-floor reception area. The reception desk, constructed from folded planes of gun-metal steel with lace wood tops, carries through the theme of the steel and veneer-wood interior furnishings.

A floating curved panel directs light through a large cut-out in the second floor toward retail showrooms below-grade. This second-level clerestory window thus highlights the entry to the retail space, and joins it to the space and light of the street.

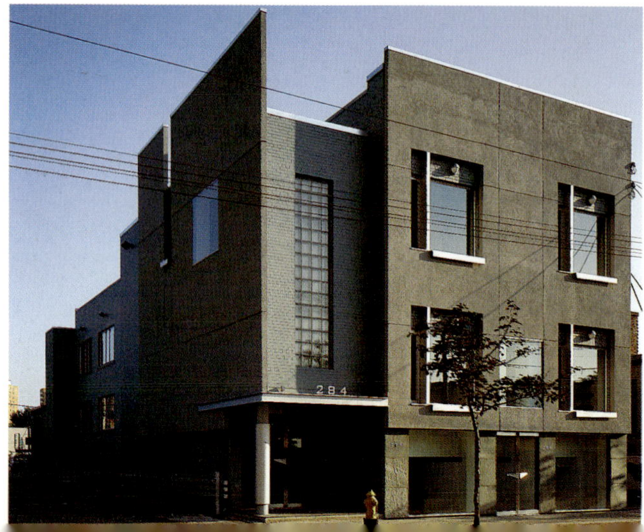

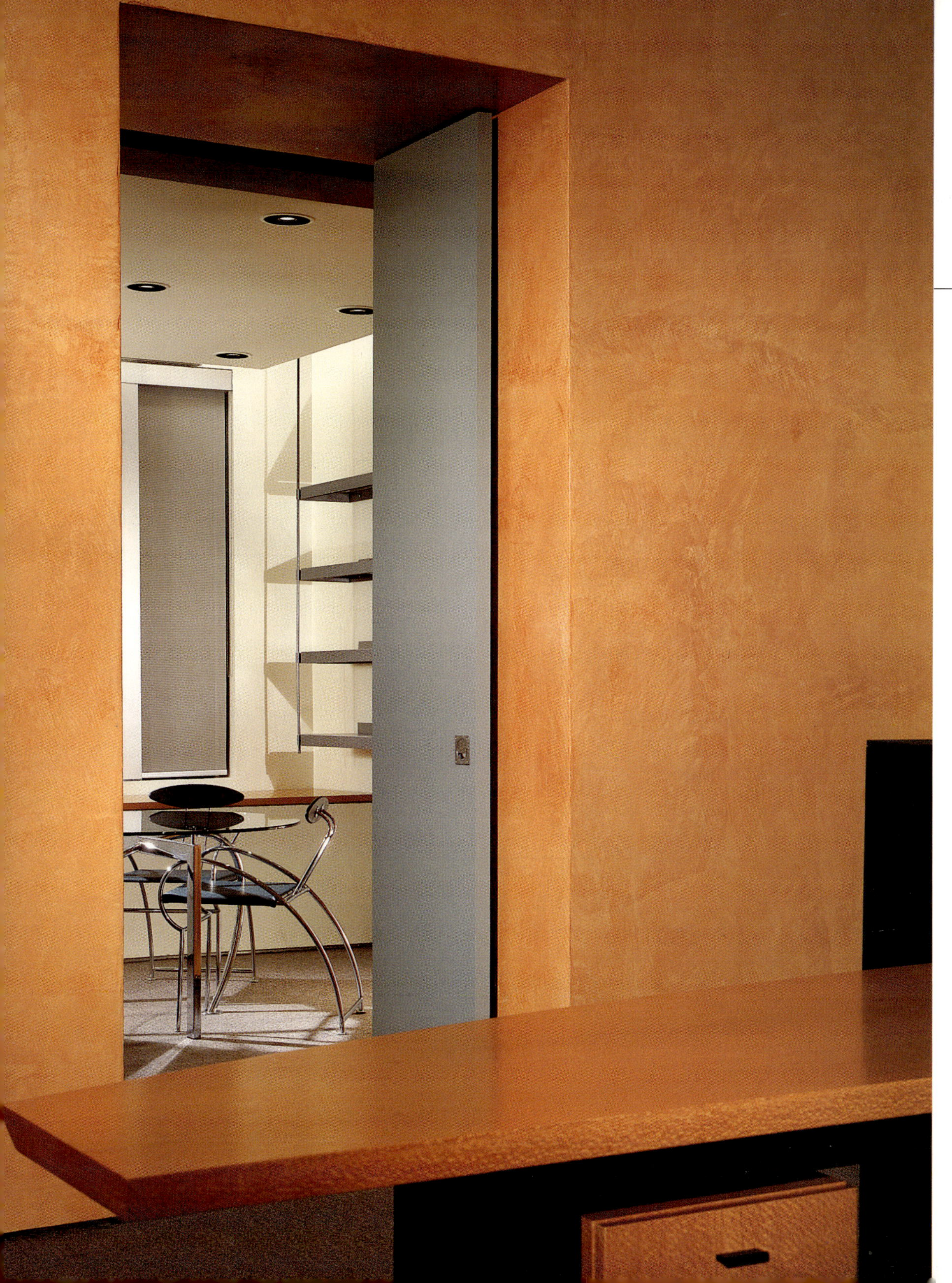

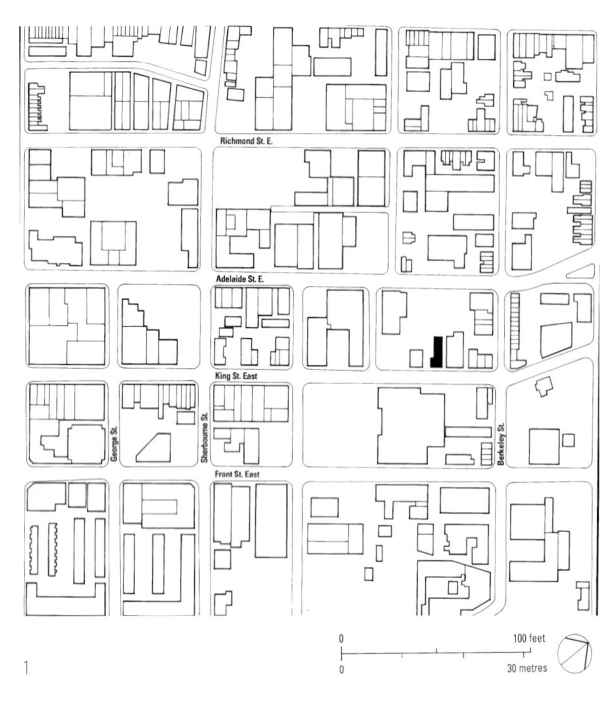

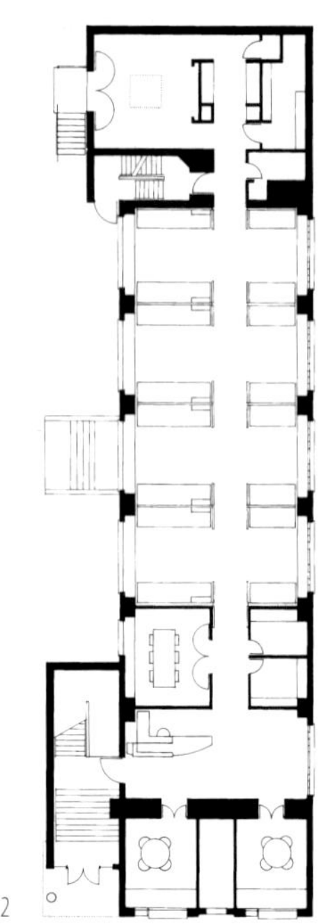

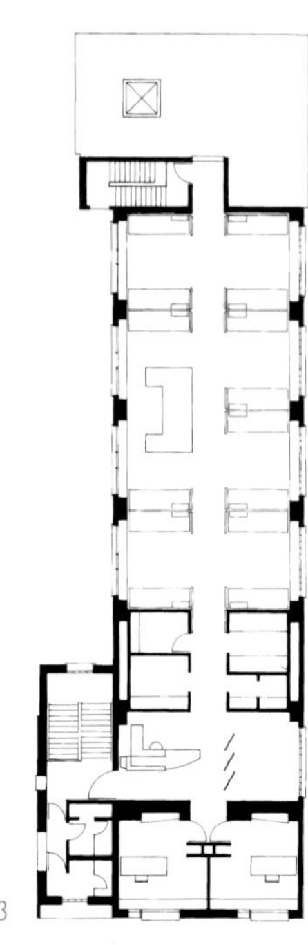

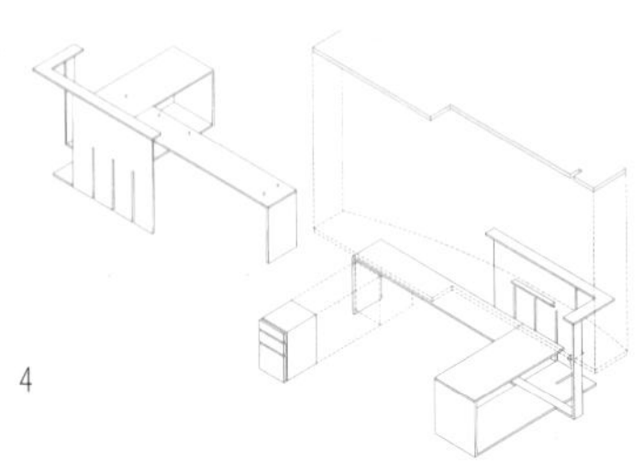

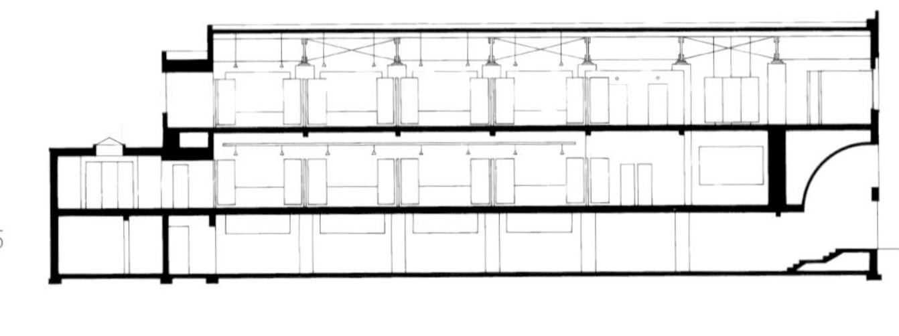

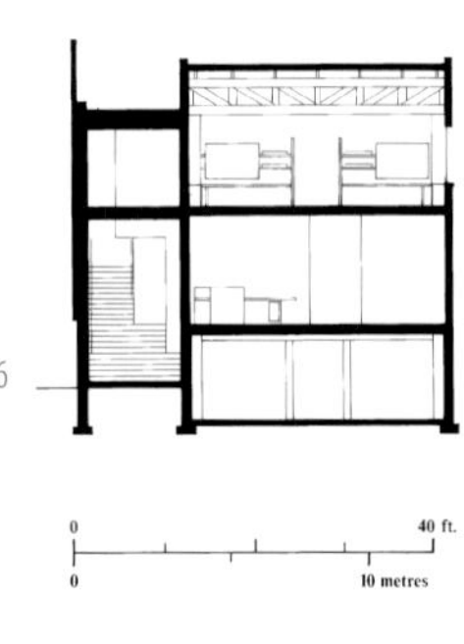

1. SITE PLAN

2. FIRST FLOOR PLAN

3 SECOND FLOOR PLAN

4. EXPLODED AXONOMETRIC STUDY OF RECEPTION DESK

5. LONGITUDINAL SECTION

6. CROSS SECTION

7. WEST ELEVATION

8. SOUTH ELEVATION

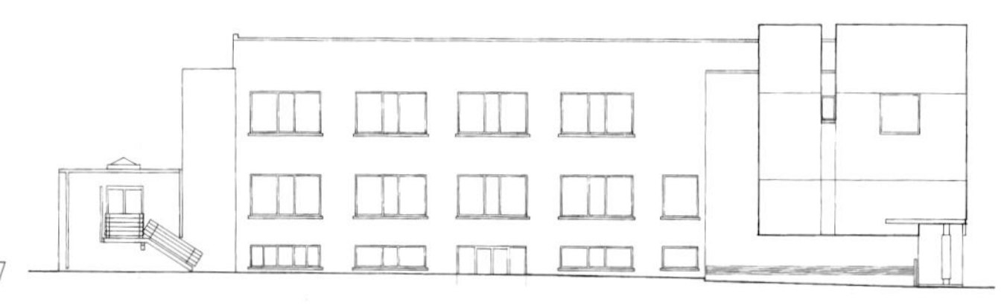

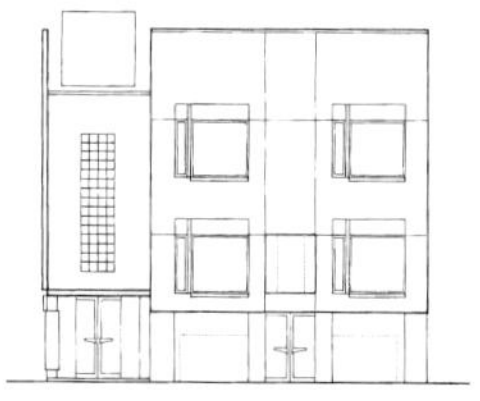

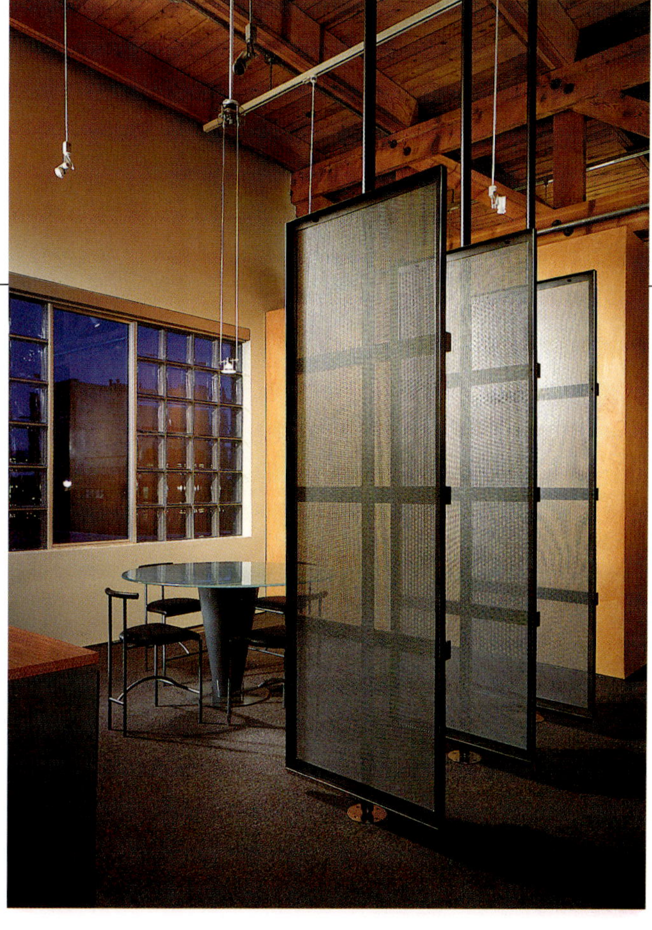

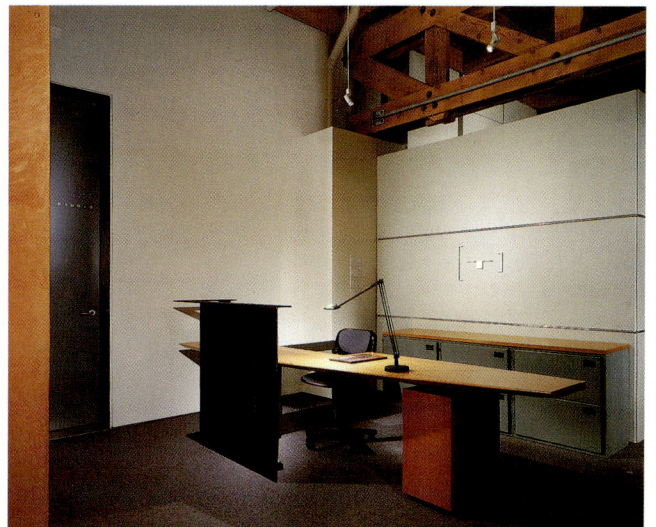

Perforated-metal screens attached to steel poles can be rotated to enclose a small meeting area lit by low voltage fixtures (top). The folded-steel panel of the custom-designed reception desk supports the desk top and conceals a computer monitor (bottom).

Dome Productions

Dome Productions, a subsidiary of The Sports Network (TSN), produces broadcast feeds of all SkyDome events for worldwide transmission, live or delayed. The new state-of-the-art facility integrates live event production and postproduction with design, construction, technology, operations, and marketing.

The rigorous technical and ergonomic design required for the event production and editing suites is combined with a dramatic sequence of movement through interconnecting corridors and stairs. Spaces of movement are developed into meeting places. Integrated into one of the staircases, the cappuccino bar creates an interactive social space for the crew, staff, and visitors. The concrete structure of the Dome Stadium is exposed within the facility. Panels of sandblasted glass in aluminum frames amplify the segmented and radiating structural order, and create memorable curving spines of movement along both floors. Electronic cabling, the lifeline of the facility, is accommodated in trays above a drywall ceiling, and large linear slots over the corridors allow for easy access. The cable system networks the facility's state-of-the-art broadcasting equipment with twelve field cameras and two large event-production control rooms.

Subtle lighting and the material palette of aluminum, granite, steel, sandblasted glass, wood veneer and paneling, and drywall create a dramatic yet soothing round-the-clock work environment.

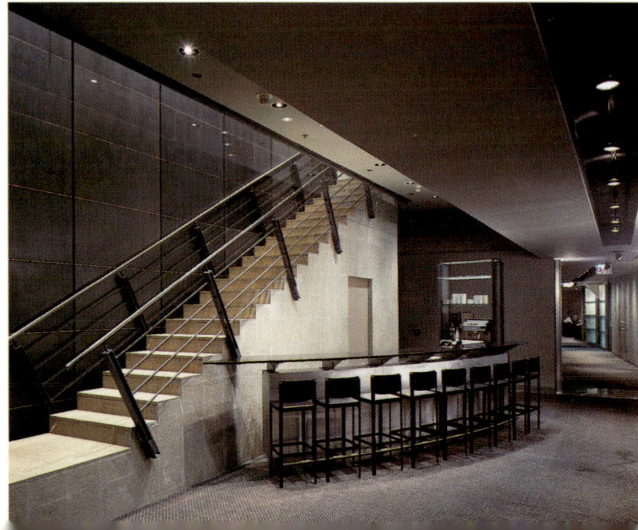

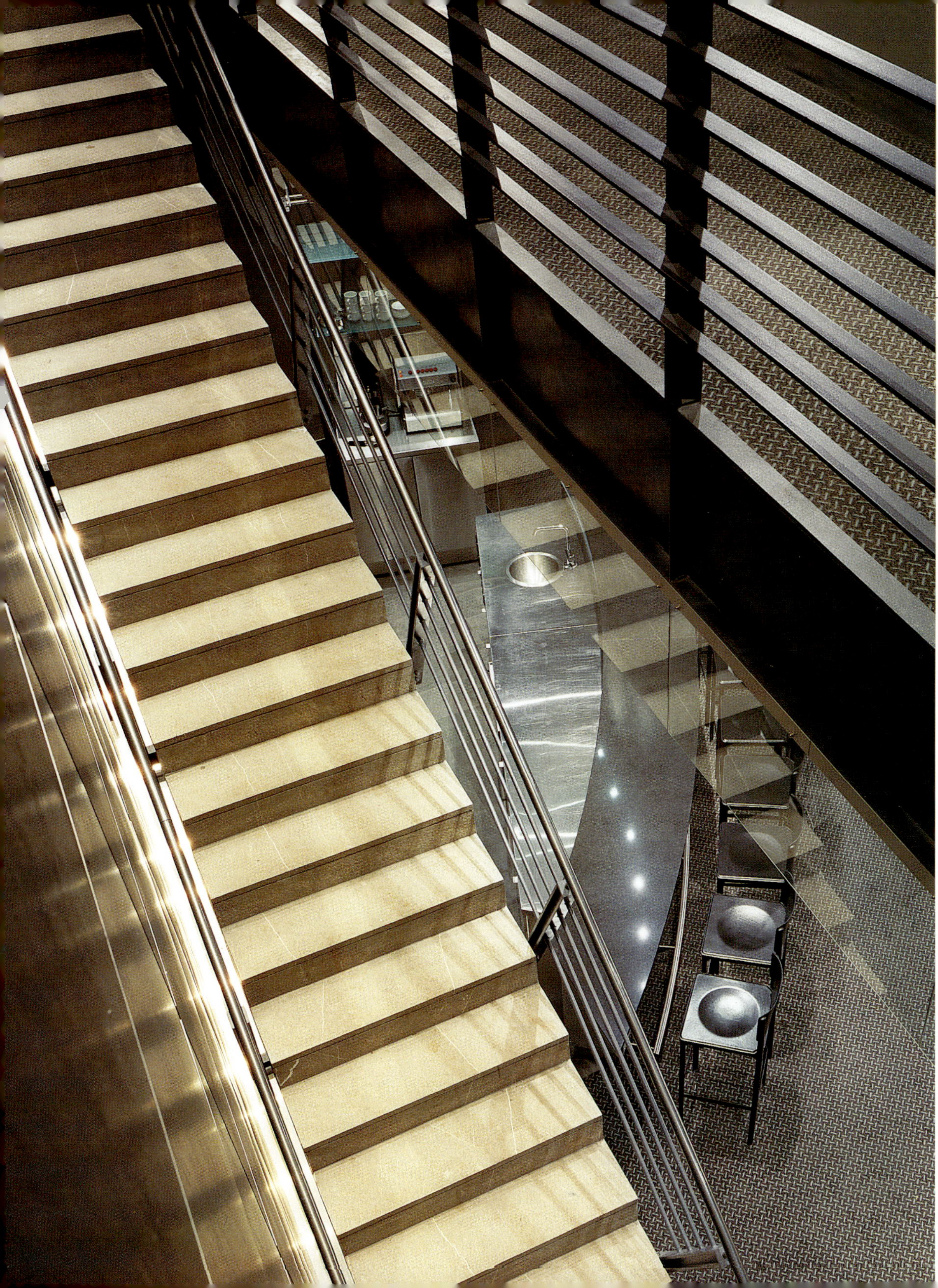

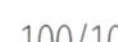

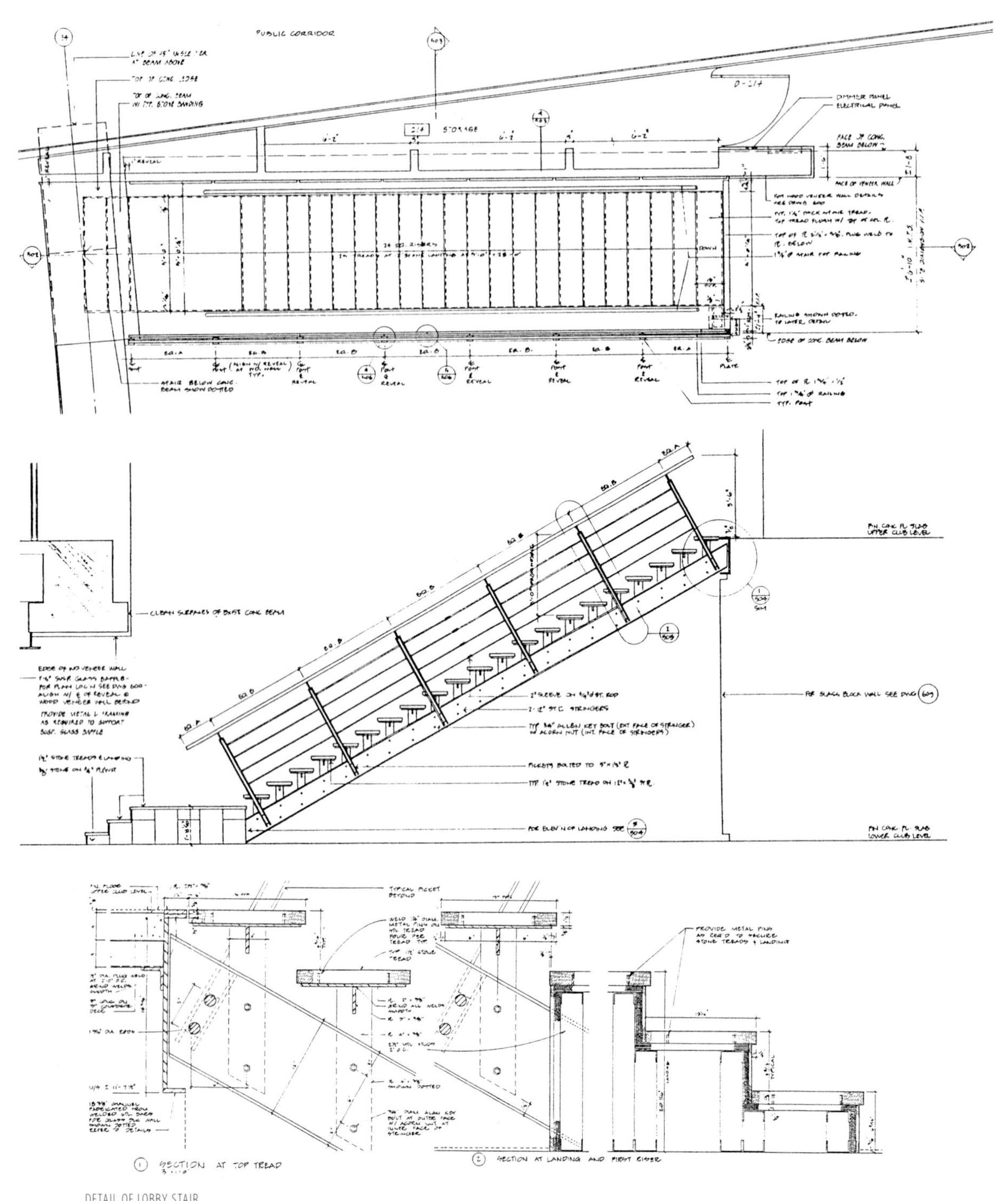

PUBLIC CORRIDOR
SECTION AT TOP TREAD
SECTION AT LANDING AND FIRST RISER
DETAIL OF LOBBY STAIR

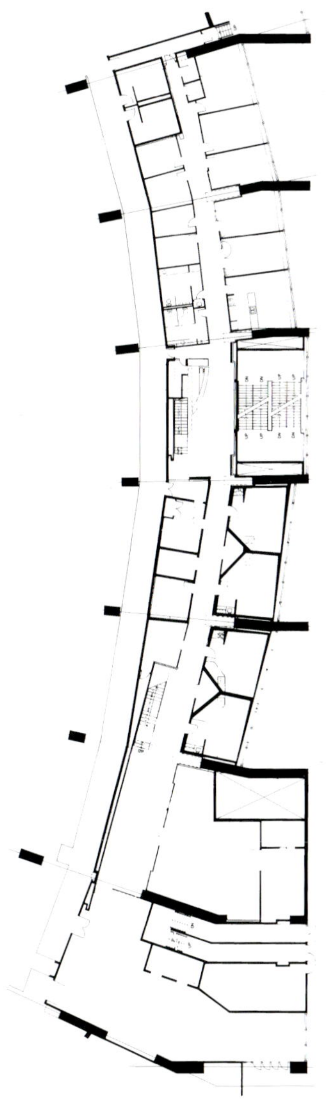

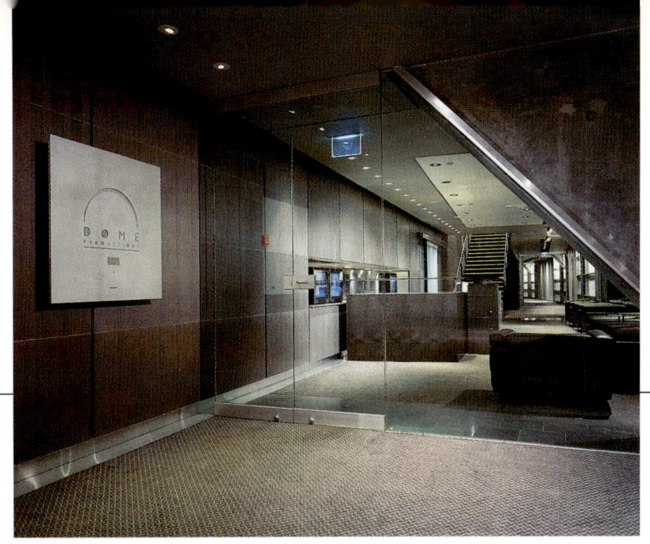

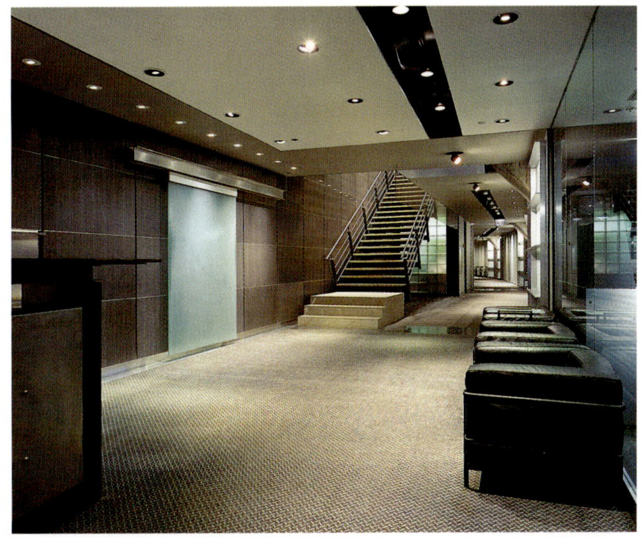

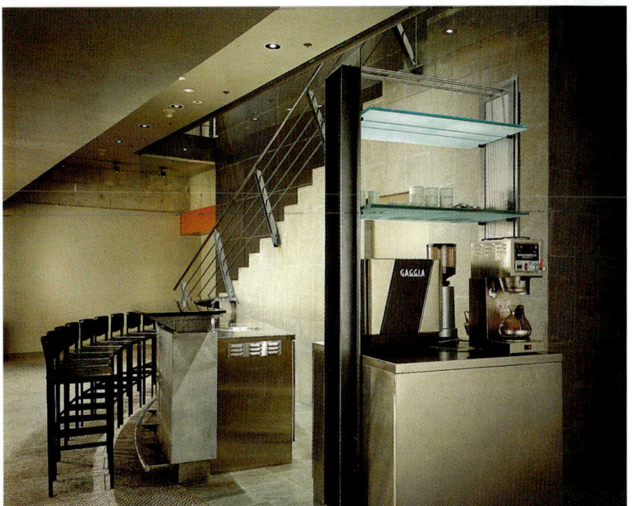

Long, curved space for the offices of Dome Productions sits beneath huge beams supporting the main structure of the SkyDome (top). The 70-foot-long (21.3-meter-long) wall of the reception area is veneered in tay wood and carpeted in a custom checkerboard pattern (center). The cappuccino bar for staff and visitors is integrated with the circulation space of the new stair (bottom).

Hasbro Inc. Headquarters

The Hasbro Inc. corporate headquarters project involved restoring and renovating a 300,000-square-foot (27,000-square-meter) masonry and cast-iron industrial structure to provide a contemporary work environment for the Fortune 500 company. Planned in three phases, the first phase was completed with Barton Myers Associates in 1986, and Phases two and three were completed by KPMB in 1994.

The plan is ordered as an urban grid, with offices, meeting rooms, and studios located along skylit "streets" and "courts." The formal expression and plan geometry contrasts the orthogonal fabric of the office studios with the existing building structure. The original concept included an elliptical exterior courtyard carved out of the center of the structure.

Phase two involved the conversion of the remaining building, with interiors constructed from polished concrete, marble dust plaster, maple plywood, MDF, aluminum, and translucent glass. The first stage of Phase two is developed as the primary public circulation through the building: a "Main Street." Constructed of steel, translucent glass, and maple screens, a series of executive offices and meeting rooms is inserted into the spaces of the existing structure, creating a lantern-like effect along the street. The project meets Hasbro's health and safety requirements for ergonomics, RSI, lighting quality, recycling, and waste management programs, in addition to local energy codes maximizing energy conservation. Features include an ice-storage system, a water-conservation policy, indoor air-quality management, and the specification of local and recycled building materials.

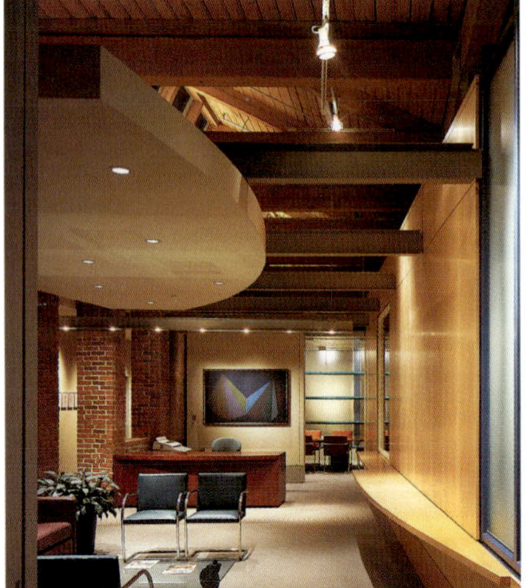

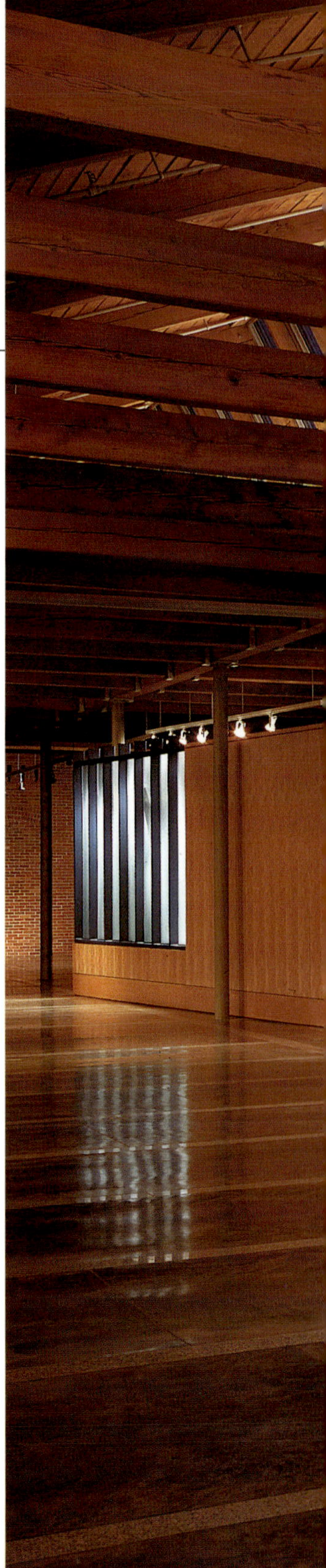

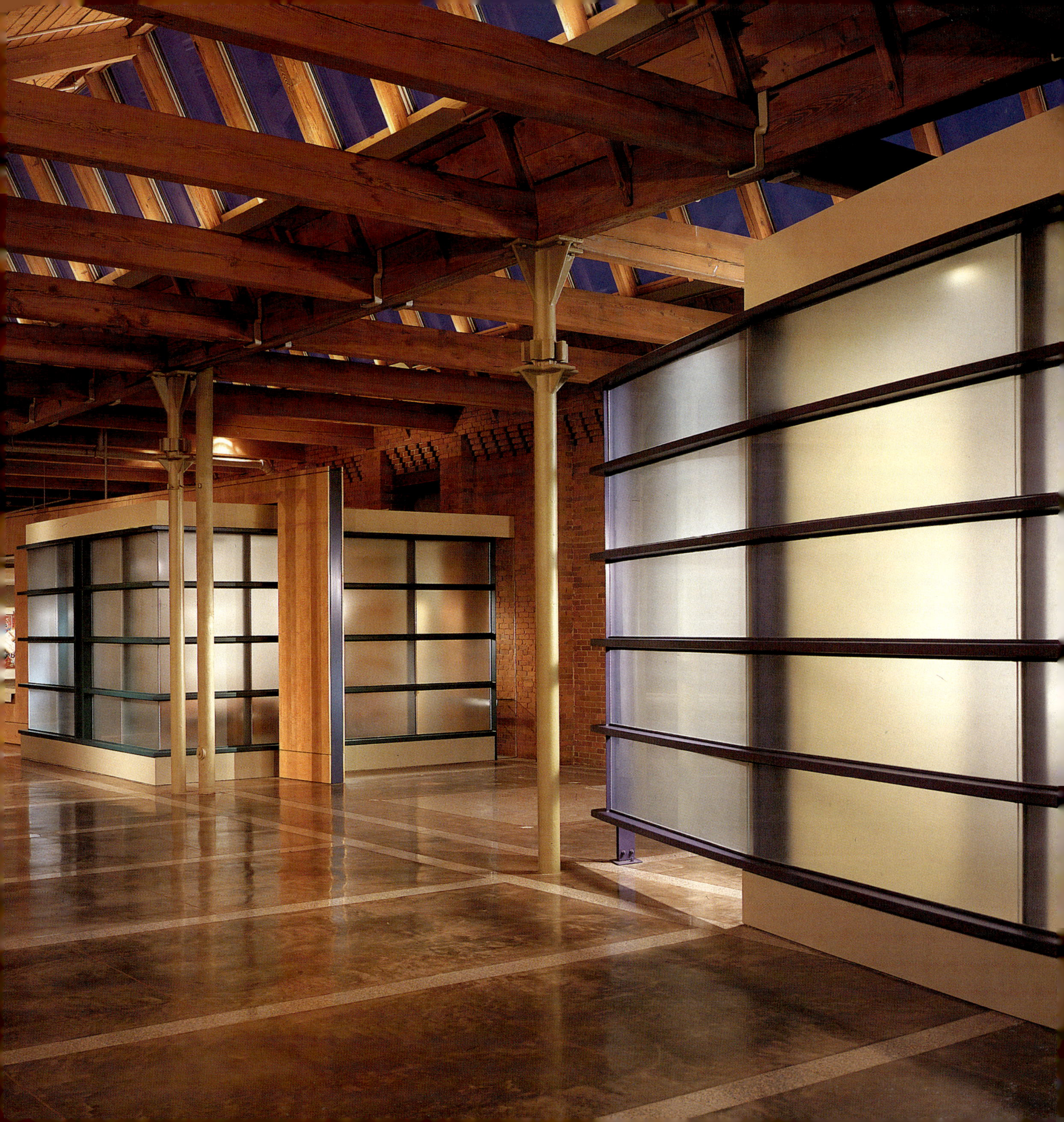

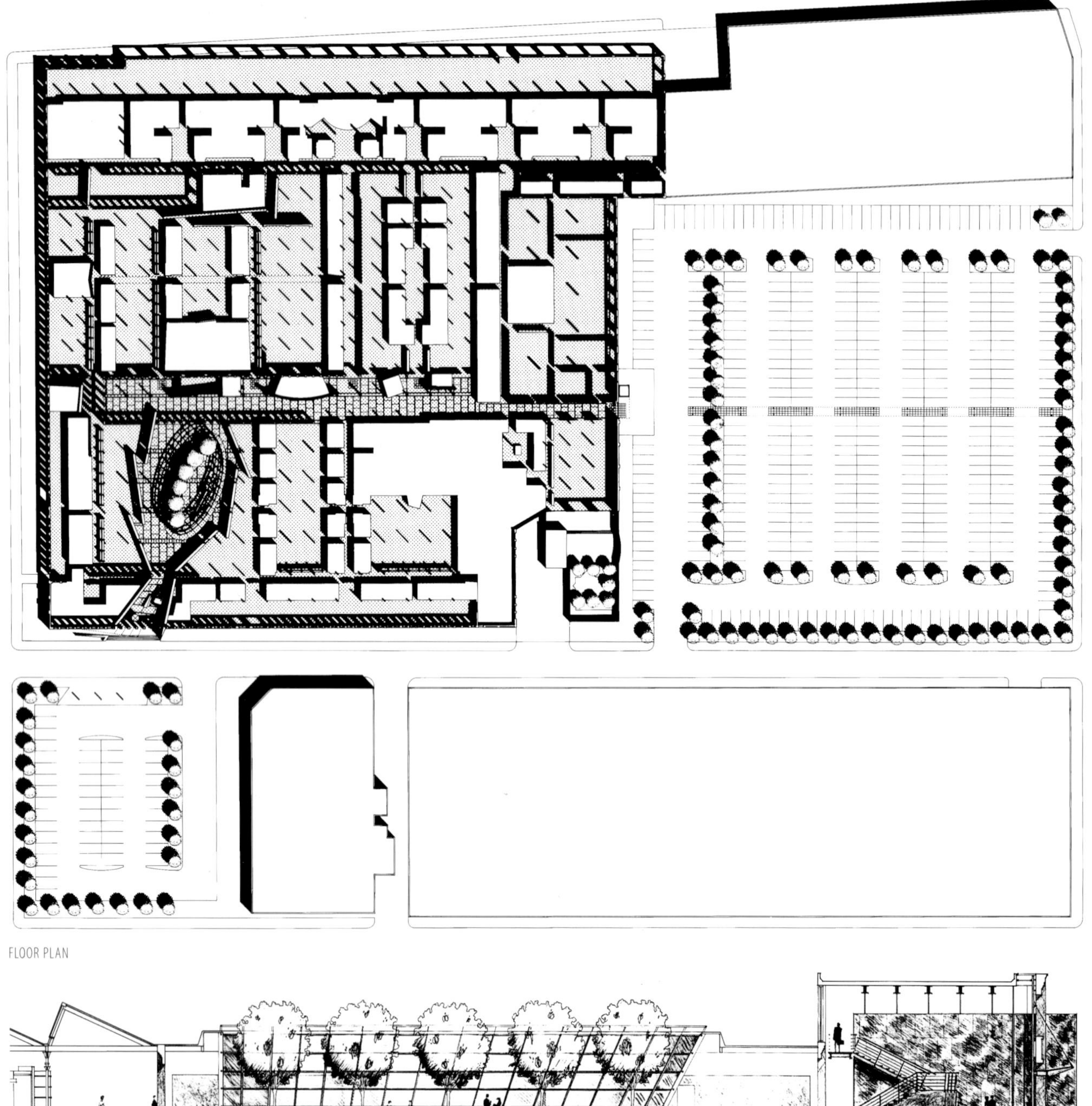

FLOOR PLAN

CROSS SECTION OF MASTER PLAN

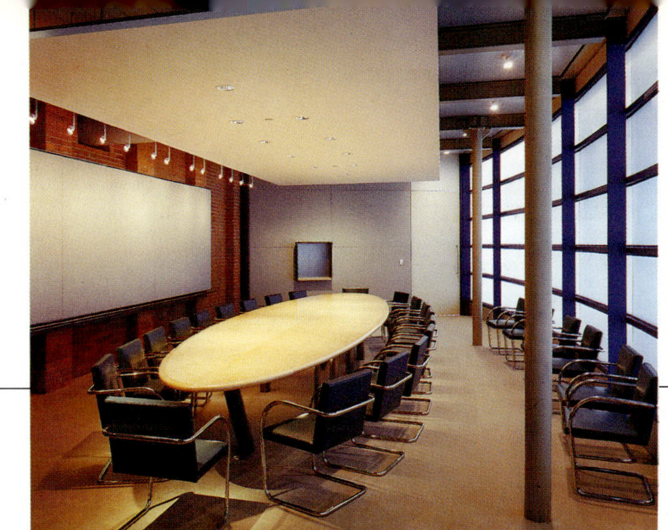

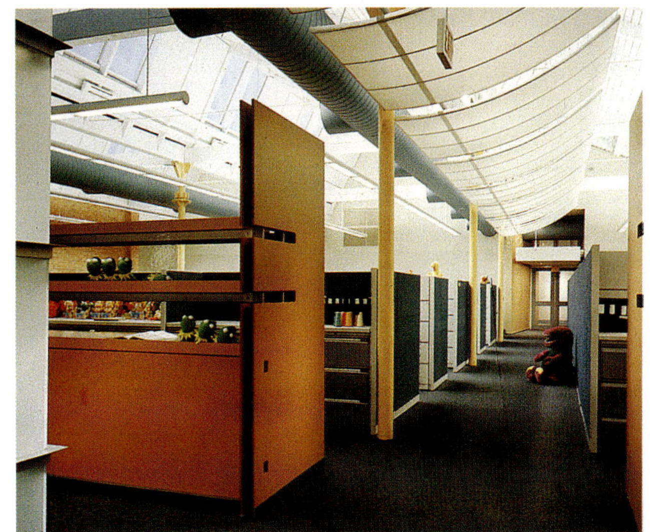

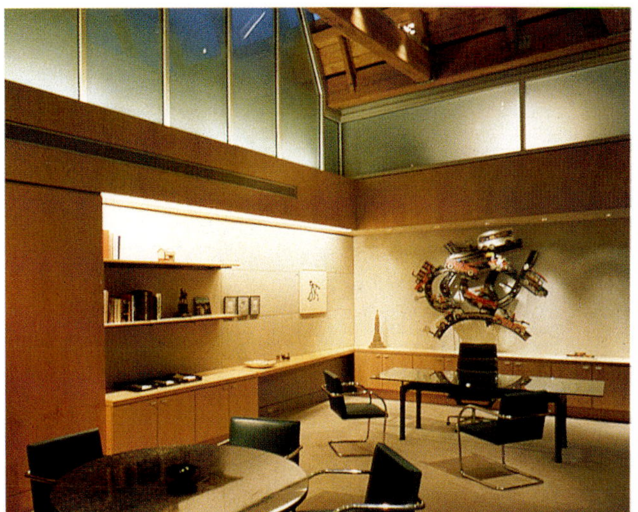

The boardroom is accessible from the new internal "Main Street "(top). Suspended fabric canopies top the corridors in studio areas (center). Existing sawtooth skylights illuminate executive offices (bottom).

Ammirati Puris Lintas

The Ammirati Puris Lintas offices express the advertising agency's philosophy of creative collaboration within a well-crafted architectural framework. The design emphasizes the vitality of the agency's creative process and the daily activities of its people, creating a clean, white, and uncluttered interior to serve the range of creative, account, and research activities.

A clear spatial sequence of entrance, reception, meeting, and work areas establishes patterns of movement and open areas. Within this order, a combination of prototypical modules for executive offices, standard offices, open workstations, and staff assistant stations create integrated team work areas, reinforcing the spirit of collaboration and teamwork that characterizes the agency's creative process.

Connections to the urban culture of Manhattan are made both visually and spatially. A series of framed views of the skyline, the East River, and the United Nations Headquarters terminates the entrance/reception sequence and primary circulation route. The city's grid of avenues, streets, and squares is adapted as a metaphor for the plan geometry. Elements that characterize a typical, industrial New York loft—white walls, high ceilings, natural light, and open space—are translated in the image of the office interiors. The material and color palette is limited to white paint for walls, columns, and ceiling planes; gray carpet

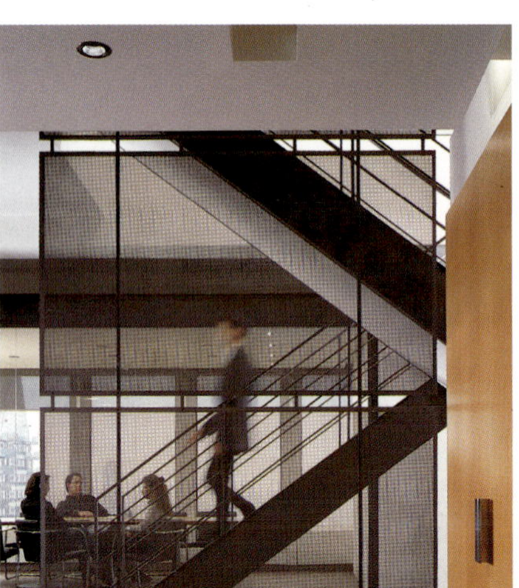

for typical floors; and hardwood flooring at selected reception and client waiting areas. Custom-designed elements in beech wood, white Carrara marble, and perforated metal act as counterpoints of materiality and texture within the regular order of the work environment.

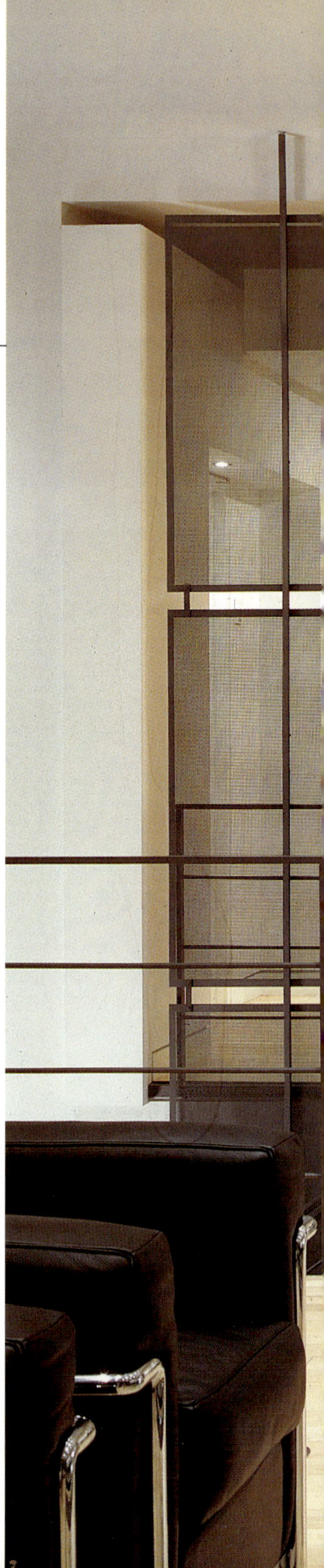

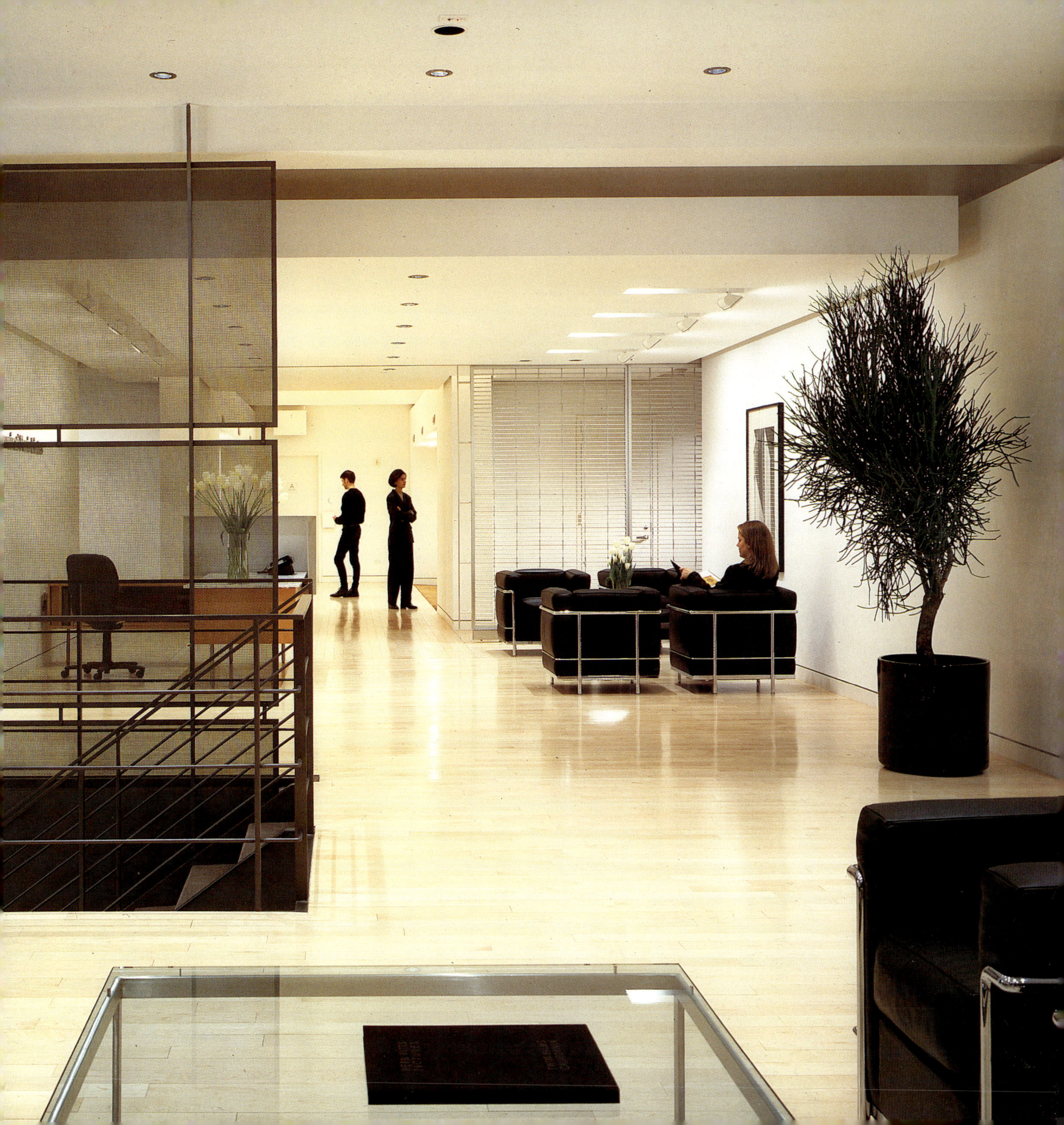

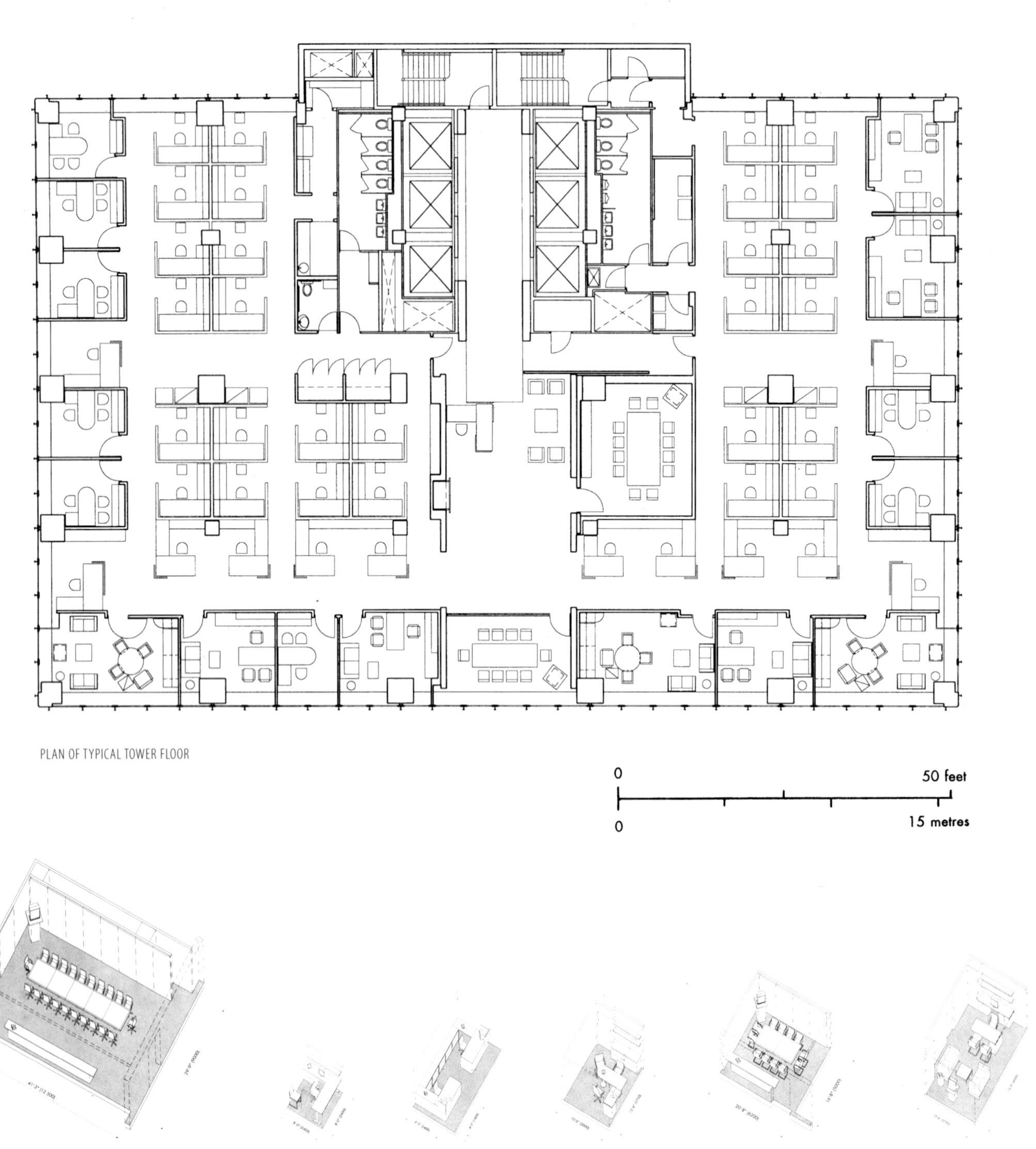

PLAN OF TYPICAL TOWER FLOOR

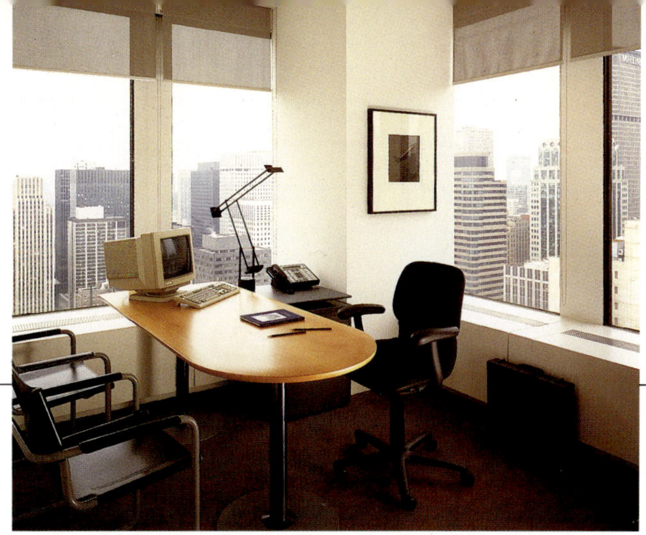

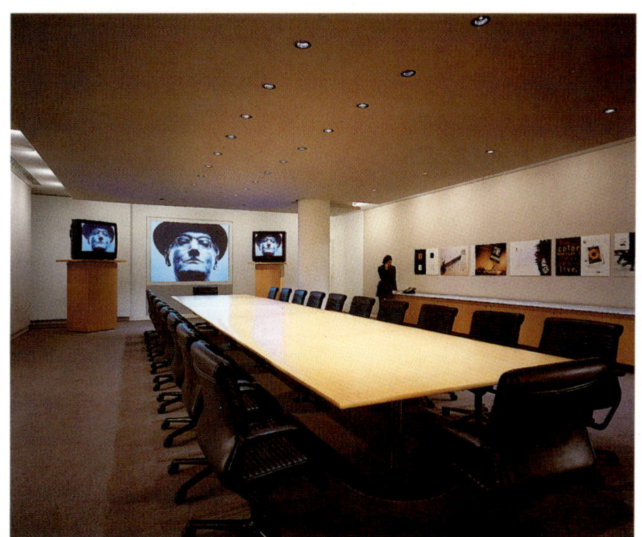

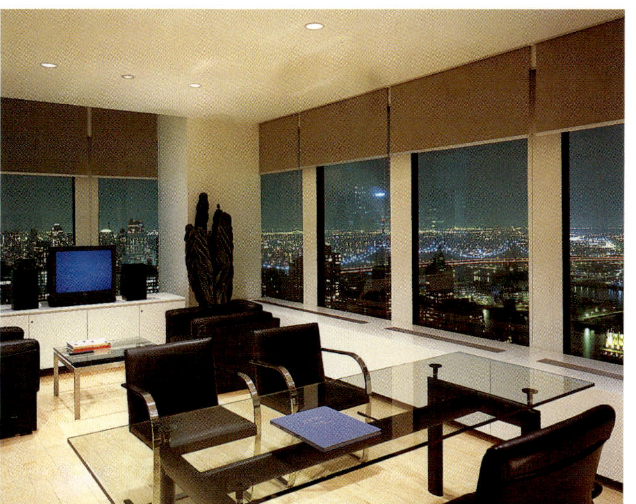

A standard office features breathtaking views of Manhattan and Brooklyn (top). Client presentation room is lined with fabric for the display of the agency's work (center). A prototype for executive offices on several floors is fitted with classic modernist furniture pieces by Mies van der Rohe and Le Corbusier (bottom).

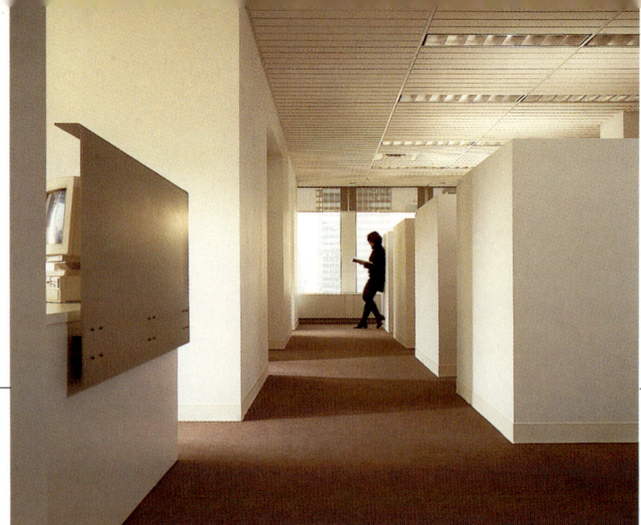

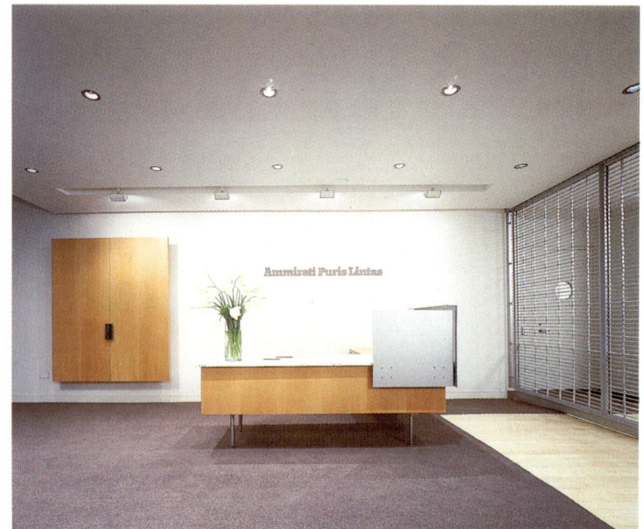

Staff workstations with low walls allow natural light to reach central areas on each floor (top). The reception area has a custom-designed aluminum security gate (center, bottom). New steel stairs are wrapped in perforated-metal screens (opposite page). The client waiting area is adjacent to a new stair (overleaf).

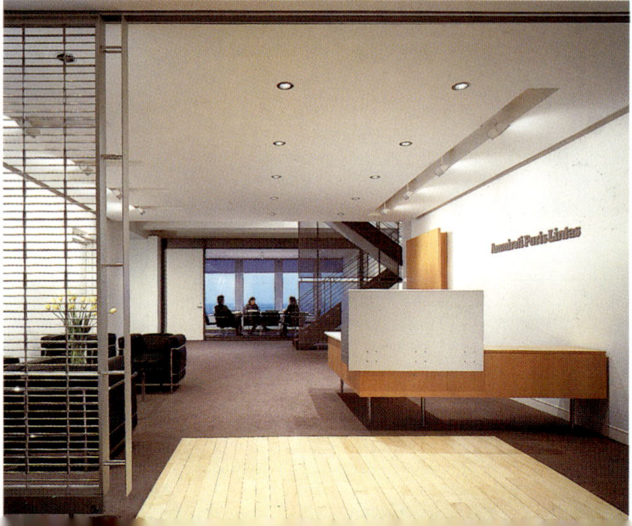

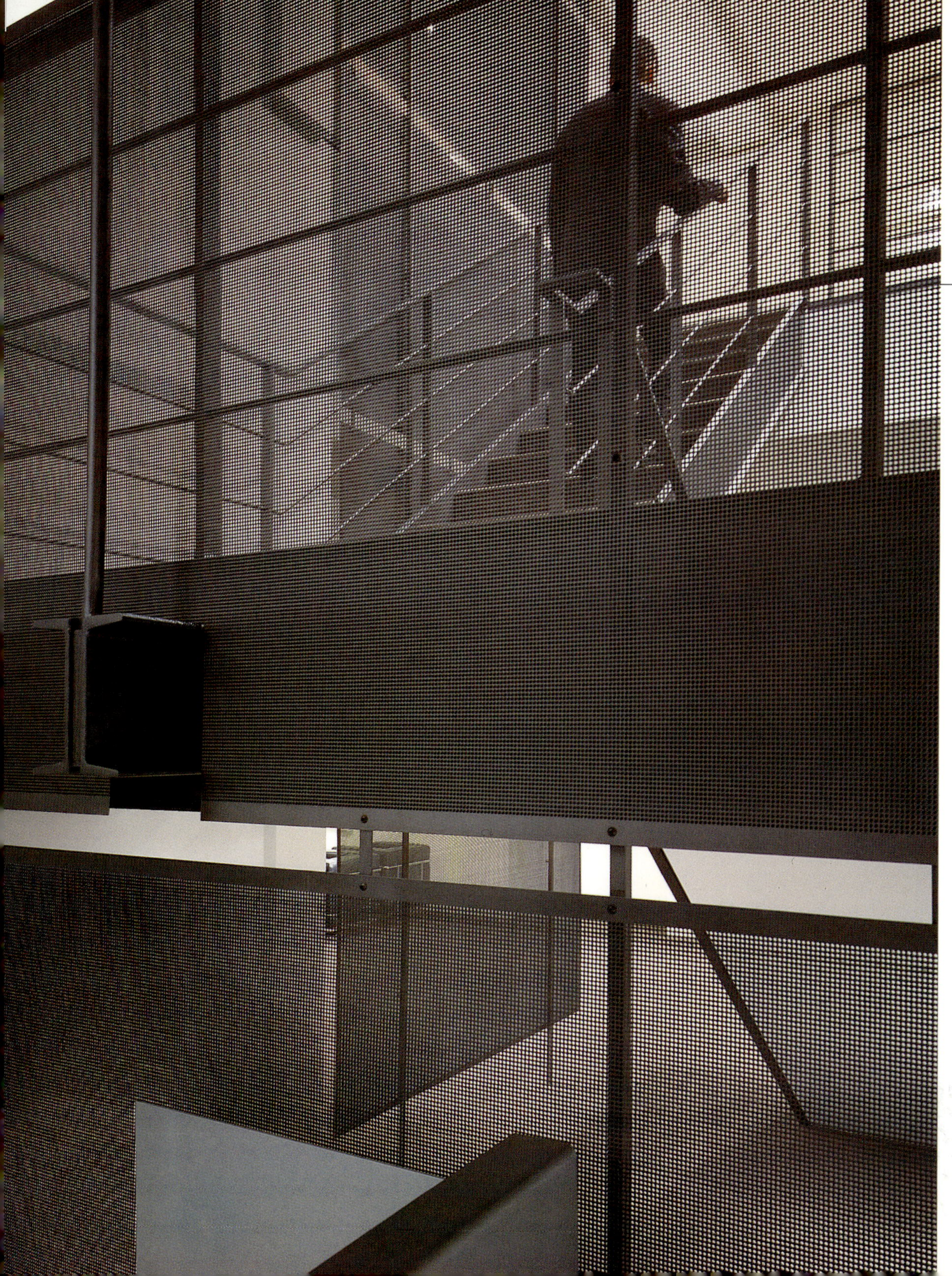

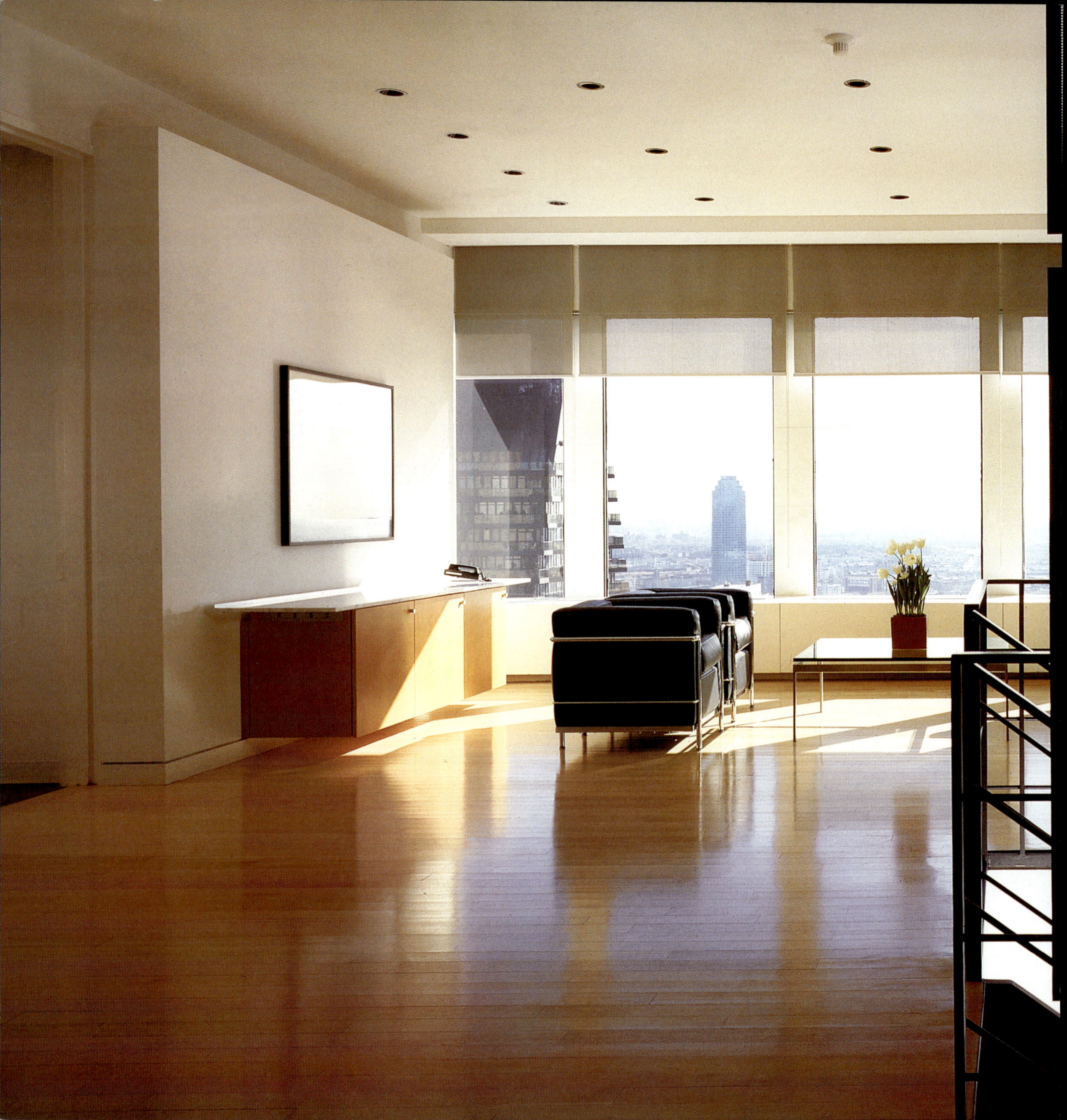

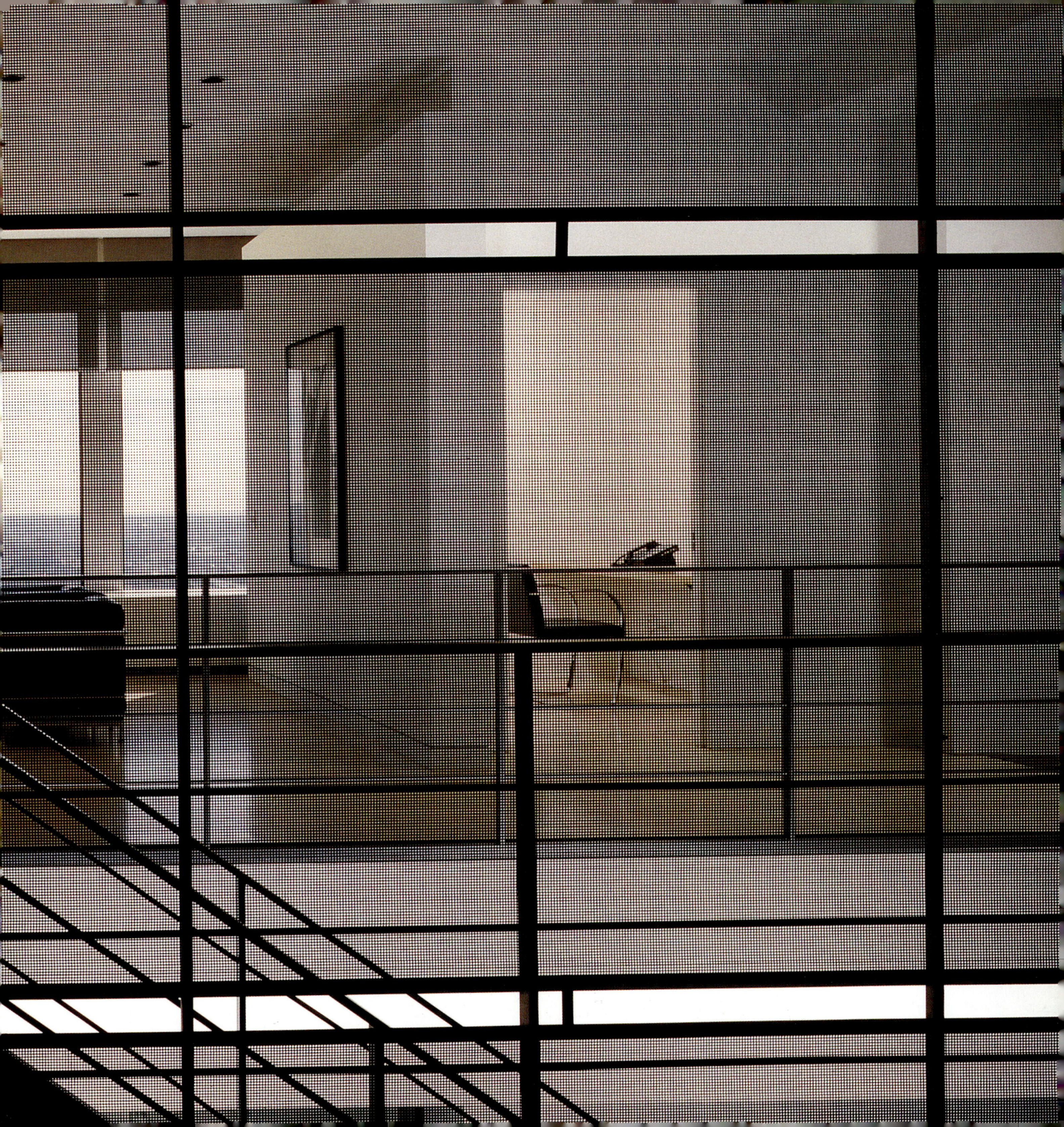

Alliance Communications Corporation

The new offices for Alliance, a major Canadian-based film and television entertainment and communications company, occupy three contiguous floors of an existing office tower in downtown Toronto.

The main reception area is located on the fifteenth floor, and is joined with the executive office floor above and the major production department below by a dramatic, interconnecting stair. A large wall, placed on a slight diagonal and paneled with cherry wood veneer, visually connects all three floors and provides immediate orientation on each floor. Unifying the work areas, an elliptical motif appears as a ceiling canopy on the upper floor, and reappears as geometric figure in the plan of the lowest floor.

Custom-designed glass and maple easel frames display large film posters throughout the offices' primary circulation spaces. A ribbon of the company's numerous industry awards lines the interior core wall. The plan balances zones of open working groups with a series of enclosed offices, maintaining selected views to the city's financial district and the Rosedale Valley residential area to the north. The materials and finishes combine the warmth of wood, the precision and industrial character of steel, and the elegance and beauty of stone in the public areas. Industrial rubber flooring, translucent glass panels, and aluminum truck siding contribute to the offices the atmosphere of an open loft. The interior spaces and sequences are designed to accommodate corporate events and presentations.

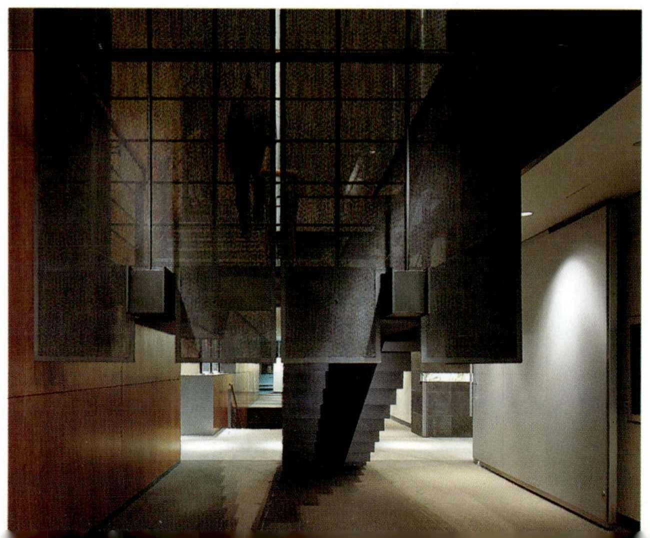

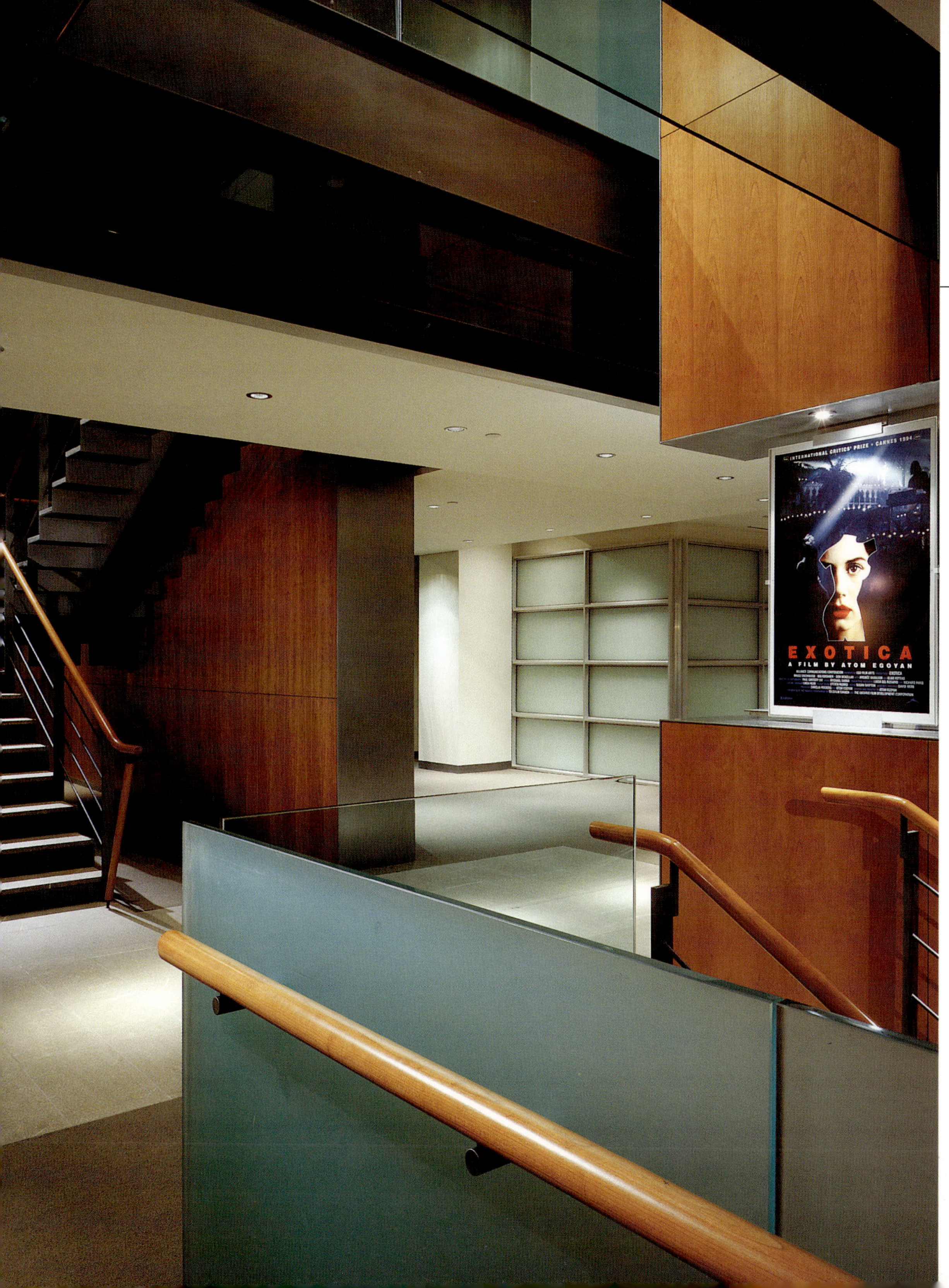

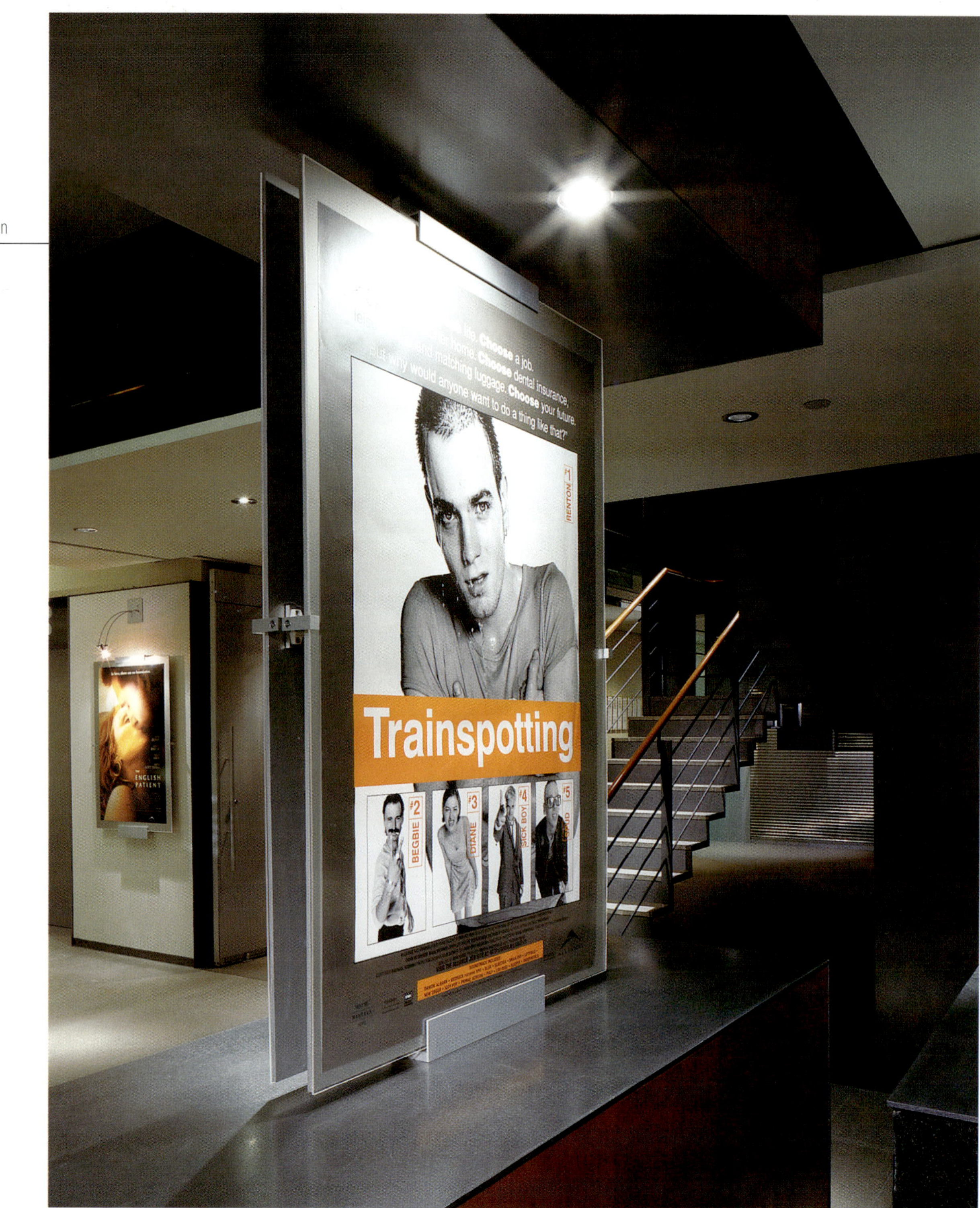
Choose a job.
Choose dental insurance,
and matching luggage. Choose your future.
But why would anyone want to do a thing like that?"
RENTON #1
Trainspotting
BEGBIE #2
DIANE #3
SICK BOY #4
SPUD #5
THE ENGLISH PATIENT

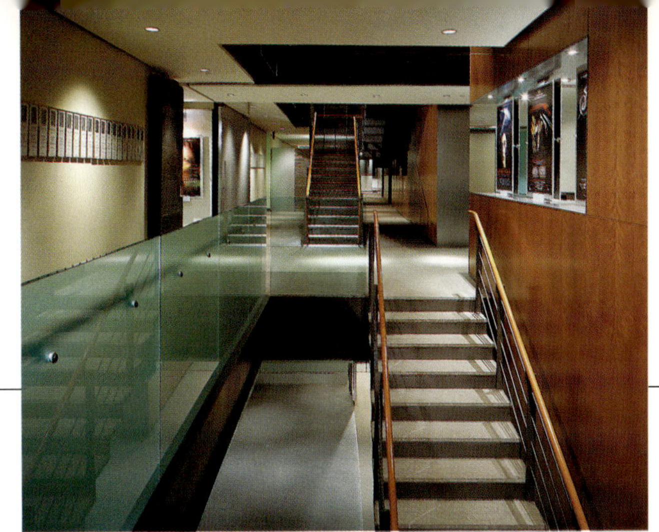

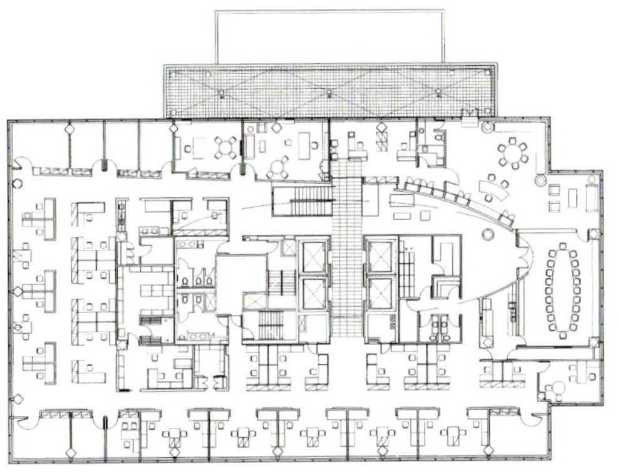

16TH FLOOR PLAN

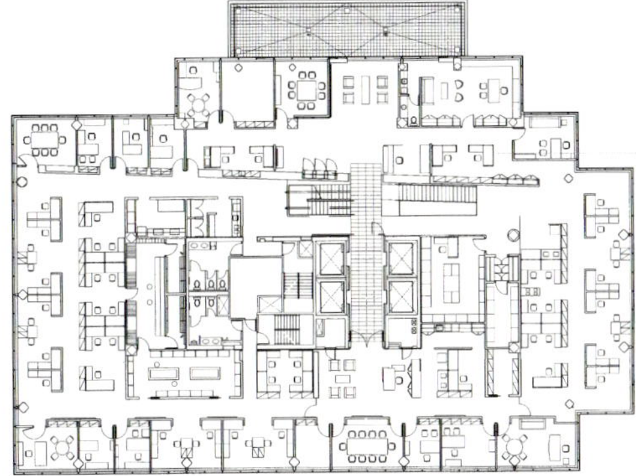

15TH FLOOR PLAN

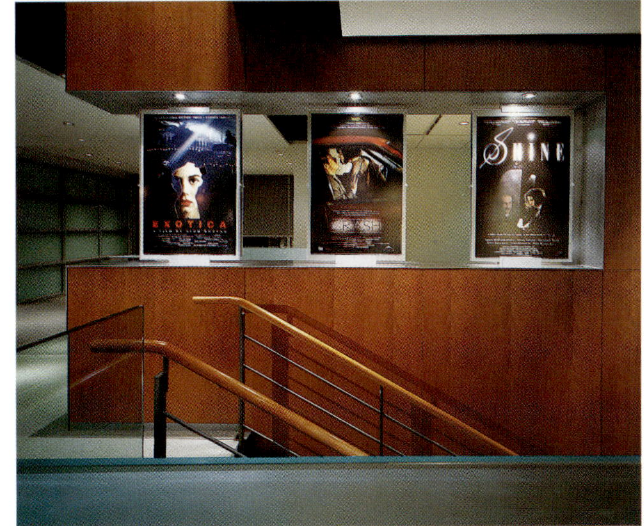

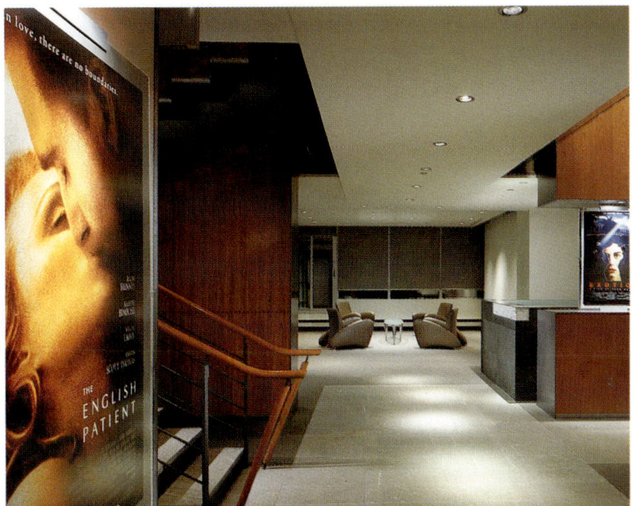

The new internal stairs, inserted through large openings cut in the existing floors, are constructed of steel and granite (top). Custom-designed display panels throughout the three floors of the offices herald the firm's latest cinematic ventures (center, bottom, opposite page).

Gluskin Sheff + Associates

Located on the forty-sixth floor of the Bay-Wellington Tower at Toronto's BCE Place, the offices of Gluskin Sheff + Associates are designed to temper the intensity of day-to-day investment activity with a serene atmosphere that is highly responsive to varying needs for privacy and interaction. A system of open and closed spaces fosters team synergy as well as concentrated individual or group performance.

The tower's floorplate of two merging octagons is conceptualized as an "urban plateau" with visual connections to Lake Ontario, the Financial Core, and the distant horizon beyond. The two high-rise cores, clad in beech wood, act as anchors for the "plateau," and deep frames for the existing floor-to-ceiling windows are designed to set off panoramic views. A different organic form—a curve, a wave, an oval, and a shell—marks each of the floorplate's four corners, identifying and orienting different departments within the overall plan, as well as the surrounding cityscape.

Throughout the offices, walls and screens create degrees of transparency. Custom-designed work enclaves are constructed of powder-coated steel frame units, sandblasted glass, and maple. Clear glass is used for the doors of enclosed spaces to provide acoustic isolation, while maintaining visibility and openness. Corporate and client-related spaces are treated with materials and colors lighter than those associated with more traditional corporate interiors. Instead of dark wood paneling, bronze, leather, and tobacco hues of color, materials such as French limestone appear on the elevator lobby floors and elm wood on the floors of the boardroom, the reception area, and major circulation spaces.

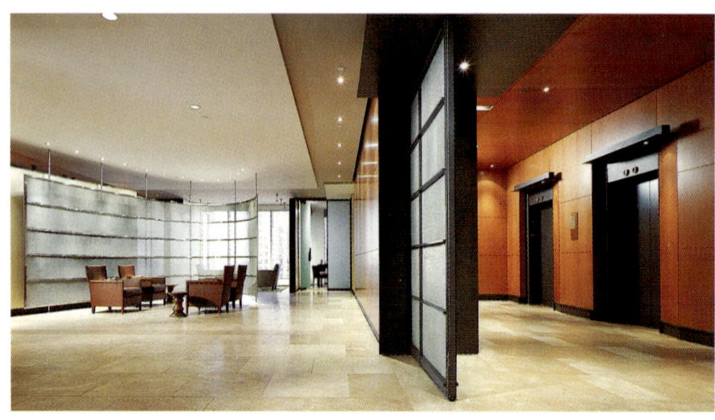

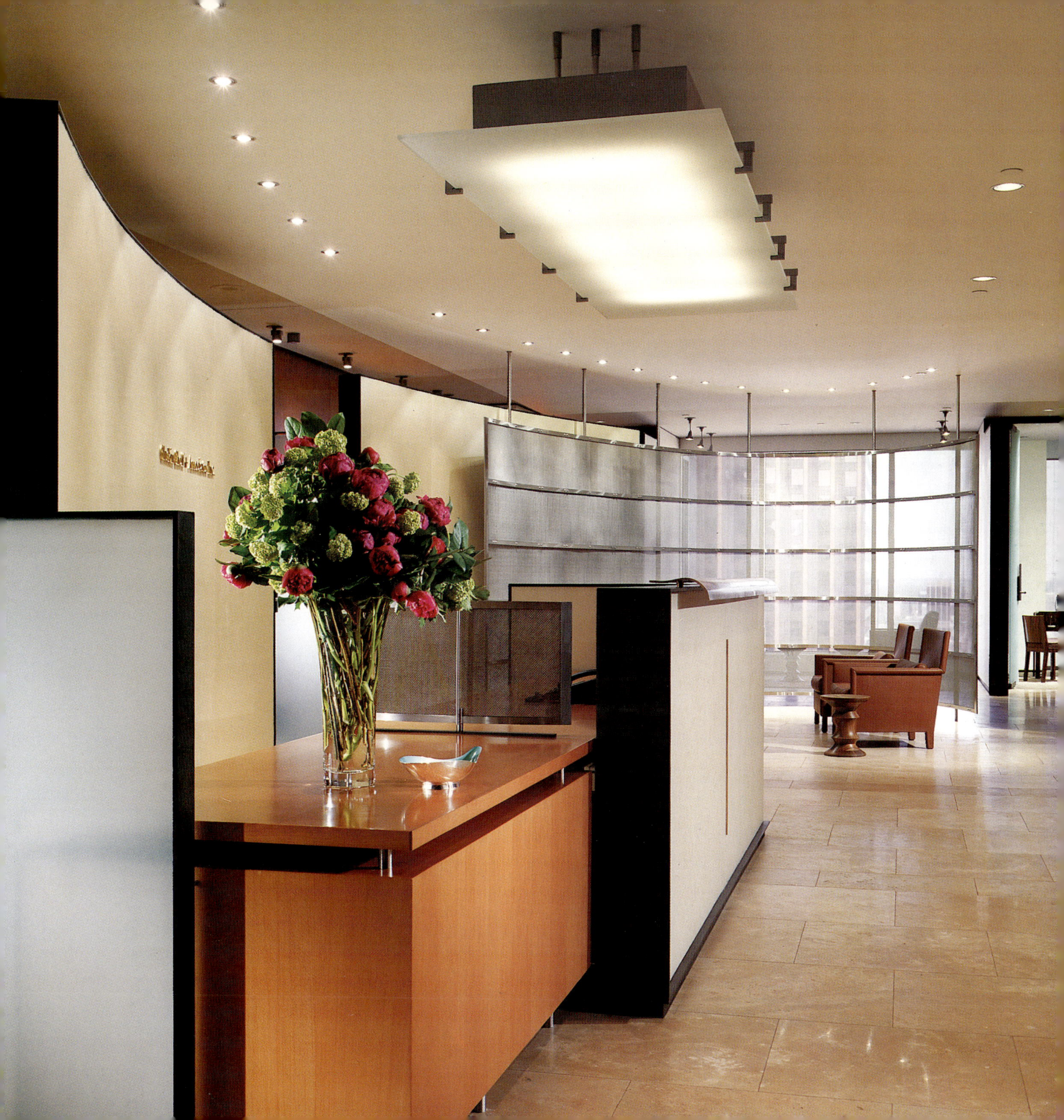

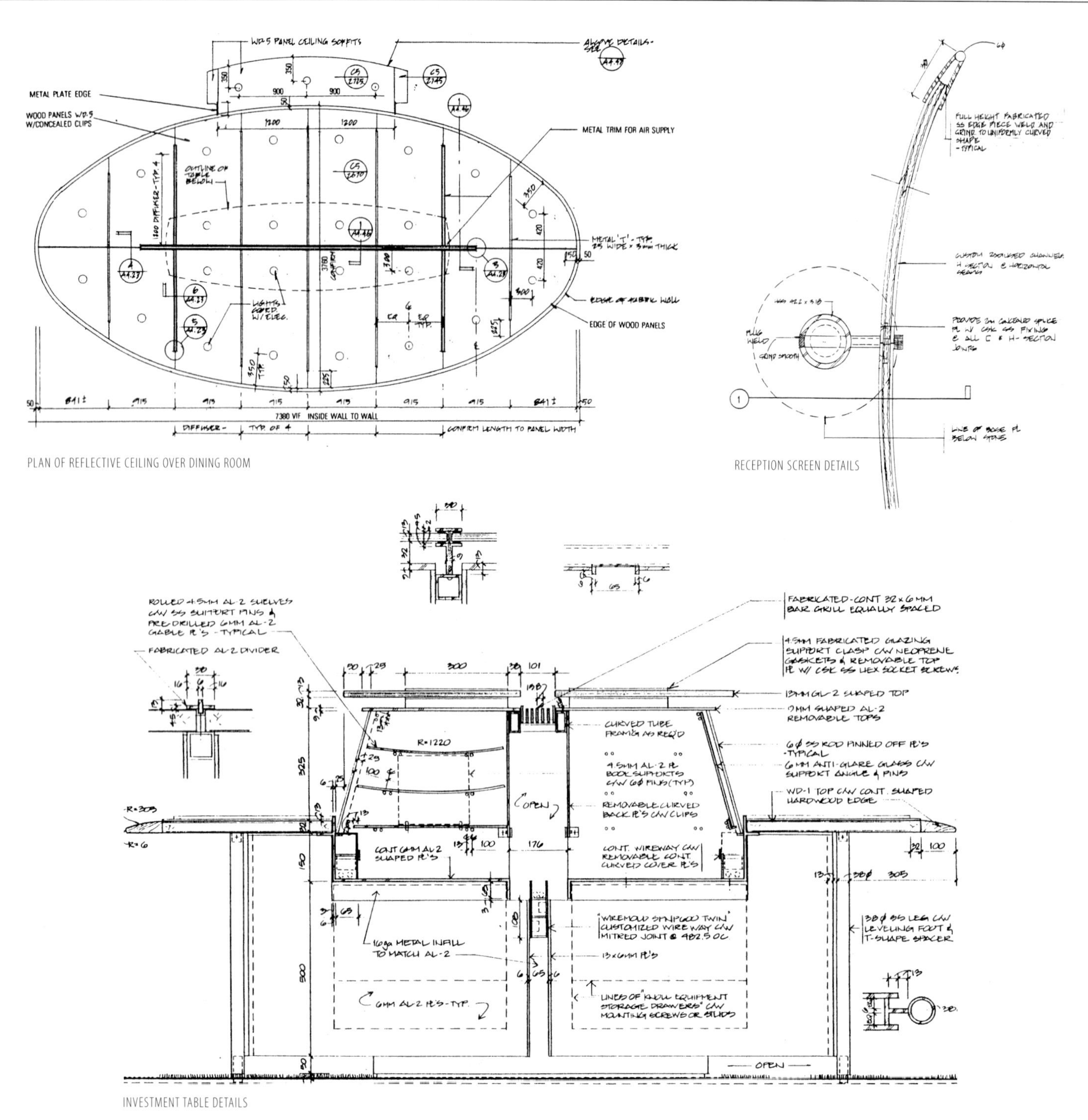

PLAN OF REFLECTIVE CEILING OVER DINING ROOM

RECEPTION SCREEN DETAILS

INVESTMENT TABLE DETAILS

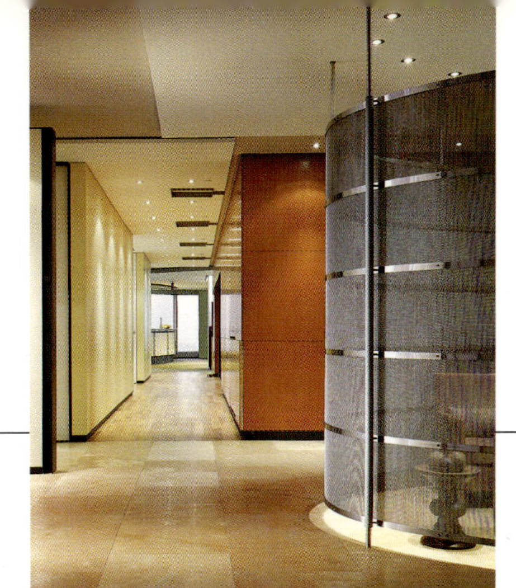

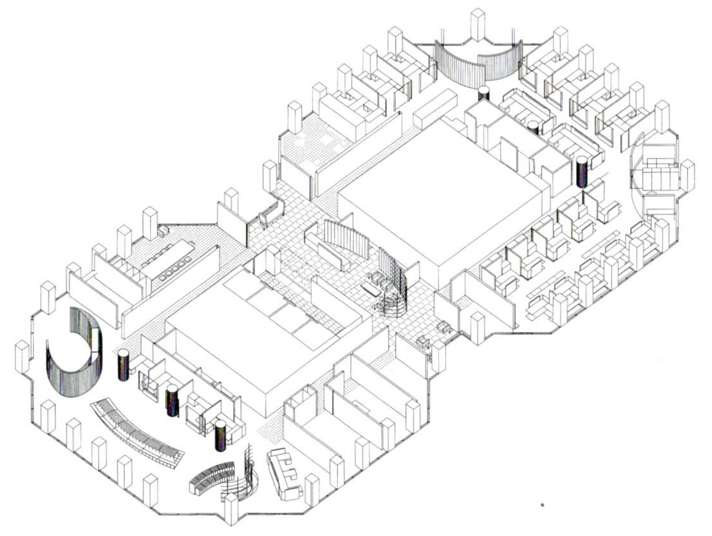

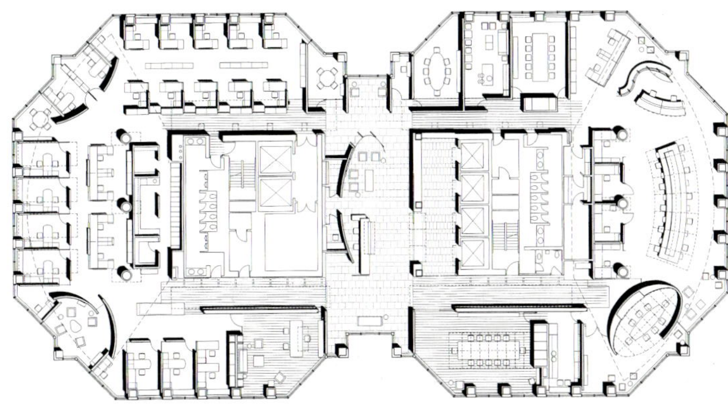

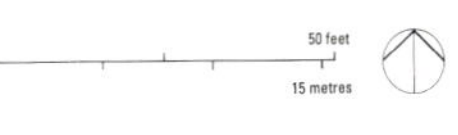

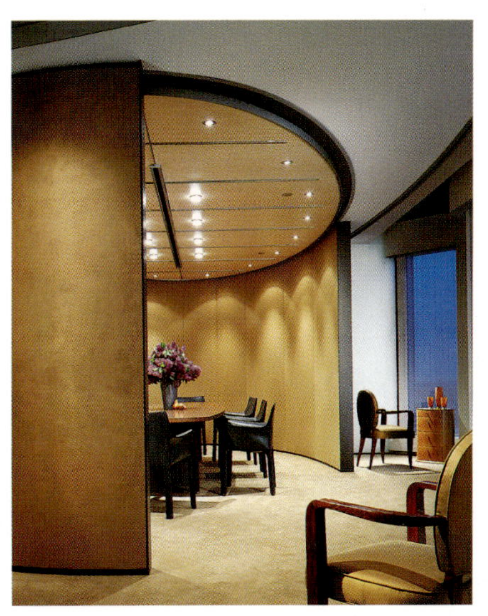

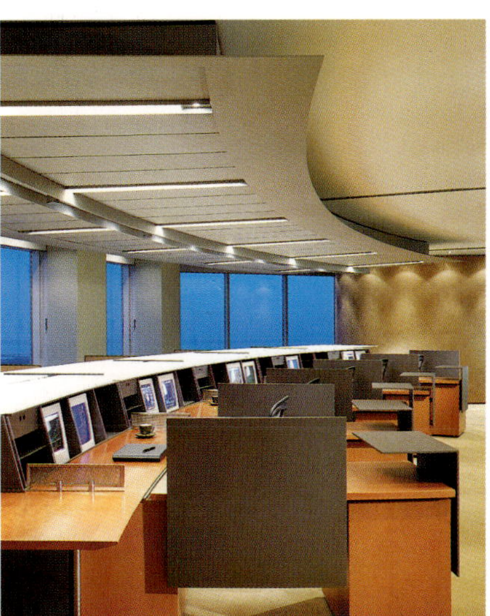

All corridors terminate with distant views of the horizon and Lake Ontario (top). The corporate dining room is a free-standing elliptical element that turns the corner in plan (center). The curved trading desk is the nerve center of the company's investment operations (bottom).

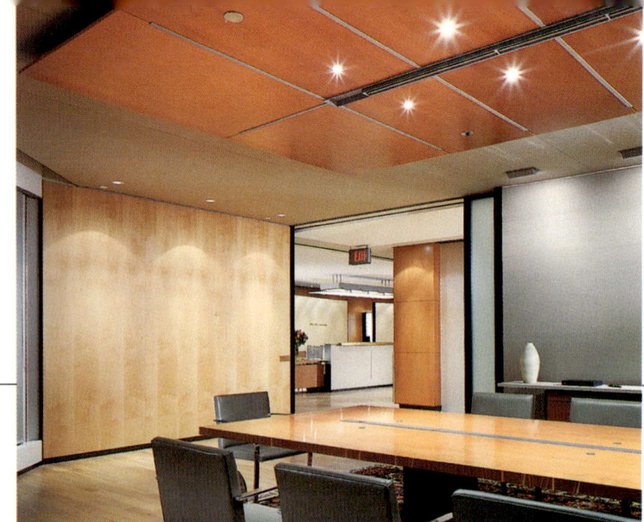

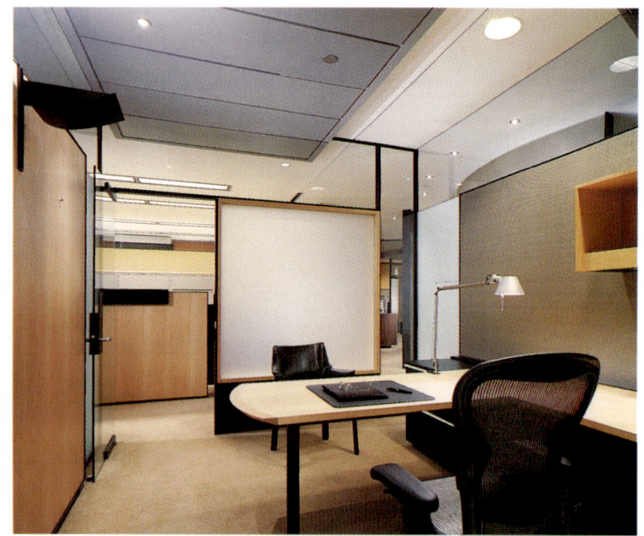

The boardroom is accessed through a rolling, motorized glass partition (top). De Stijl influences are evident in the composition of desk units and glazed partitions (center, opposite page). A quiet lounge for visitors and staff offers uninterrupted views across the city (bottom). The visitor reception area and spacious corridors leading east and west (overleaf).

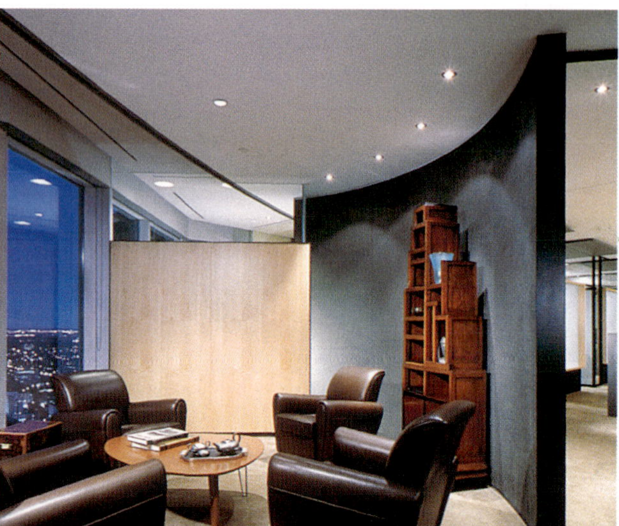

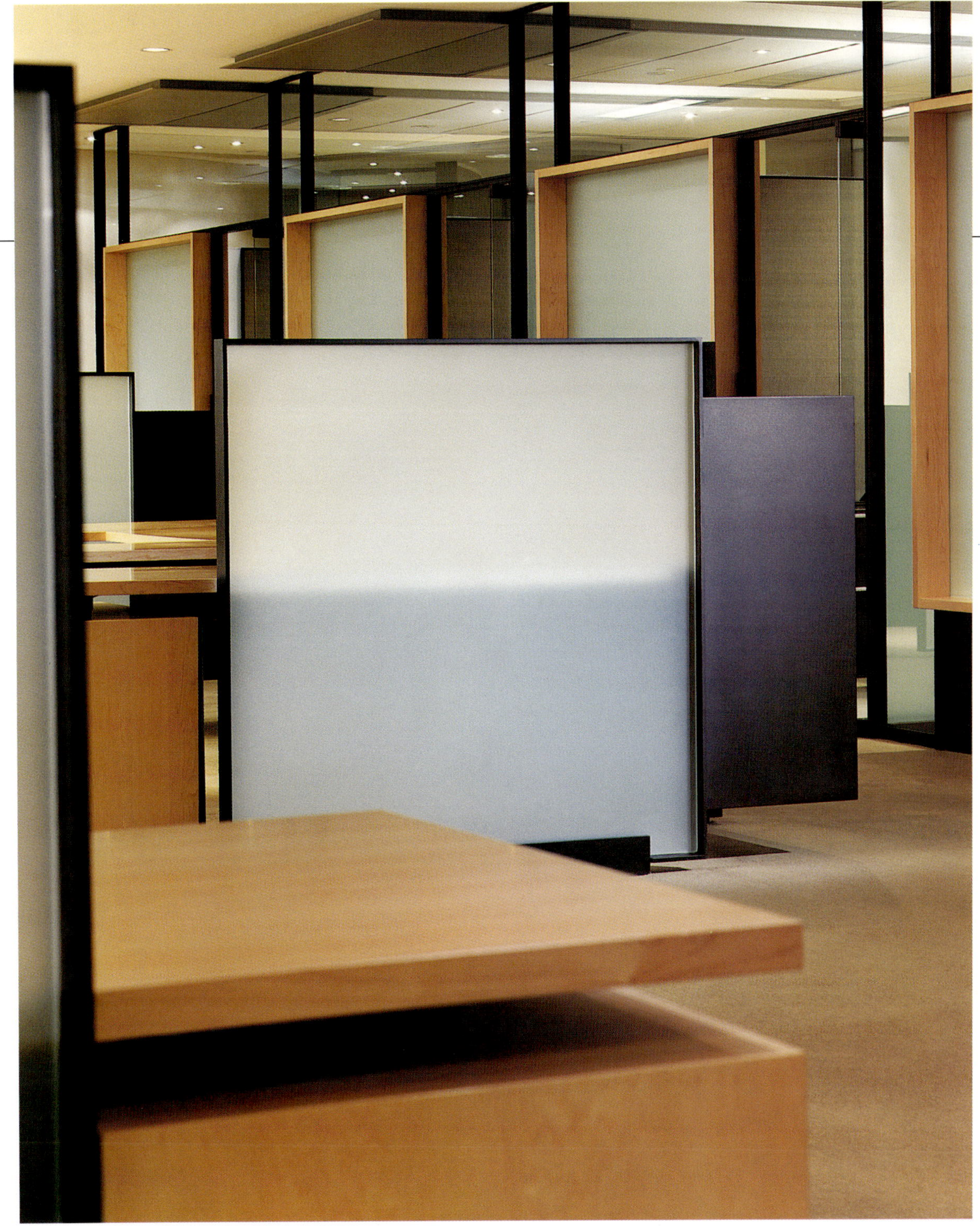

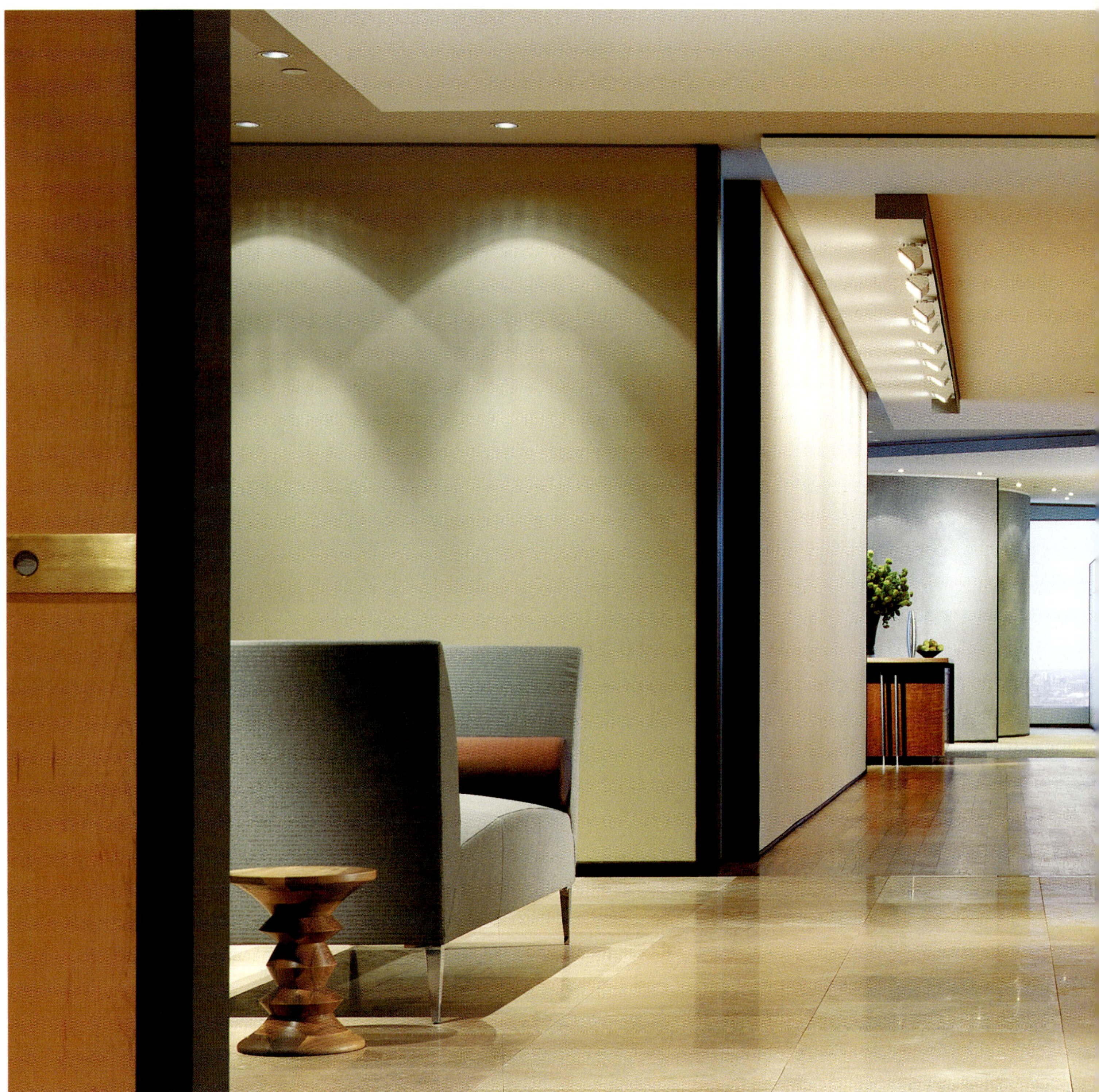

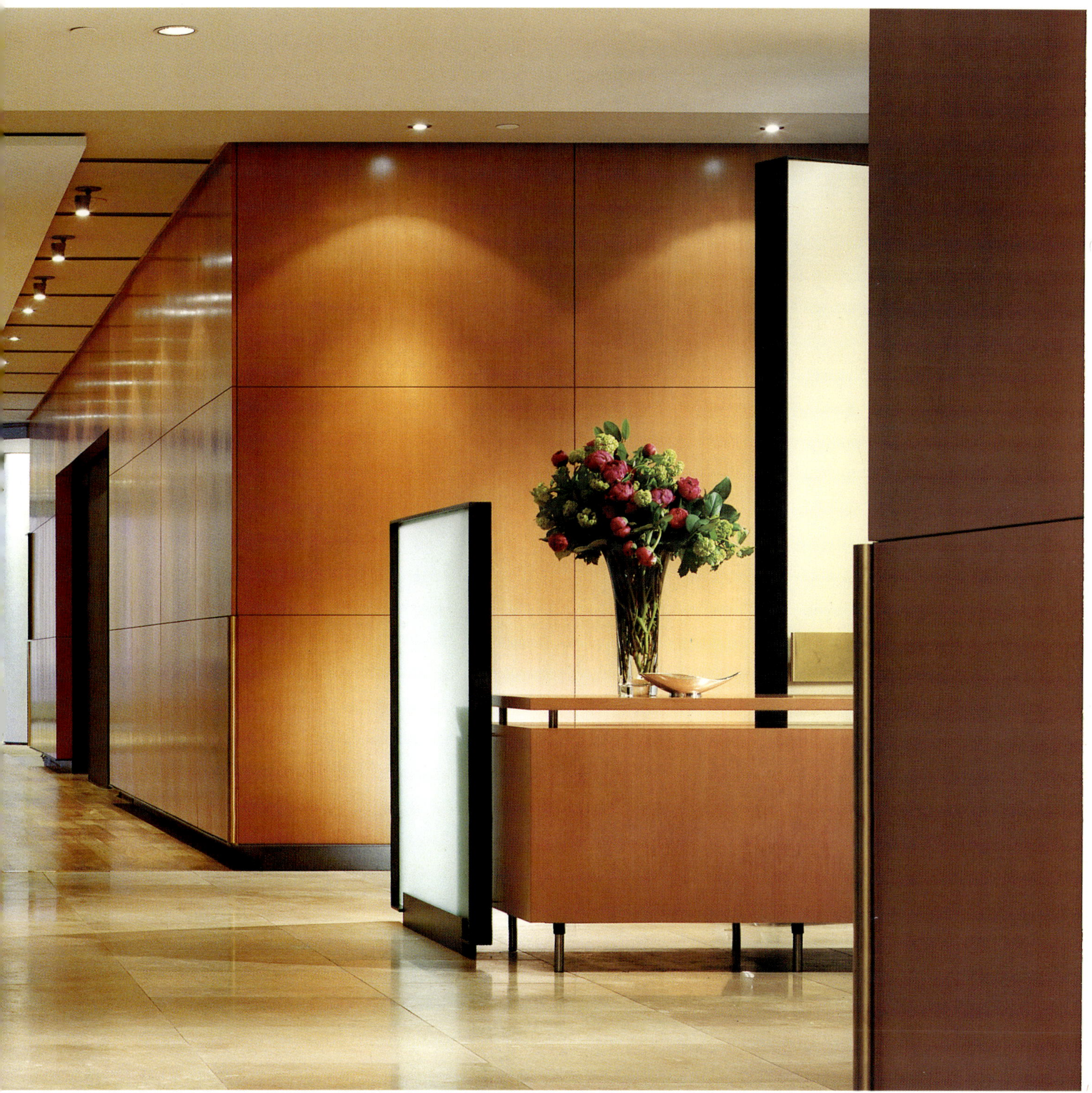

Reisman-Jenkinson House

The Reisman-Jenkinson residence and studio combines living and working space for a family of four in a suburb north of Toronto. Challenging conventional expectations about domesticity, and celebrating the parallel existence of artistic practices and the rituals of daily life, the architecture creates an alternative to typical suburban living.

The four light-gray, split-faced concrete block buildings are linked together by three glazed elements to form a forecourt and garden court. One edge of the forecourt is the sculpture studio, which receives indirect northern light through clerestory windows. Opening onto the court, Douglas fir double doors frame views from the studio toward a spectacular outdoor landscape of silver maple trees. A light-filled entrance volume forms the other flank of the forecourt, connecting the studio and main loft buildings.

The main "living loft" is anchored at either end by two fireplaces, and composed of simple volumes with high ceilings, large door and window openings, and maple hardwood floors. A pyramidal skylight establishes the space of the kitchen as a third interior court.

Bedrooms and writing studios are located deeper in the lot and grouped around a landscaped garden court. Large sliding panels in the "living loft" and the master bedroom buildings allow adjustable degrees of privacy within a flexible living arrangement. Figural roofs above the sculpture studio and main living building are fabricated from anodized, preformed aluminum panels.

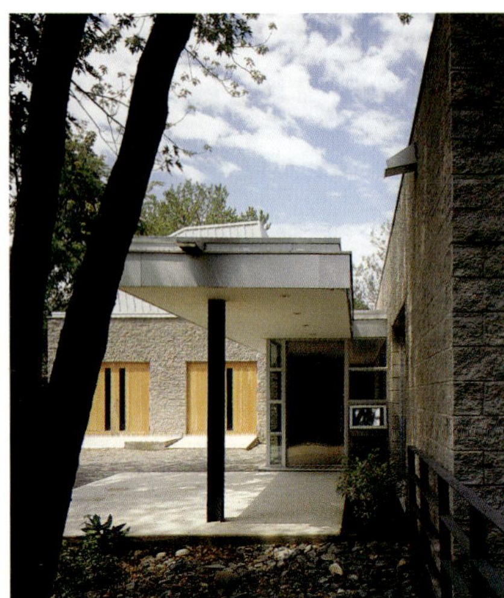

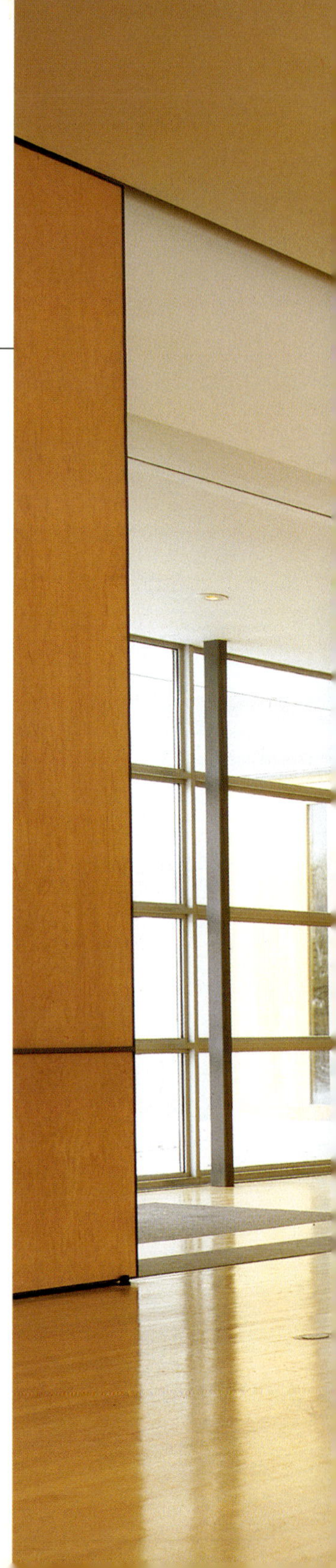

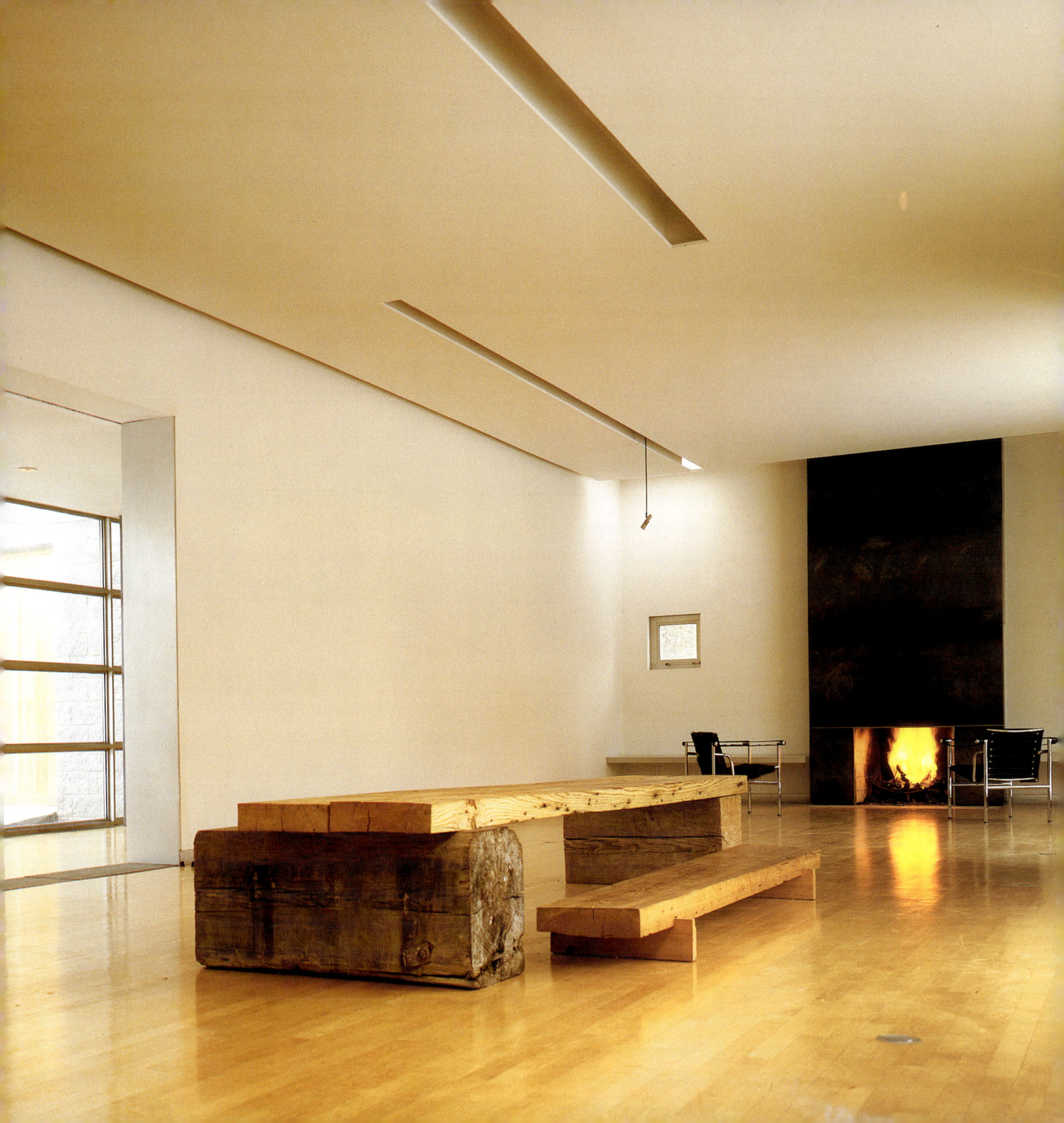

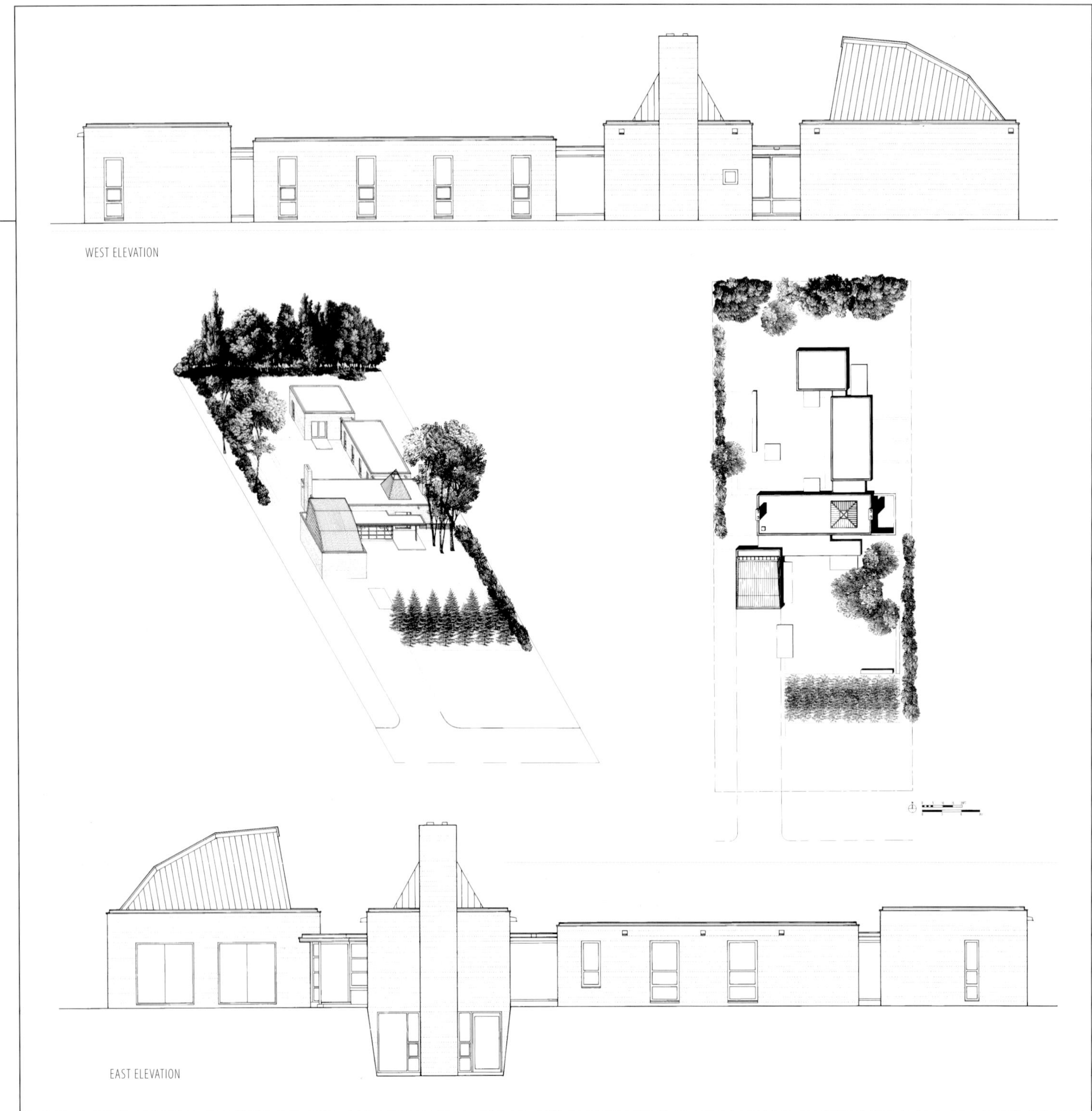

WEST ELEVATION
EAST ELEVATION

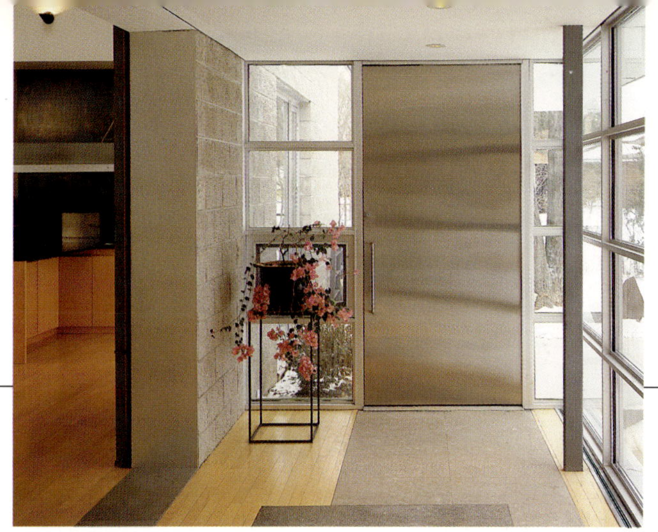

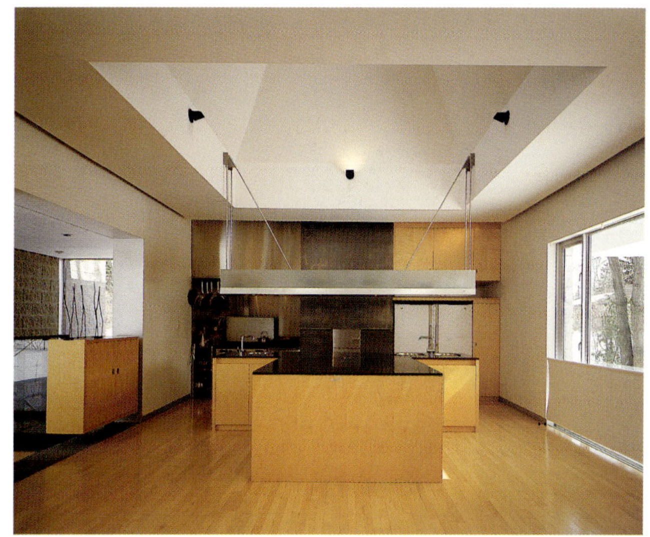

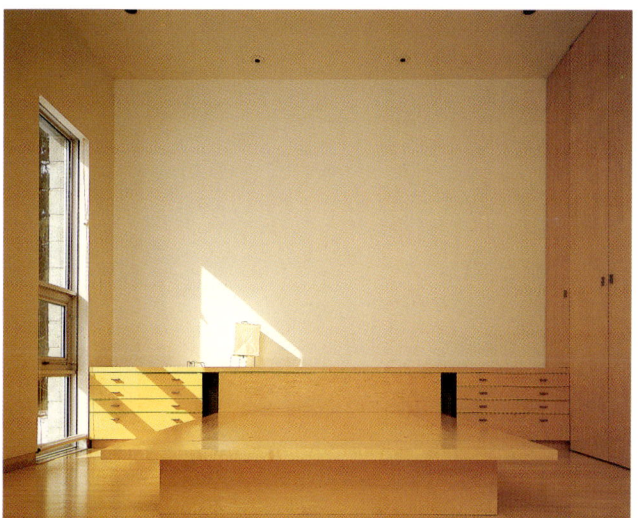

The entrance to the house is a distinct volume separating the sculptor's studio from the living room (top). An overhead pyramidal void, topped by a skylight, is centered on the monumental kitchen counter (center). The master bedroom overlooks the garden court (bottom).

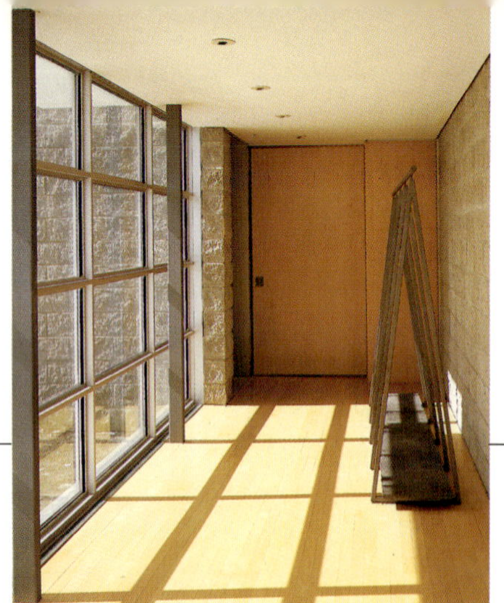

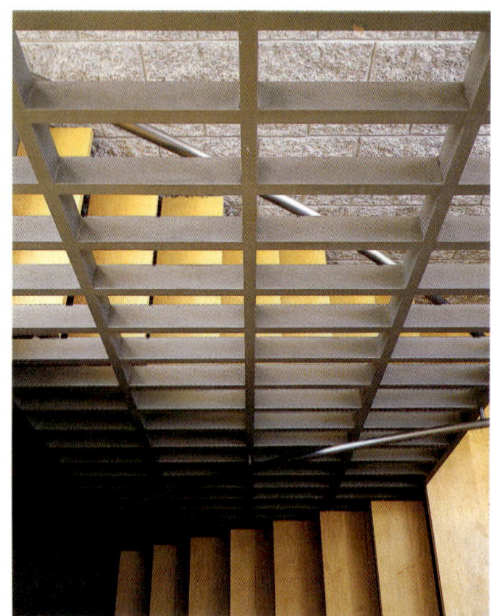

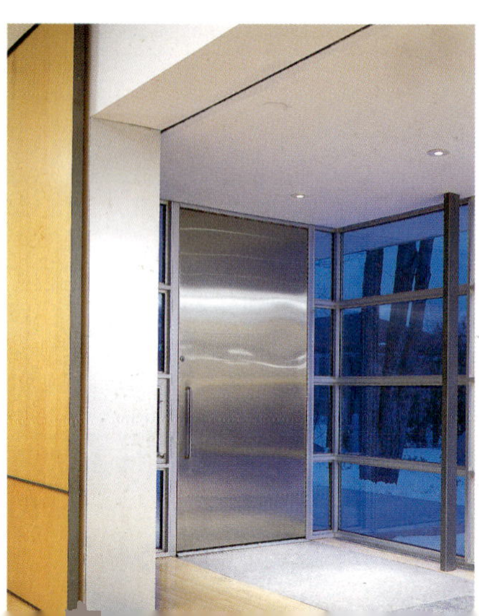

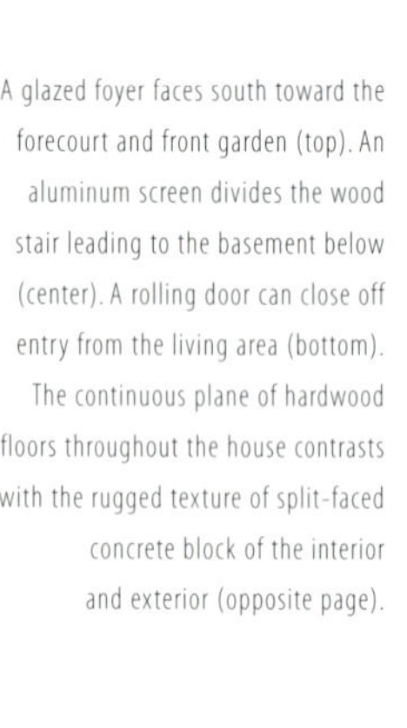

A glazed foyer faces south toward the forecourt and front garden (top). An aluminum screen divides the wood stair leading to the basement below (center). A rolling door can close off entry from the living area (bottom). The continuous plane of hardwood floors throughout the house contrasts with the rugged texture of split-faced concrete block of the interior and exterior (opposite page).

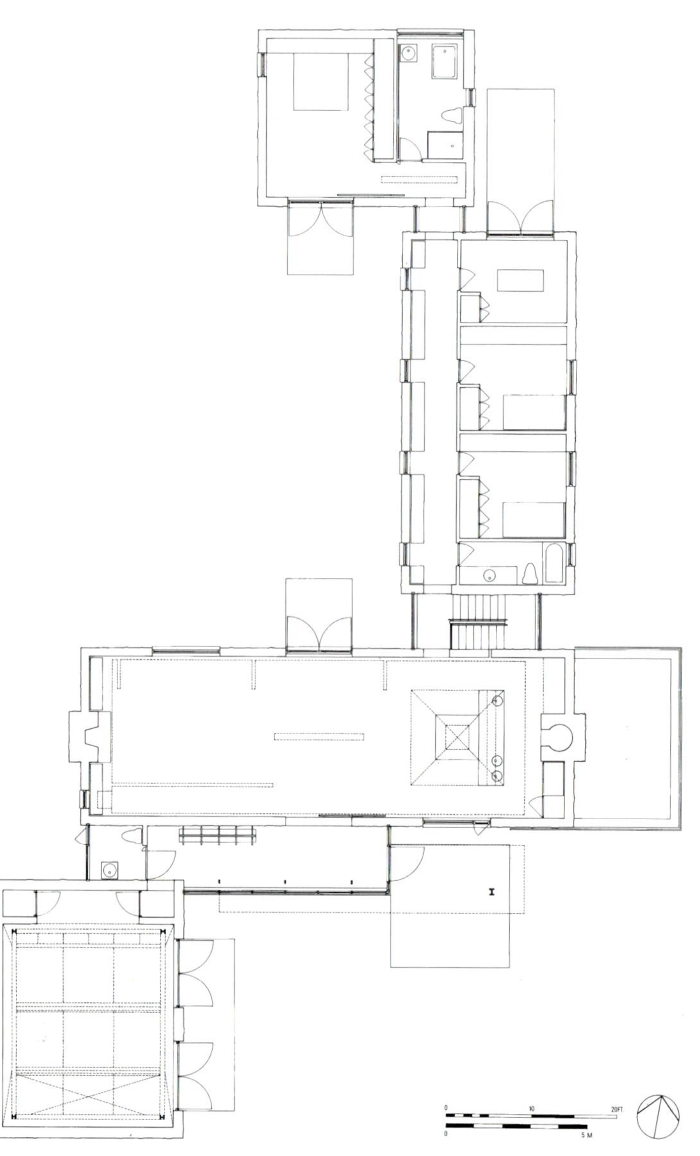

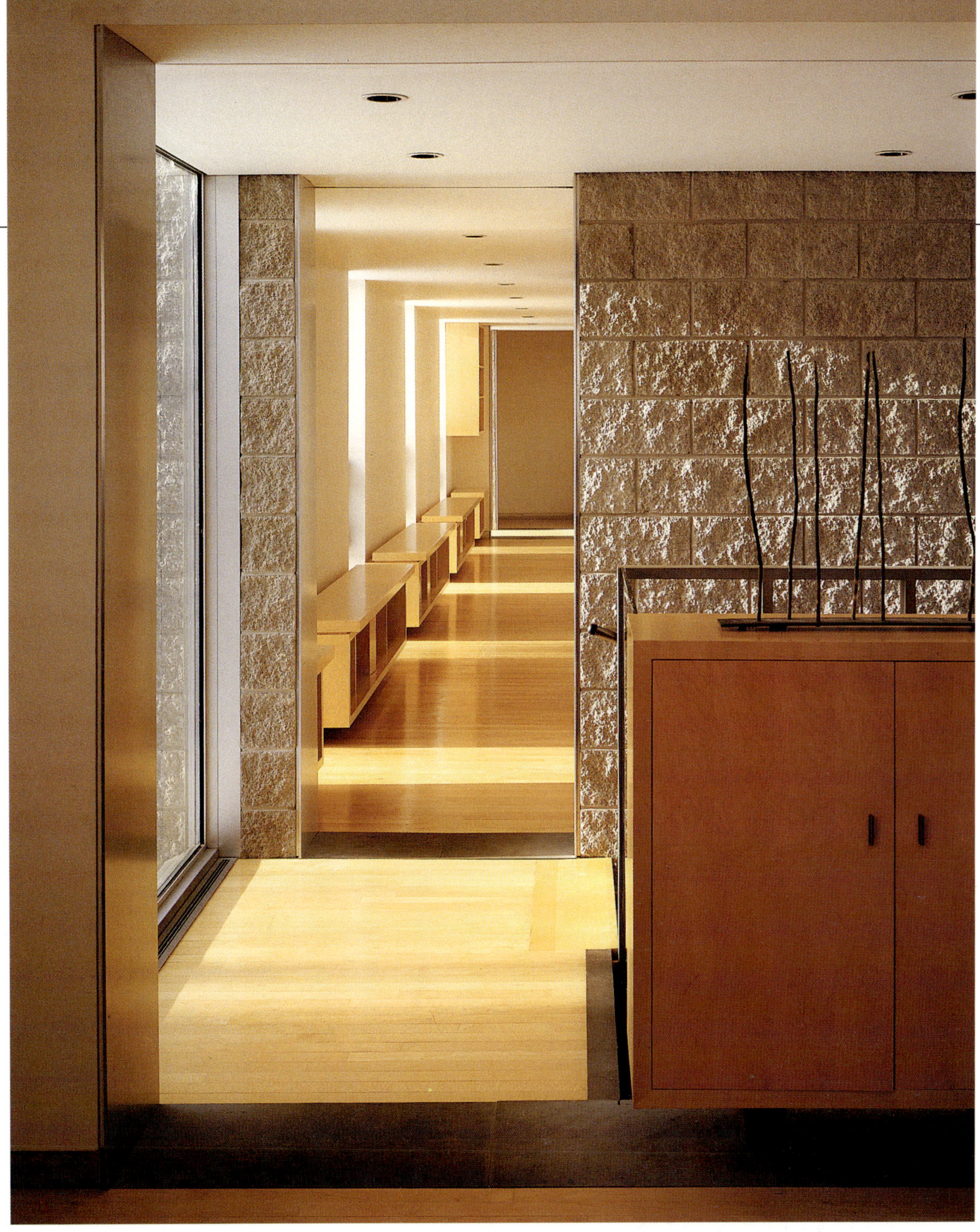

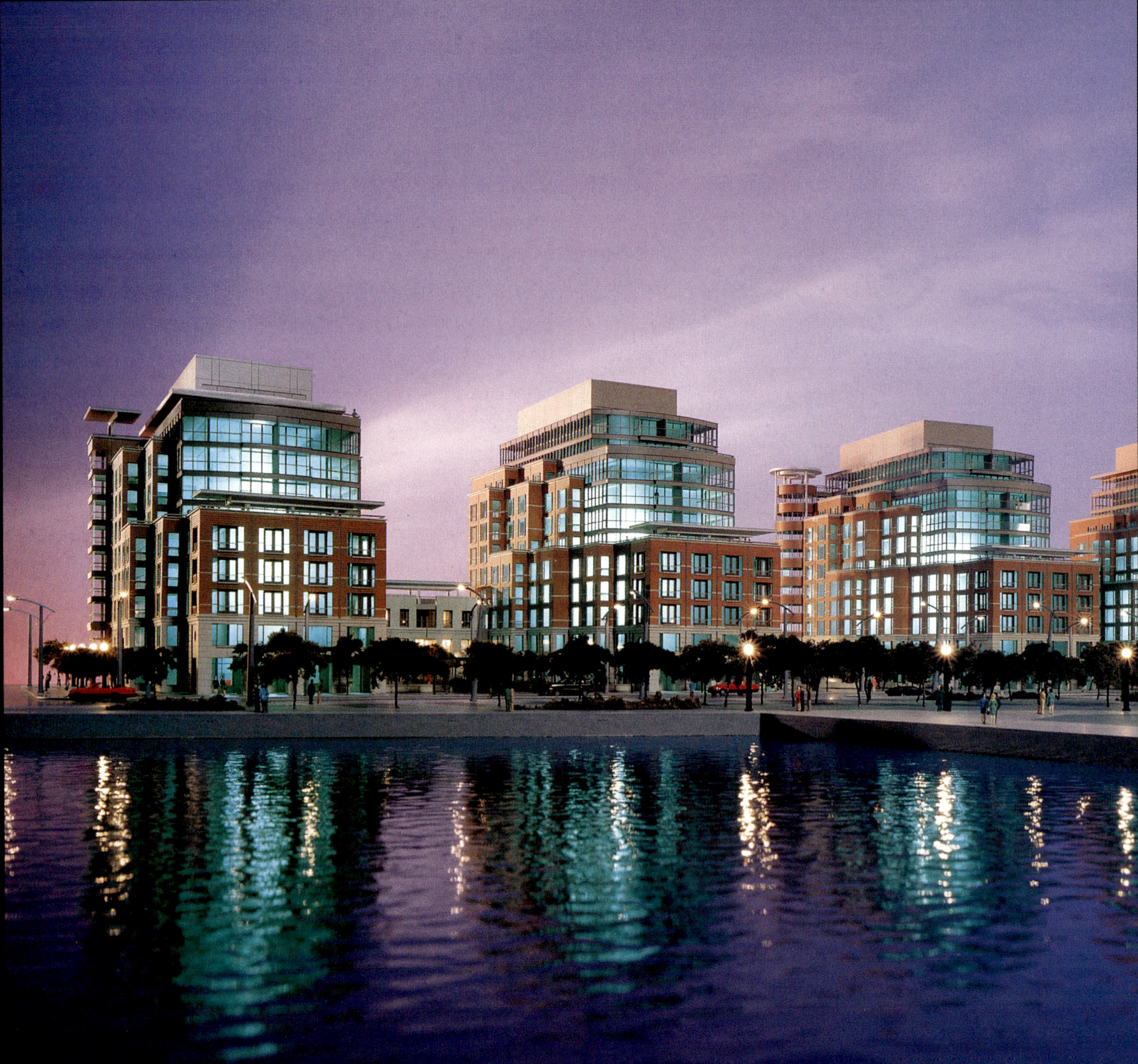

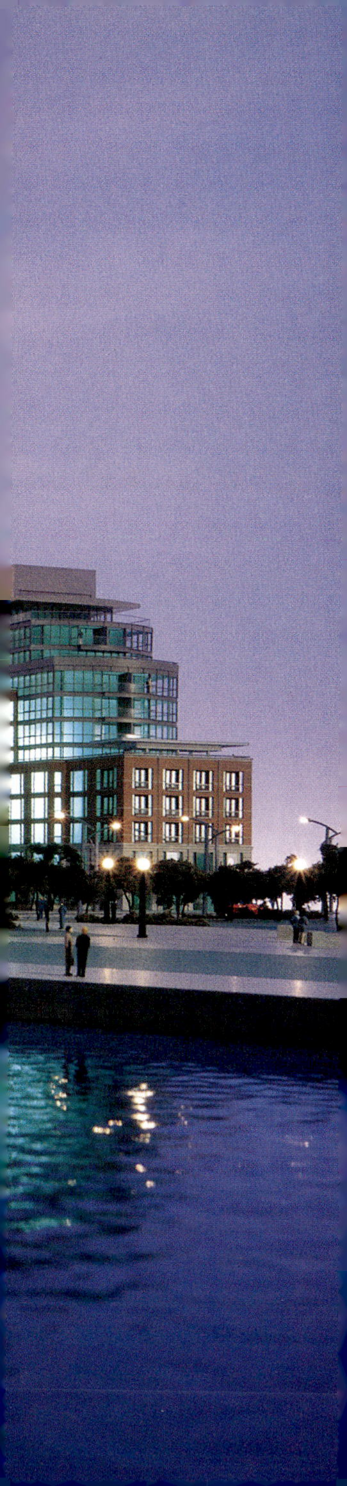

Selected Buildings

1987
Ottawa City Hall
Ottawa, Ontario, Canada
(invited competition entry in joint venture with
Adamson & Associates)

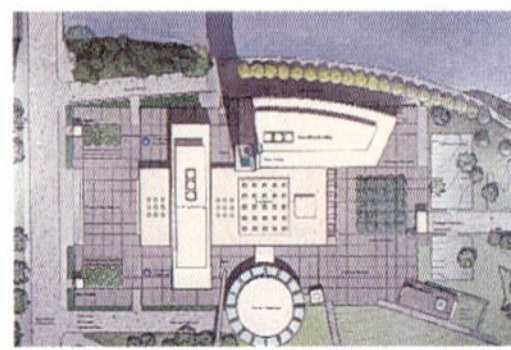 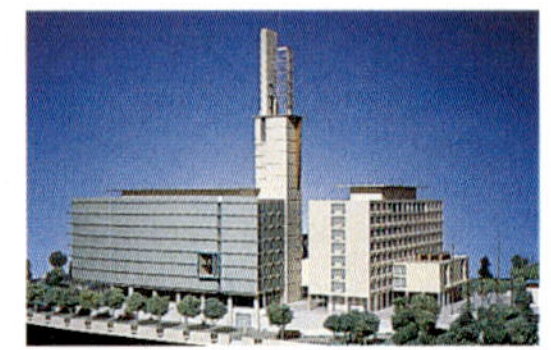 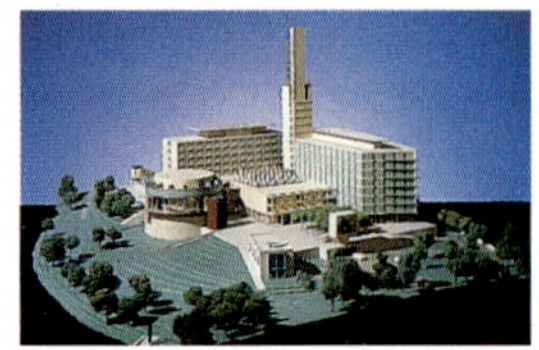

1991
Vancouver Public Library
Vancouver, British Columbia, Canada
(invited competition entry awarded Second
Prize in joint venture with James K. M. Cheng
Architects Inc. and Musson Cattell Mackey
Partnership)

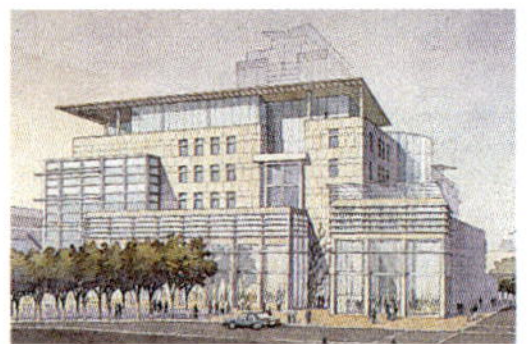 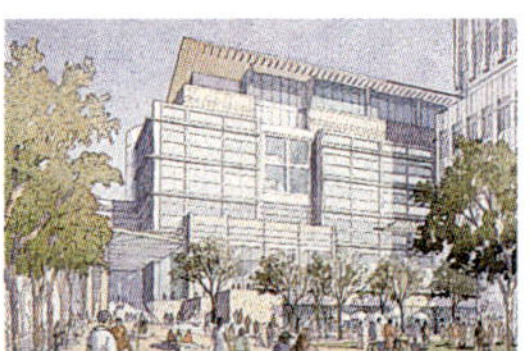 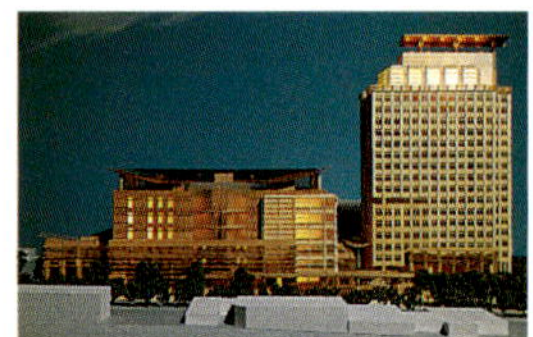

1992
Rahimi Developments
Hamburg, Germany
(project)

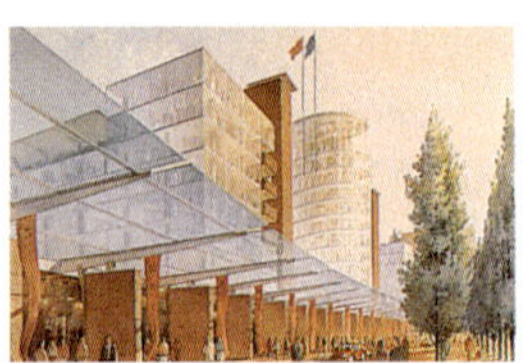 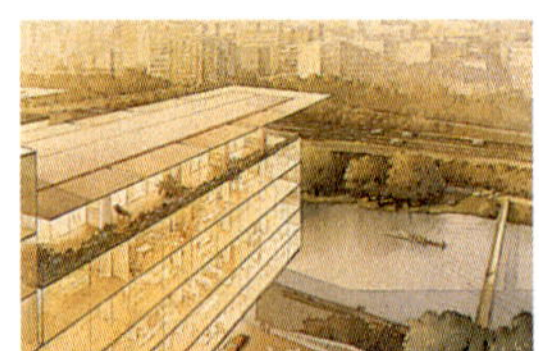 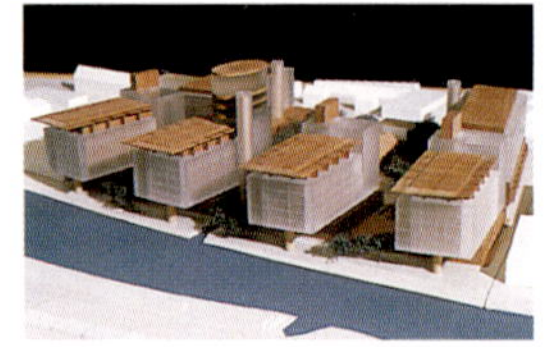

1994
Tip Top Tailors Building
Toronto, Ontario, Canada
(competition entry)

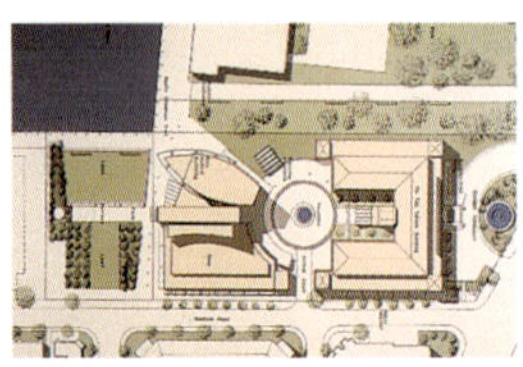 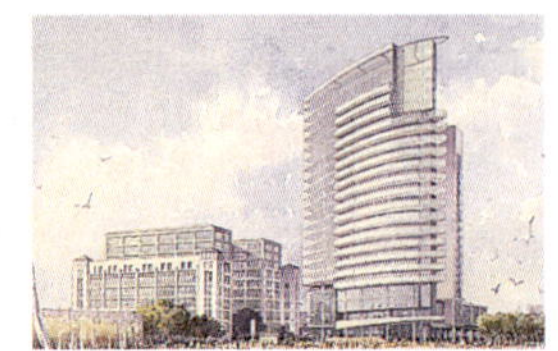 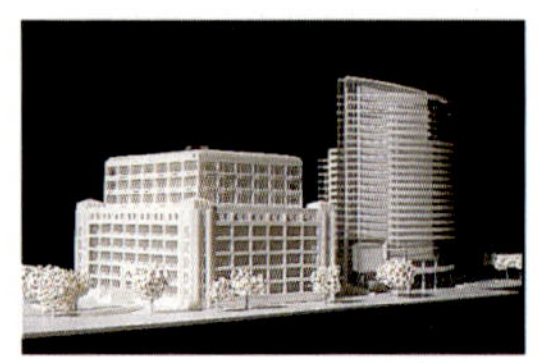

1995 – 1996
Metronome
Toronto, Ontario, Canada
(ongoing work)

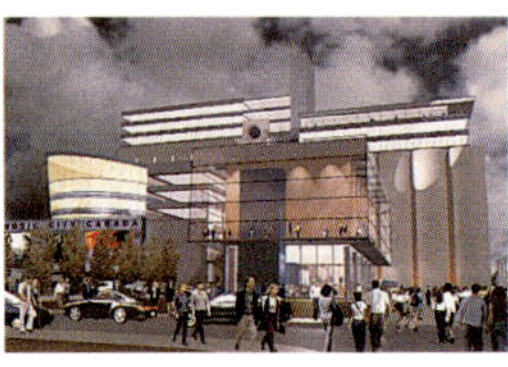 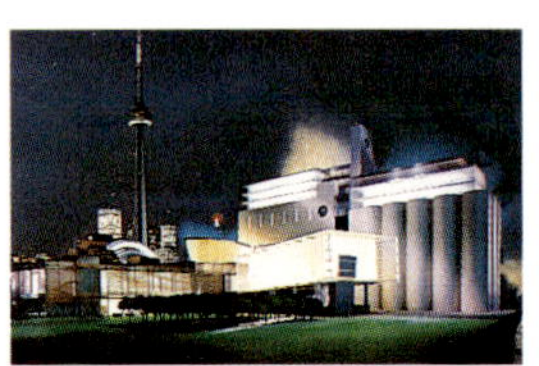 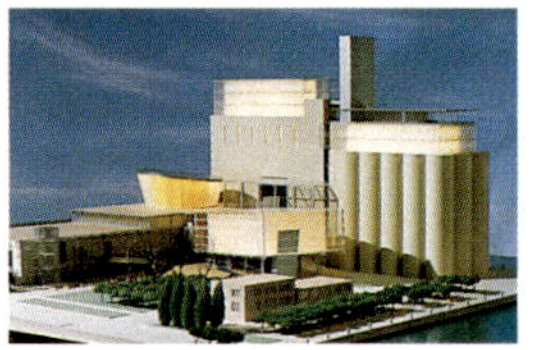

1989
Graywood Developments Tower
Toronto, Ontario, Canada
(project)

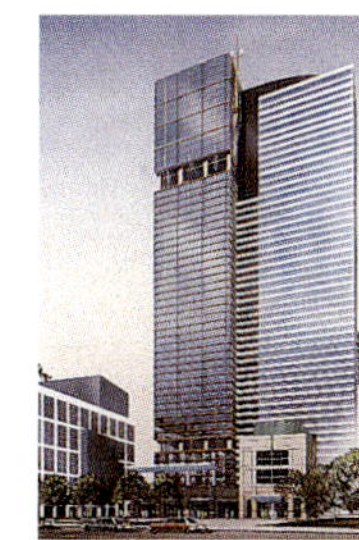
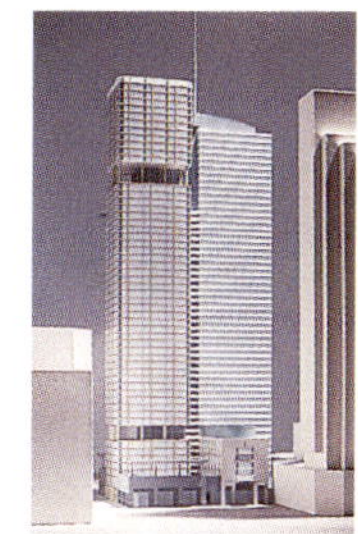
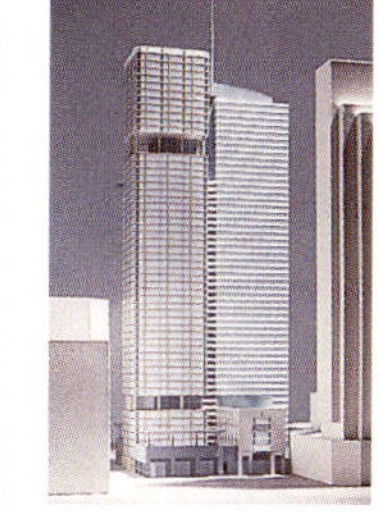

1994
University of Minnesota Master Plan
Minneapolis, Minnesota, USA
(project)
(in collaboration with Berridge
Lewinberg Greenberg)

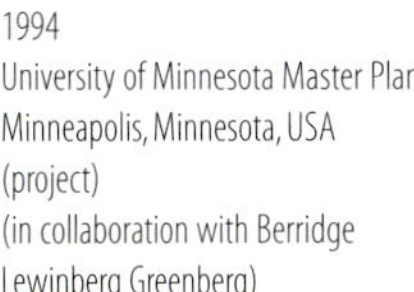
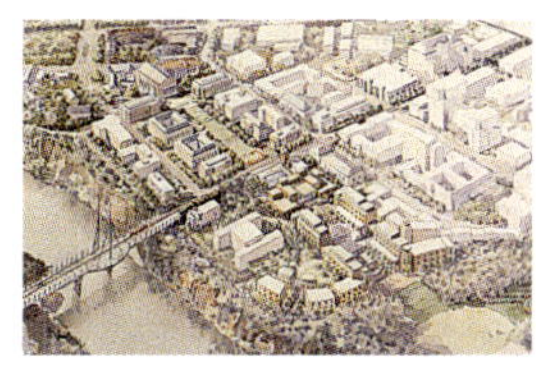
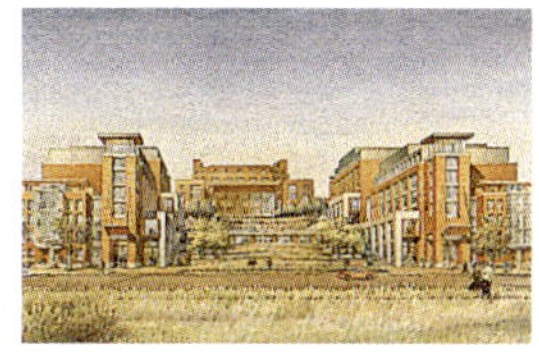
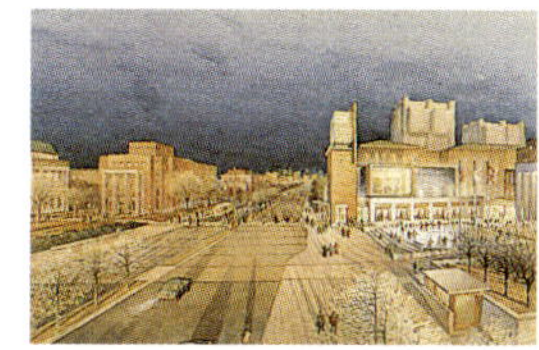

1995
Korean Museum of Art and Culture
Los Angeles, California, USA
(honorable mention in international
competition)

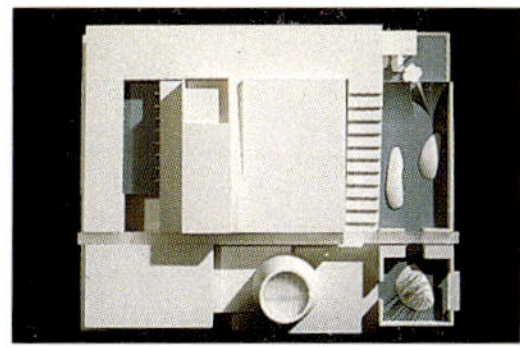
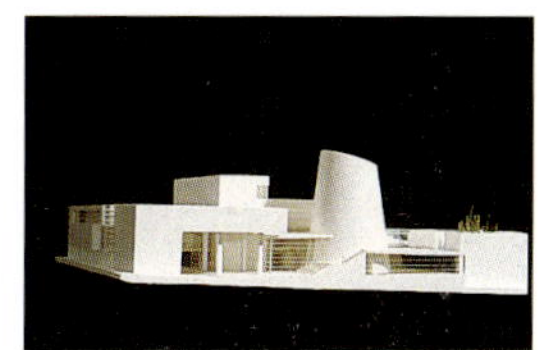
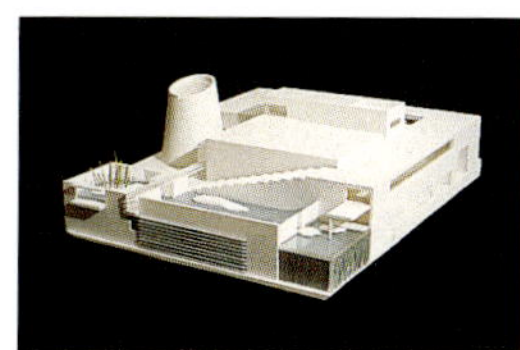

1995
Centre for Environmental Engineering
and Sciences
University of Waterloo
Waterloo, Ontario, Canada
(competition entry in joint venture with Pellow
Smith Carter Architects, Inc.)

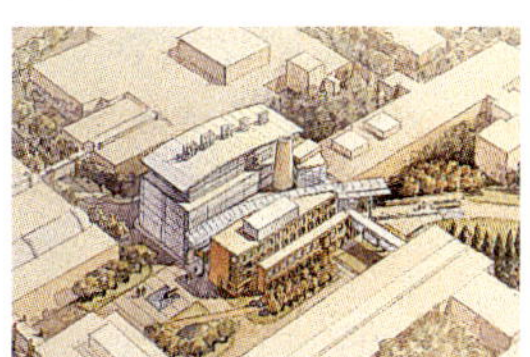
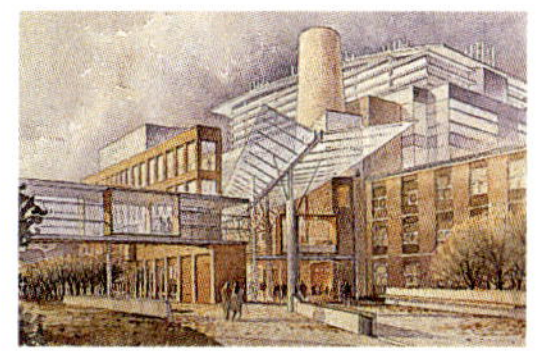
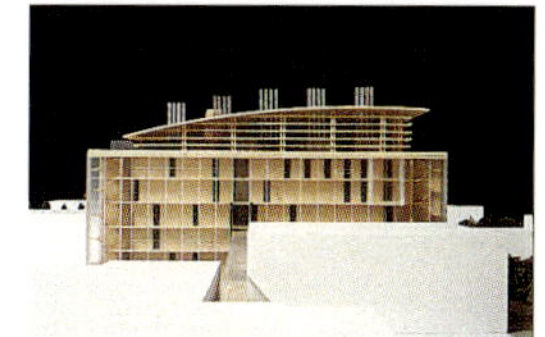

1995
Providence Centre Health Care Complex
Scarborough, Ontario, Canada
(to be built 1997)
(in joint venture with
Montgomery & Sisam Architects)

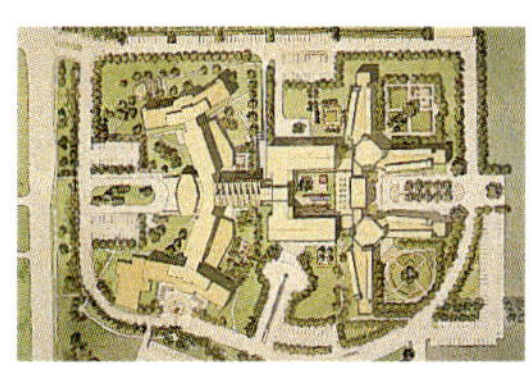
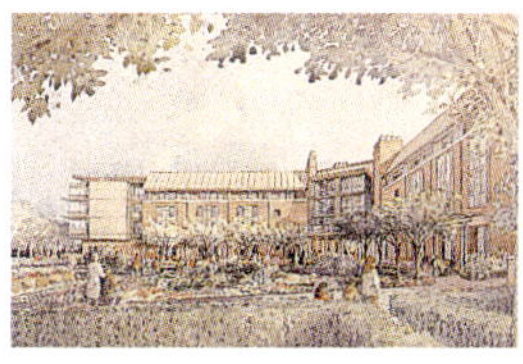
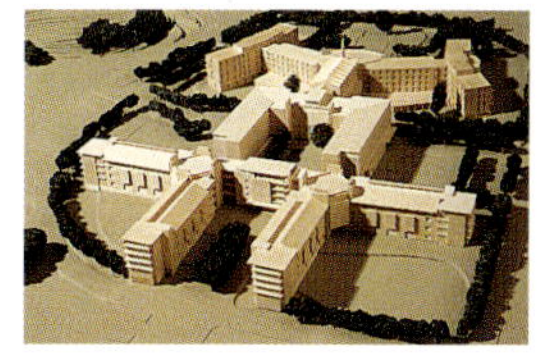

1994 – 1996
Goodman Theatre
Chicago, Illinois, USA
(to be built 1997)

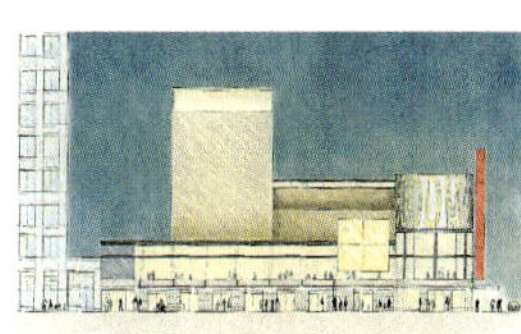
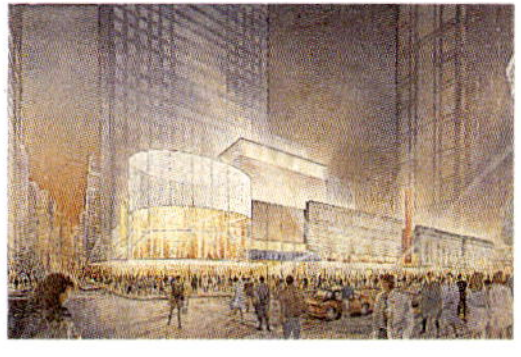
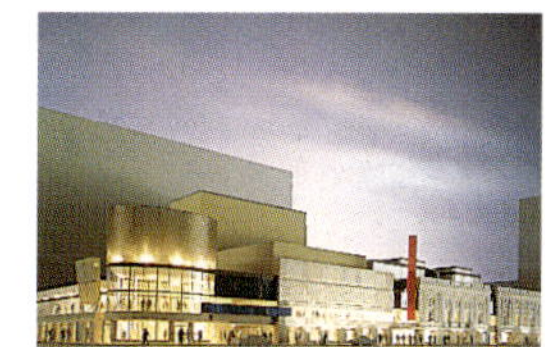

1993–1996
Chinese Cultural Centre
Scarborough, Ontario, Canada
(under construction 1997; in joint venture with
Patrick T. Y. Chan Architect)

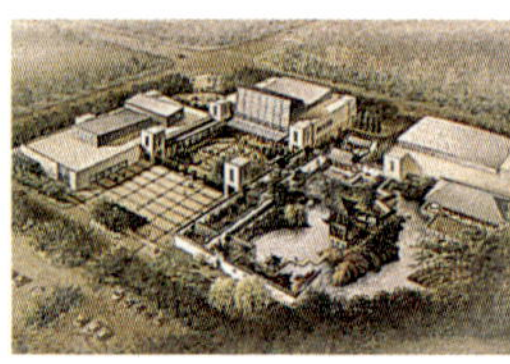
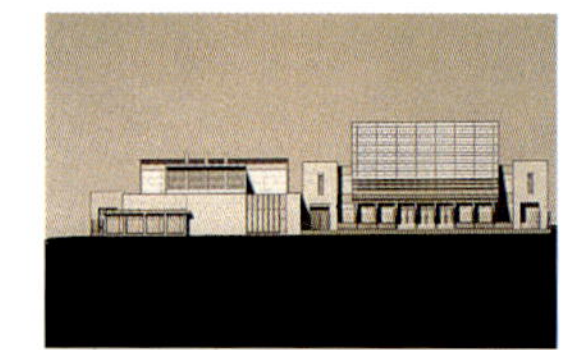
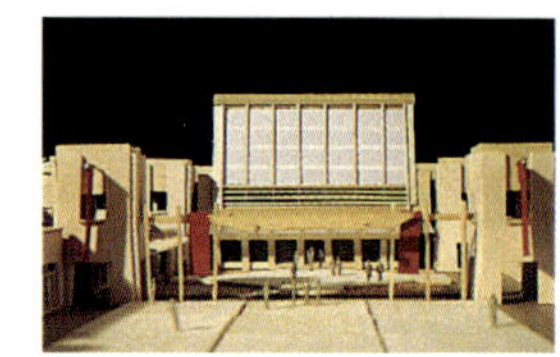

1994
Kensington Parking Garage
Kensington Market, Toronto, Canada
(under construction 1997; design consultants
to Read Jones Christoffersen Ltd.)

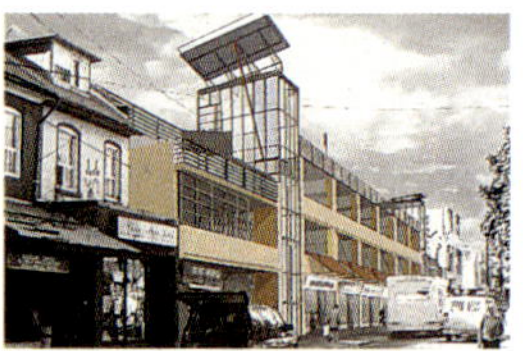
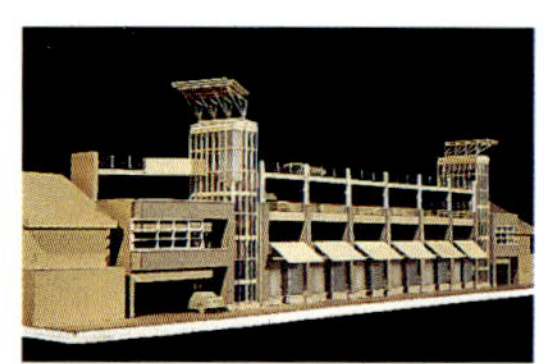
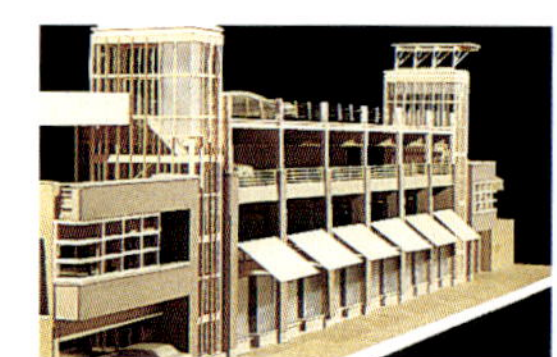

1994
Uptown Core Park
Oakville, Ontario, Canada
(Phase I under construction; with Milus
Bollenberghe Topps Watchorn and
Environmental Artworks Ltd.)

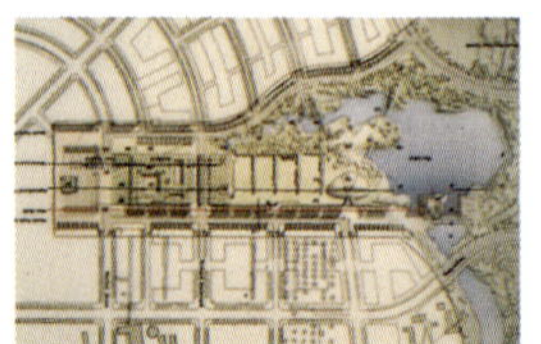
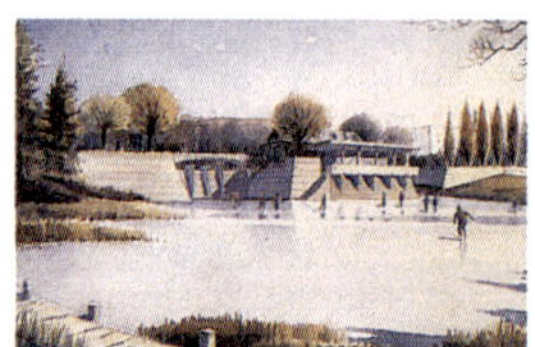
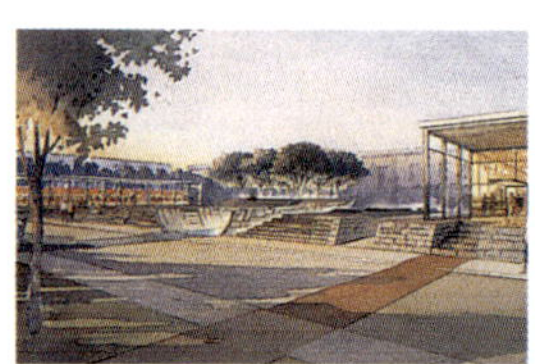

1994–1995
Stratford Festival Theater Renovation
Stratford, Ontario, Canada
(completed 1997)

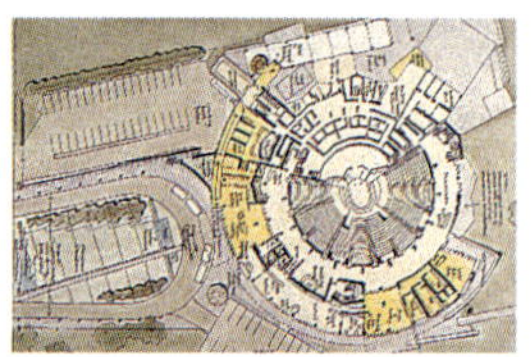
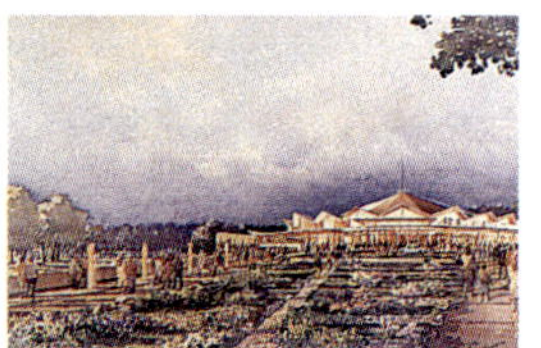
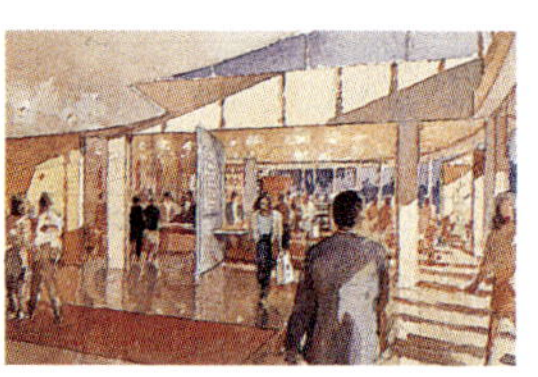

1995
500 Queen's Quay West Condominiums
Toronto, Ontario, Canada
(with Stone Kohn McQuire Vogt Architects;
under construction 1996–1997)

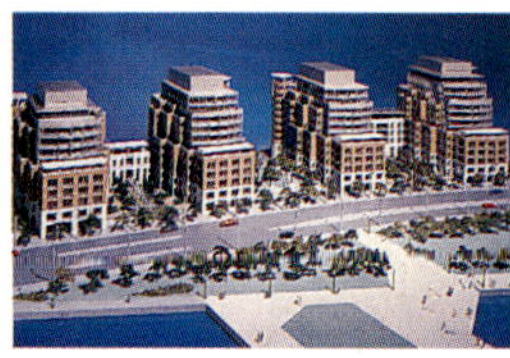
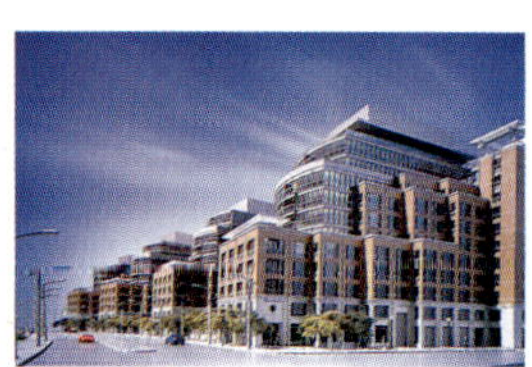
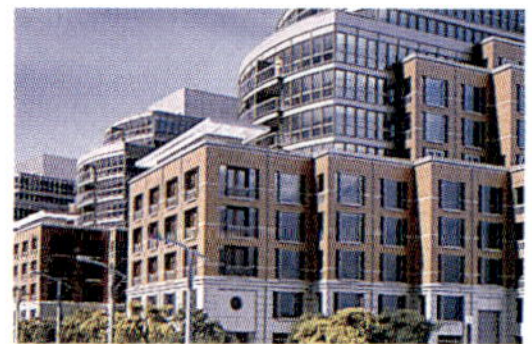

1987–1988
Dorchester Offices
Chicago, Illinois, USA
(completed 1989)

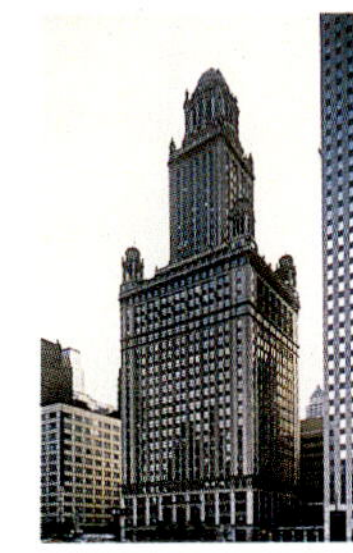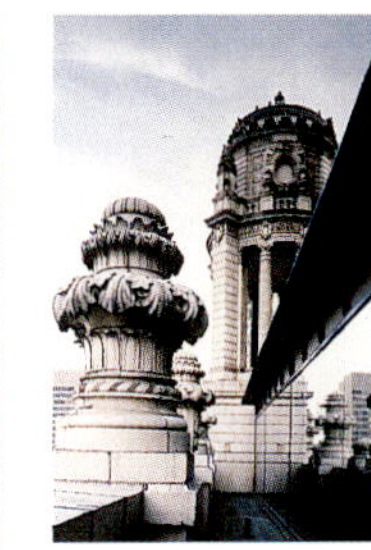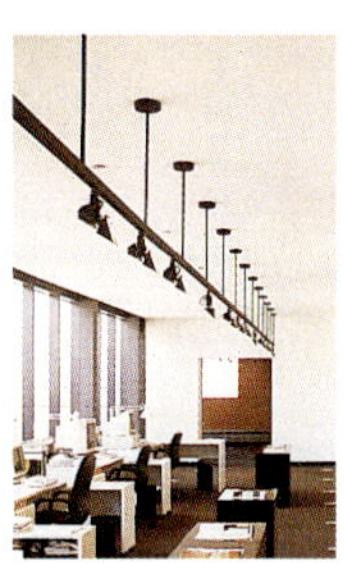

1993
Ammirati Puris Lintas Offices
BCE Place, Toronto, Canada
(completed 1994)

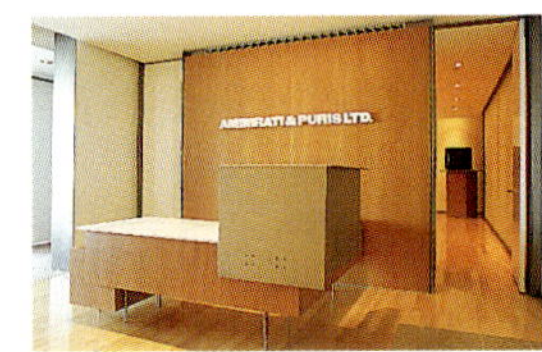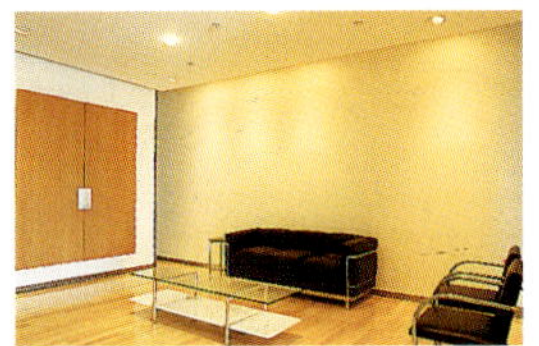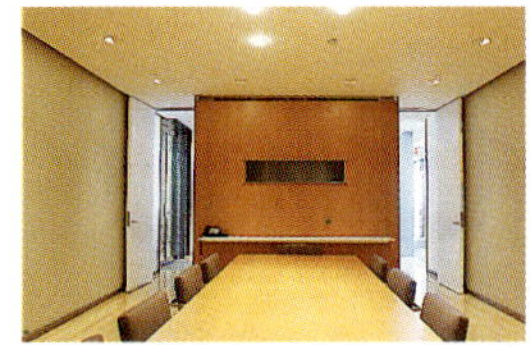

1992–1993
Victoria University Student Residence
Toronto, Canada
(completed 1994; design consultants to Victoria
University; Keith Becker, Architect of record)

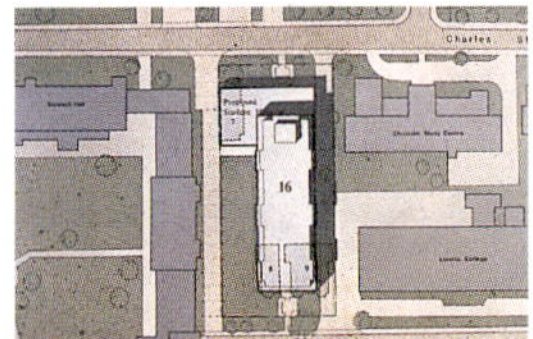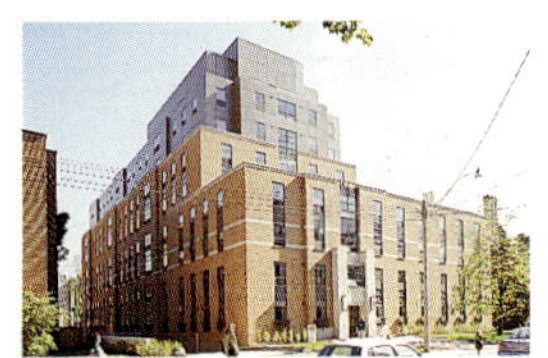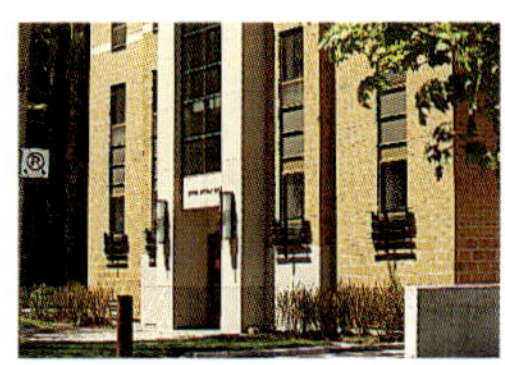

1994
Ministry of Culture, Tourism, and Recreation
Niagara Falls, Ontario, Canada
(completed in 1995)
(in joint venture with Dunlop Farrow Inc.)

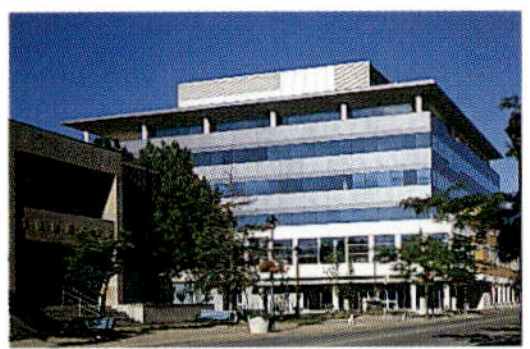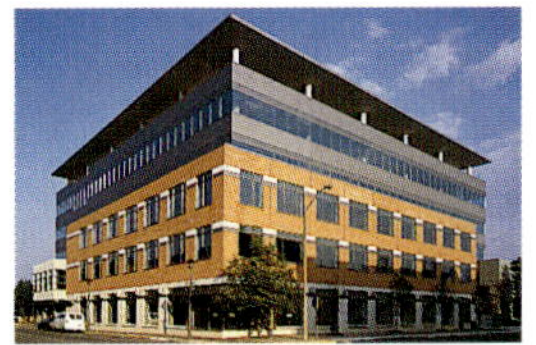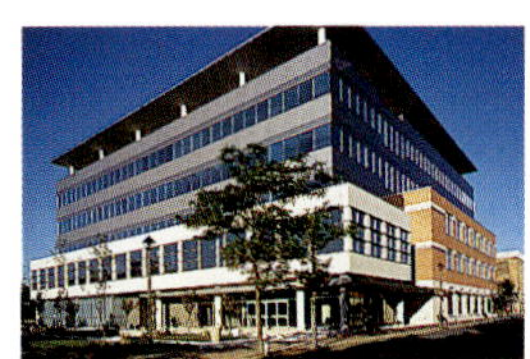

1996
Fort Lasalle, Royal Military College
Kingston, Ontario, Canada
(completed 1997)

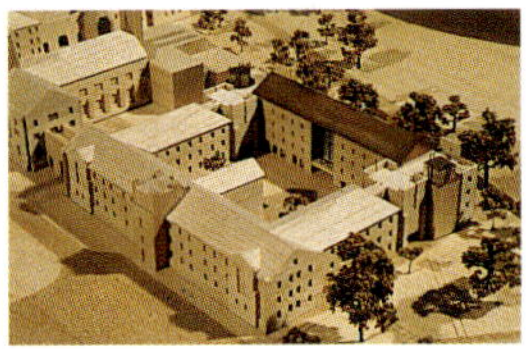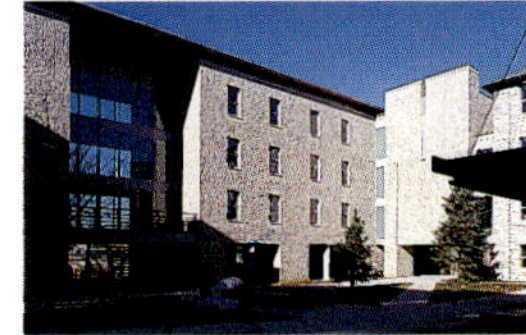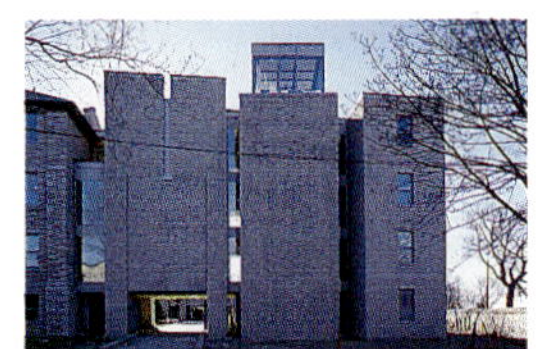

1996
Hummingbird Centre Renovations
Toronto, Ontario, Canada
(completed 1997)

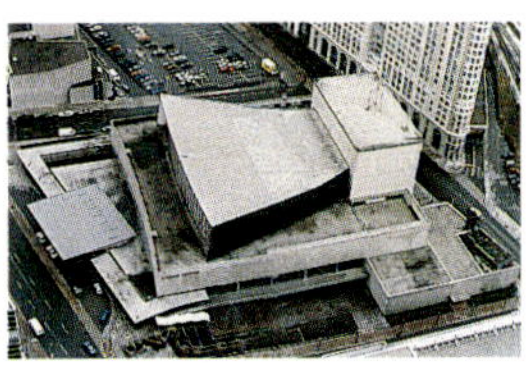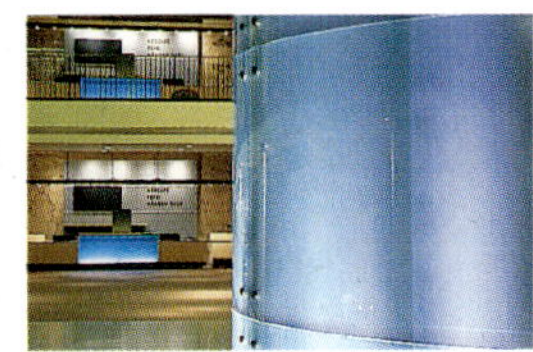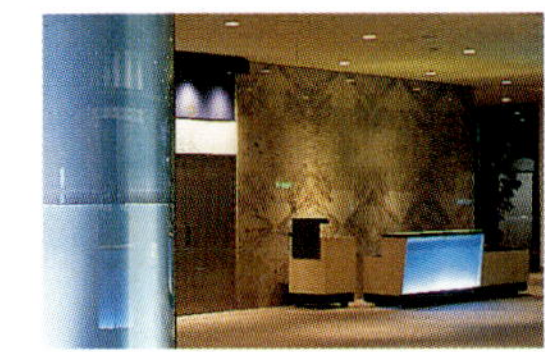

List of Works and Credits

ITCHENER CITY HALL
1990–1993, Kitchener, Ontario
Awards: Winning design in a national competition, 1989
      Award of Excellence, Canadian Architect, 1991
      Governor General's Medal for Architecture, 1994
      Client: City of Kitchener
      Pan-American Biennale of Architecture—Honorable Mention 1996
Project Team: Bruce Kuwabara; Marianne McKenna, Luigi LaRocca, Howard Sutcliffe, David Pontarini, Judy Taylor, Andrew Dyke, Mitchell Hall, Evan Webber, John Allen, Mike Poitras, Glenn MacMullin
Structural Engineer: M. S. Yolles & Partners Ltd.
Electrical Engineer: Mulvey & Banani International Inc.
Mechanical Engineer: Merber Corporation
Landscape Consultant: Milus Bollenberghe Topps Watchorn
Contractor: Ellis-Don Construction Ltd.
Model: Richard Sinclair
Photographer: All photos except as noted by Steven Evans. Timothy Hursley/The Arkansas Group (pp. 18–19)

JOSEPH S. STAUFFER LIBRARY
QUEEN'S UNIVERSITY
1991–1994, Kingston, Ontario
Awards: Winning design in a national design competition, 1990
      Governor General's Award for Architecture, 1997
Client: Queen's University
Project Team: Thomas Payne; Chris Couse; David Pontarini, Judy Taylor, Victoria Gregory, Goran Milosevic, Mike Poitras
Consulting Architect: Moffat Kinoshita Associates Inc.
Structural Engineer: Robert Halsall & Associates Ltd.
Mechanical Engineer: JSA Energy Analysts
Electrical Engineer: Mulvey & Banani International Inc.
Landscape Architect: Ferris & Quinn Associates Inc.
Cost Consultant: James F. Vermeulen Ltd.
Library Consultant: McAdams Planning Consultants Inc.
Contractor: Eastern Construction Company Ltd.
Photographers: ESTO/Jeff Goldberg (pp. 26, 29 top and bottom, 30, 31 center, 33–35); Steven Evans (pp. 27, 29 center, 31 top)

WOODSWORTH COLLEGE
UNIVERSITY OF TORONTO
1990–1992, Toronto, Ontario
Awards: Governor General's Medal for Excellence, 1992
      O.A.A. Architectural Excellence Award, 1993
      A.I.A. Brick in Architecture Award, 1993
      Toronto Historical Board Commendation, 1993
      City of Toronto Urban Design Award, 1995
Client: University of Toronto
Associated Architects: Barton Myers Architect Inc. and Kuwabara Payne McKenna Blumberg
KPMB Project Team: Thomas Payne; Siamak Hariri; David Pontarini, Victoria Gregory, John Cook, Goran Milosevic, Bob Sims, Josef Neuwirth, Mitchell Hall, Birgit Siber
Structural Engineer: Yolles Partnership Ltd.
Mechanical and Electrical Engineer: Merber Corporation
Landscape Consultant: Ferris McCluskey Quinn & Associates
Cost Consultant: A. J. Vermeulen Inc.
Contractor: Jaltas Inc.
Photographer: Steven Evans

FIELDS INSTITUTE
UNIVERSITY OF TORONTO
1994–1995, Toronto, Ontario
Client: University of Toronto; The Fields Institute
Project Team: Thomas Payne, Lexi Kolt, Luigi LaRocca, Michael Taylor, Bill Colaco, Victoria Gregory, Ian Izukawa, David Jesson, Jeff Wagner, Meg Graham
Structural Engineer: Yolles Partnership Ltd.
Mechanical Engineer: Merber Corporation
Electrical Engineer: Crossey Engineering
Landscape Consultant: Milus Bollenberghe Topps Watchorn
Contractor: PCL Constructors Eastern Inc.
Photographer: ESTO/Jeff Goldberg

WALTER CARSEN CENTRE FOR THE NATIONAL BALLET OF CANADA
1995–1996, Toronto, Ontario
Client: The National Ballet of Canada
Project Team: Thomas Payne; Chris Couse, Todd Macyk, Matthew Wilson, Dmytriy Pereklita, Bill Colaco, Karen Petrachenko, Anthony Provenzano
Structural Engineer: Halsall Associates Ltd.
Mechanical and Electrical Engineer: Rybka Smith Ginsler Ltd.
Contractor: Dalton Engineering
Photographers: Michael Awad (pp. 46, 49 center, bottom); ESTO/Jeff Goldberg (pp. 47, 49 top)

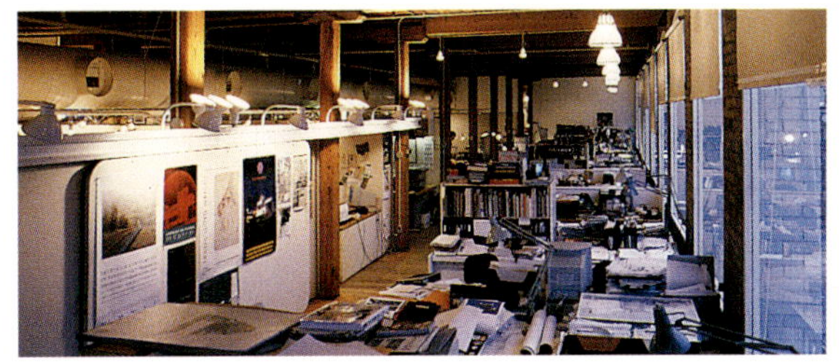

THE DESIGN EXCHANGE
1992–1994, Toronto, Ontario
Awards: Governor General's Award for Architecture, 1997
Client: The Design Exchange
Project Team: Shirley Blumberg; Bruce Kuwabara, Siamak Hariri, Todd Macyk; David Jesson, Karen Petrachenko, Kelly Lem, Mike Poitras, Anthony Provenzano
Structural Engineer: Yolles Partnership Ltd.
Mechanical Engineers: Merber Corporation
Electrical Engineers: Carinci Burt Rogers Engineering
Cost Consultant: James F. Vermeulen Ltd.
Color Consultant: Donald Kaufman Color
Signage and Graphics: Gottschalk & Ash International
General Contractor: Jackson-Lewis Company Ltd.
Photographer: Robert Burley/Design Archive (pp. 50, 56, 57 top, middle); Steven Evans (pp. 51, 53–55, 57 bottom)

KING JAMES PLACE
1989–1991, Toronto, Ontario
Awards: Governor General's Award for Architecture, 1992
Toronto Masonry Award, Overall Winner, 1992
City of Toronto Urban Design Award, Honorable Mention, 1993
Award of Merit, Toronto Historical Board, 1994
Client: Equifund York Developments Ltd.
Project Team: Shirley Blumberg, Bruce Kuwabara, Michael Taylor, Byron Carter, Mike Poitras, Joseph Neuwirth, Elaine Didyk
Structural Engineer: Read Jones Christoffersen
Mechanical Engineer: Merber Corporation
Electrical Engineer: Carinci Burt Rogers Engineering
Contractor: Buttcon Ltd.
Photographer: Steven Evans

MARC LAURENT
Phase one: 1986; Phase two: 1988; Phase three: 1990; Phase four: 1991; Phase five: 1995, Toronto, Ontario
Client: Harry Bendayan
Project Team: Bruce Kuwabara, Thomas Payne, Lexi Kolt, Larry Chow, Jason King, Todd Macyk, Anthony Provenzano
Mechanical and Electrical Engineer: Merber Corporation
Contractor: Phases one to four: H. Bendayan; Phase five: Gorman Mazzon Ltd.
Photographer: Michael Awad (pp. 62, 69 bottom); Steven Evans (pp. 63–66, 69 top, bottom)

CREED'S INTERIORS
1990, Toronto, Ontario
Client: Creed's Ltd., Toronto
Project Team: Bruce Kuwabara; Karen Petrachenko, Larry Chow, Mark Jaffar, Shaun O'Reilly
Structural Engineer: Yolles Partnership Ltd.
Electrical Engineer: M.H. Engineering
Contractor: Hazelton Construction Ltd.
Photographer: Steven Evans

NICOLAS
1991, Toronto, Ontario
Client: Nicolas Kalatzis
Project Team: Bruce Kuwabara, Thomas Payne, Todd Macyk
Mechanical and Electrical Engineer: Merber Corporation
Contractor: Millworks Custom Fabricators
Photographer: Steven Evans

OASIS PARFUMERIE
1992, Oakville, Ontario
Awards: A.R.I.D.O. Gold Award, 1993
Client: Oasis Parfumerie Inc.
Project Team: Bruce Kuwabara and Shirley Blumberg, Karen Petrachenko, Todd Macyk, David Jesson
Contractor: Millworks Custom Fabricating
Photographer: Steven Evans

CREATIVE COPY & DESIGN
1992, Toronto, Ontario
Awards: A.R.I.D.O. Silver Award, 1993
Client: Nick Manos
Project Team: Shirley Blumberg, Bruce Kuwabara, Michael Taylor, Karen Petrachenko
Contractor: Owner
Photographer: Steven Evans

SEGA CITY @ PLAYDIUM
1995–1996, Mississauga, Ontario
Awards: Mississauga Urban Design Award, 1996
Client: Playdium Entertainment Corporation
Project Team: Bruce Kuwabara; Luigi LaRocca; Mike Poitras, Anita Matusevics, Don Collins, Marco Magarelli
Structural Engineer: Yolles Partnership
Mechanical Engineer: MCW Consultants Inc.
Electrical Engineer: Carinci Burt Rogers Engineering Inc.
Interiors: II BY IV Design Associates Inc.
Contractor: Vanbots Construction Corporation
Photographer: Michael Awad

GRAND VALLEY INSTITUTION FOR WOMEN

1995–1996, Kitchener, Ontario
Awards: Governor General's Award for Architecture, 1997
Client: Public Works Canada and Correctional Services Canada
Project Team: Marianne McKenna; Bruce Kuwabara; Bob Sims; John Allen;
Howard Sutcliffe, David Pontarini
Structural Engineer: Read Jones Christoffersen
Mechanical and Electrical Engineer: Crossey Engineering Ltd.
Landscape Architect: Milus Bollenberghe Topps Watchorn
Photographer: Steven Evans (pp. 88–92); Peter Gill (p. 93)

TUDHOPE STUDIOS

1987–1989, Toronto, Ontario
Client: Tudhope Associates Inc.
Project Team: Marianne McKenna, Bruce Kuwabara, Howard Sutcliffe, Luigi LaRocca,
Beverley Horii, Neil Morfitt
Structural Engineer: M. S. Yolles & Partners
Mechanical Engineer: Merber Corporation
Electrical Engineer: Carinci Burt Rogers Engineering
Photographer: Wolfgang Hoyt

DOME PRODUCTIONS IN THE SKYDOME

1989, Toronto, Ontario
Client: The Sports Network/Labatts Brewery Ltd.
Project Team: Bruce Kuwabara; Luigi LaRocca, Howard Sutcliffe, Lexi Kolt,
Steven Robinson
Structural Engineer: M. S. Yolles & Partners
Electrical Engineer: Carinci Burt Rogers Engineering
Mechanical Engineer: Merber Corporation
Construction Manager: Dalton Engineering
Photographer: Steven Evans

HASBRO INC. HEADQUARTERS

1991, Pawtucket, Rhode Island
Phase 2 (Main Street/Executive Offices); 1992, Phase 2A; 1994, Phase 2B
Awards: New England Construction Users Council Award
Client: Hasbro Inc.
Project Team: Shirley Blumberg, Bruce Kuwabara, Walter Daschko, Peter McMillan,
Kelly Lem, Ian Izukawa, David Poloway, Bob Sims, Mitchell Hall, Glenn MacMullin
Structural Engineer: M. S. Yolles & Partners
Mechanical Engineer: J. C. Higgins Corporation
Electrical Engineer: Boulos/Robinson
Construction Manager: Dimeo Construction Company
Photographer: Steve Rosenthal

AMMIRATI PURIS LINTAS

1994–1995, New York, New York
Client: Ammirati Puris Lintas
Project Team: Bruce Kuwabara; Shirley Blumberg, Kevin Mast; David Jesson;
Brian Main, Prish Jain, Heather Dubbeldam, Mark Berest, Mike Poitras, Matthew
Wilson, Leah Maguire, Anthony Provenzano
Associated Architect: John C. Fondrisi, A.I.A.
Structural Engineer: Severud Associates
Mechanical and Electrical Engineer: Jaros Baum & Bolles
Construction Manager: Structure Tone Inc.
Photographer: ESTO/Jeff Goldberg

ALLIANCE COMMUNICATIONS CORPORATION

1995–1996, Toronto, Ontario
Client: Alliance Communications Corporation
Project Team: Bruce Kuwabara and Shirley Blumberg; Luigi LaRocca; Karen Petrachenko,
Michael Krus, Marco Magarelli, David Poloway, Karen Cvornyek
Structural Engineer: Read Jones Christoffersen
Mechanical Engineer: Smith & Anderson
Electrical Engineer: Mulvey & Banani International
Lighting Consultant: Suzanne Powadiuk
Construction Manager: Urbacon Ltd.
Photographer: Robert Burley/Design Archive

GLUSKIN SHEFF + ASSOCIATES

1995, Toronto, Ontario
Client: Gluskin Sheff + Associates
Project Team: Bruce Kuwabara; Marianne McKenna; Mitchell Hall, David Poloway,
Karen Petrachenko, Glenn MacMullin
Mechanical and Electrical Engineer: Merber Corporation
Audio Visual Consultant: Brian Arnott Associates
Lighting Consultant: Suzanne Powadiuk
Construction Manager: Govan Brown Associates Ltd.
Photographer: ESTO/Jeff Goldberg

REISMAN-JENKINSON HOUSE

1990–1991, Richmond Hill, Ontario
Awards: Governor General's Award for Architecture, 1994
Client: Stephen Jenkinson, Dolly Reisman
Project Team: Bruce Kuwabara, Evan Webber
Structural Engineer: M. S. Yolles & Partners
Building Envelope Consultant: Michel Perrault
Contractor: Lora Lane Group Inc.
Photographer: Steven Evans

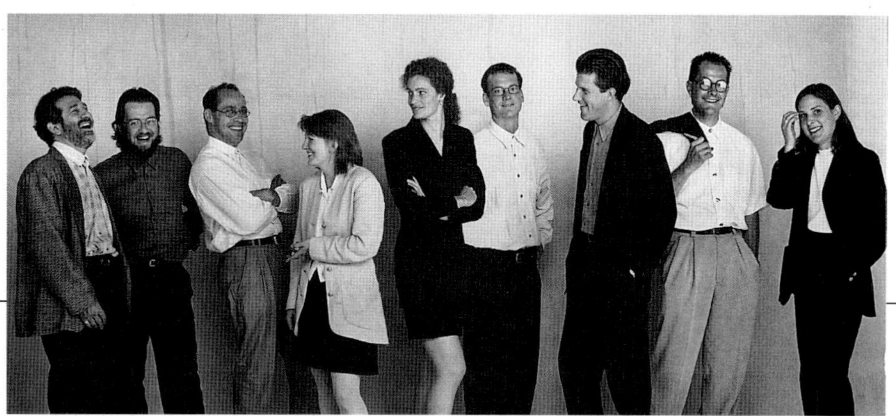

KPMB ASSOCIATES AND INTERNS 1987–1997

John Allen
Fred Allin
Ebrahim Amin
Andrew Alzner
Michael Awad
Rob Beraldo
Mark Berest
Adrian Blackwell
Andrew Blackwood
Kevin Bridgman
Jill Calvert
Byron Carter
Allison Carr
Vince Catalli
Rosa Chang
Donald Chong
Larry Chow
Chester Chu
Kyra Clarkson
Bill Colaco
Donald Collins
John Cook
Christopher Couse
Karen Cvornyek
John Czechowski
Lisa d'Abbondanza
Andre D'Elia
Walter Daschko
Matthew Dawson
Elaine Didyk
David Dow
Heather Dubbeldam
Andrew Dyke
Michael Epp
Shaun Fernandes
Mary Jane Finlayson
Anne-Marie Fleming

Dominic Gagnon
Rick Galezowski
Joan Gardner
Shauna Gilles-Smith
Rob Gilvesy
Kelvin Goddard
Meg Graham
Bill Greaves
Victoria Gregory
David Griffin
Greg Guerra
Don Gulay
Radek Guzowski
Mitchell Hall
Siamak Hariri
Daphne Harris
Courtney Henry
Robert G. Hill
Monica Hlozanek
Tina Hollingshead
Rick Hopkins
Beverly Horii
Desmond Hui
Grant Hutchinson
Michael Issac
Ian Izukawa
Mark Jaffar
Prish Jain
David Jesson
Andrew Jones
Wendy Kaiser
Jason King
Tom Koehler
Lexi Kolt-Wagner
Michael Krus
Jennifer Kuwabara
Gerry Lang

Luigi LaRocca
Jeff Latto
Kelly Lem
Alan Leung
Mary Lou Lobsinger
Andrea MacElwee
Glenn MacMullin
Todd Macyk
Marco Magarelli
Leah Maguire
Brian Main
Karen Mak
Drew Mandel
Ky Maruyama
Kevin Mast
John McFarland
Shannon McGaw
Peter McMillan
Dan McNeil
Michelle Mearns
Gianni Meogrossi
Goran Milosevic
Neil Morfitt
Joe Moro
Joseph Neuwirth
Yusuke Obuchi
Sean O'Reilly
Katherine Pankratz
Glenn Parker
Juliette Patterson
Jason Pearson
Dmytriy Pereklita
Karen Petrachenko
Mike Poitras
David Poloway
David Pontarini
Frank Portelli

Suzanne Powadiuk
Anthony Provenzano
Andres Quinlan
Johanna Radix
Ron Renters
Corry Ricci
Howard Rideout
Steven Robinson
Paulo Rocha
Jerry Rubin
John Shnier
Amanda Sebris
Birgit Siber
Marc Simmons
Robert Sims
Cal Smith
Matt Smith
Naoki Stepanek
Howard Sutcliffe
Sherene Tay
Judy Taylor
Michael Taylor
Simon Taylor
Janet Town
Jennifer Turner
Charmaine Underwood
Claudio Venier
Alan Vihant
Jeff Wagner
John Wall
Evan Webber
David Weir
Matthew Wilson
Michael Wong
Michael Yuen
Nick Zigomanis

Kuwabara Payne McKenna Blumberg
Architects Associates from left to right:
Luigi LaRocca, Goran Milosevic, Evan
Webber, Lexi Kolt-Wagner, Judy Taylor,
Robert Sims, Mitchell Hall, Christopher
Couse, and Victoria Gregory.

ACKNOWLEDGMENTS

We have always been interested in the narrative function of architecture to create meaningful places and appropriate symbols of our time. The event of this publication celebrates ten years of making architecture here in our Toronto office.

The preparation of a monograph is a complex undertaking and would not have been possible without the foresight and confidence of our clients in Canada and the United States, and we are deeply indebted to them. The execution of the projects shown here is also a testament to the sustained enthusiasm and dedication of those staff members who have helped us to realize our designs over the past ten years. The consistently high standard of their efforts has given us great pride.

Special thanks are due to George Baird of Harvard University, and to Detlef Mertins of the University of Toronto who have kindly taken the time to interpret our work and to write about it with considerable eloquence. We are grateful to Oscar Riera Ojeda for first putting our name forward for publication, and for applying his perceptive eye to the graphic layout of this book. The advice and guidance of G. Stanley Patey, Martha Wetherill, Winnie Danenbarger, and Rosalie Gratarotti at Rockport Publishers has been invaluable. We owe a special debt of gratitude to the many talented photographers who have managed to successfully capture the essence of our work. Several editors and journalists have shown an early interest in, and continued support for, the innovative quality of our work, including Lindsay Bierman, Brian Carter, Adele Freedman, Tom Fisher, Christopher Hume, David Lasker, Bronwen Ledger, Lorenzo Pignatti, Lisa Rochon, and Karen Stein.

Finally, we are extremely thankful to those family members and personal friends who have consistently supported us, in fair weather and foul, as we have struggled to realize our goal of an enduring and memorable architecture.

Bruce Kuwabara
Thomas Payne
Marianne McKenna
Shirley Blumberg